IMAGES
of America

TROUT VALLEY, THE HERTZ ESTATE, AND CURTISS FARM

On the cover: This picture of the main barn was taken during the time period when John D. Hertz owned the estate and surrounding farmland, sometime between 1920 and 1925. He used it to house show horses, polo ponies, and brood mares. It was referred to as the calf barn during the Curtiss Farm era, and was primarily used to raise the prize-winning Curtiss cows. Chicken coops were also assembled here. There was a small apartment, which was sometimes used as an employee residence during both the Hertz and the Curtiss eras. The barn is currently in use by Trout Valley residents to stable horses on the lower level, while the upper level is used as a gathering place for meetings and social events. (Courtesy of Shirley Beene.)

IMAGES
of America

TROUT VALLEY, THE HERTZ ESTATE, AND CURTISS FARM

Lisa Damian Kidder
Introduction and Afterword by
Trout Valley Mayor Bob Baker

ARCADIA
PUBLISHING

ISBN 978-0-7385-6160-8

Published by Arcadia Publishing
Charleston SC, Chicago IL, Portsmouth NH, San Francisco CA

Printed in the United States of America

Library of Congress Catalog Card Number: 2008924110

For all general information contact Arcadia Publishing at:
Telephone 843-853-2070
Fax 843-853-0044
E-mail sales@arcadiapublishing.com
For customer service and orders:
Toll-Free 1-888-313-2665

Visit us on the Internet at www.arcadiapublishing.com

Royalties from this book are being used in part to help fund the Trout Valley Preservation and Restoration Society and to assist with the start-up and funding of the Trout Valley Museum project.

Contents

ACKNOWLEDGMENTS

This book is by no means an exhaustive collection of Trout Valley's rich and varied history, but rather I have attempted to provide an overview of the key influences that helped to form this community, particularly focusing on the Hertz era and the Curtiss era. I have also tried my best to represent the scenic beauty and hometown community traditions that flourish to this day.

This book would not have been possible without the assistance and support of several people who generously donated their time and expertise to the project, namely Shirley Beene, along with Nancy and Dave Helmer, who provided the majority of the images included in this book, as well as countless hours of fact checking through the information written herein. Their lifetime commitment to preserving our local history and willingness to share it with others has truly been an inspiration.

Special thanks to Sally Henderson, who selflessly volunteered her time to conduct research, as well as track down additional documents and photographs used for this book. As one of the original residents in Trout Valley, her expertise was an invaluable asset to this project.

Lorette Dodt, who serves on the graphic design and photography faculty and is the coordinator for visual communication and mass communication at Triton College, arranged the Hertz and Curtiss era chapters. I am proud to feature many of her artistic photographs within these pages.

Also thank you to Bob Harper for providing many of the photographs featured in the Hertz era chapter, and to the Trout Valley residents who allowed their photographs and other memorabilia to be reproduced within the pages of this book. Most importantly, I am grateful to present and former residents who have helped to create and preserve such a memorable community.

INTRODUCTION

I turn from the busy highway onto a winding, country road. The pressures of the day begin to seep away. I watch horses grazing, kids fishing, and neighbors taking a walk. Although only 40 miles from Chicago and along a suburban corridor of big-box numbness, I have been transported to another world, another time.

Trout Valley is a storied place, rich with colorful history, filled with wonder and bedecked with natural splendor. Like a modern-day Shangri La, it is a small valley hidden away from the eroding influence of the modern world. Trout Valley—even the name evokes bucolic images. It is a green oasis that has drawn the fancy of entrepreneurs and artists for nearly a century.

As I enter, I am enveloped by a sense of nostalgia. Trout Valley is a throwback to a different era—the ivy-covered barn, the spring-fed trout streams, the canopy of towering oaks—it is as if someone gathered the best postcard scenes of Americana and dropped them into one location. Even today, I can understand what may have attracted taxicab and rental car magnate John D. Hertz to these soft, rolling hills along the Fox River.

With his desire to raise horses and play polo, he may have been attracted to its open pastures; perhaps he was drawn to the series of small ponds that run through the land that are perfect for fishing, or, with the manner that he carefully tended the fertile grounds, it may have been the lure of the landscape and abundant wildlife. Whatever originally brought Hertz to this locale, his presence has been fueling the community ever since.

As I drive along the same paths Hertz carved into the countryside, I view many of his original structures—the arched gateway, the landscaped grounds, the daughter's mansion, and the art deco pool. Leona Farms, as Hertz called it, was a pastoral retreat from the teeming city life of the 1920s where he was amassing his fortune. In many ways, it has remained this same retreat. Those who make Trout Valley their home today come to appreciate its open spaces, delight in its natural wealth, and foster a strong desire to preserve its history and resist change.

The Curtiss years are also reflected in the current prism of Trout Valley. Otto Schnering, the founder of the Curtiss Candy Company, was a kindred spirit to Hertz. Both self-made millionaires, they also shared an earthy love and respect for farm work. When they wanted to relax and escape the daily grind of their empire-building, they turned to hard manual labor—raising cows, bulls, horses, hogs, and poultry. The agrarian life was embraced and celebrated by both men. When Schnering purchased the Hertz estate, he transformed the horse ranch into a full-fledged farming operation and made his home there.

The lavish parties and prestige of the Hertz years gave way to the down-to-earth and family styling of the Curtiss era. Schnering invited his employees to live with him on the estate grounds, offered riding and swimming lessons to the children, and sponsored holiday parties and special events in the community. Many of the traditions begun during that time—children's Christmas party, Fourth of July picnic, pool parties—continue today.

Both of these men created unique legacies that live on more than 50 years later through the actions and dispositions of the current residents. Hertz bestowed his vision and affection for the land upon Trout Valley and it is still keenly felt today. This passion is why the village of Trout Valley was born.

Once an unincorporated area in McHenry County governed by a homeowner's association, the residents banded together and formed a village when the last pristine piece of the Hertz estate was threatened with development. This open area of bluffs, fen, and riverfront access was under siege, but access through Trout Valley was needed to make it a reality. The residents had been through similar battles before and resisted the efforts of the home developer and the neighboring municipality. In fact, not only was an offer of thousands of dollars per homeowner turned down, but the residents paid to bring suit to preserve this unique area. John D. Hertz would have been proud.

Schnering's philanthropy and contributions to the local community were renowned. He supported church groups, civic organizations, and the boys and girls clubs. In fact, one of his last acts before he died was a sizable contribution to the Boy Scouts of America. He understood and impressed upon those around him the importance of giving back to the communities they serve. Schnering's motto of "All of us" is the touchstone that unites modern day Trout Valley as well.

As a small community, our residents are expected to contribute. They freely give of their time and talents and we have many examples in our midst of donated hard work and labor. My ride takes me past the pool, the dams, the bridges, the park, the community center—all of these entities have been built, managed, or updated through the volunteer efforts of the residents. It is this spirit and dedication that further knits together the fabric of this area and carries on the traditions borne during the Hertz and Curtiss days.

We are unique because of our reliance on community, we know the neighbors on our block, and the next block over, and several blocks away. Since the early days of Hertz and Curtiss, we have taken communal pride when members of the Trout Valley family have risen to great heights—including famous bandleader Frankie Masters and his wife and singer Phyllis Miles, "Oscar Mayer Wiener" jingle writer Richard Trentlage, and Jimmy John Liautaud, the founder of Jimmy John's gourmet sandwiches. As we watch each generation grab for its golden ring, we want to believe that somehow our strong connections to the past and the rarefied air of the valley can spur on creativity and inspiration.

Darkness is descending on the valley and its unlit streets. The moon hangs low in the sky and casts a pale gleam on the pasture. In my mind's eye I can see the ghostly apparitions of the polo players, the racehorses, the prize bulls, and the young Little Leaguers who have all shared this space. I am thoughtful. I have spent the last several moments on my own private journey touring the memorable events and incredible history of the secret treasure I call my home. I want to share it with you now in photographs. I invite you to turn the page and join me on this ride.

Bob Baker
Mayor of Trout Valley

An elevated view looks down onto one of the original Hertz polo fields. John Hertz, an avid polo player, not only raised polo ponies at Leona Farms, but also had two regulation polo fields on his estate. (Photograph by Lorette Dodt.)

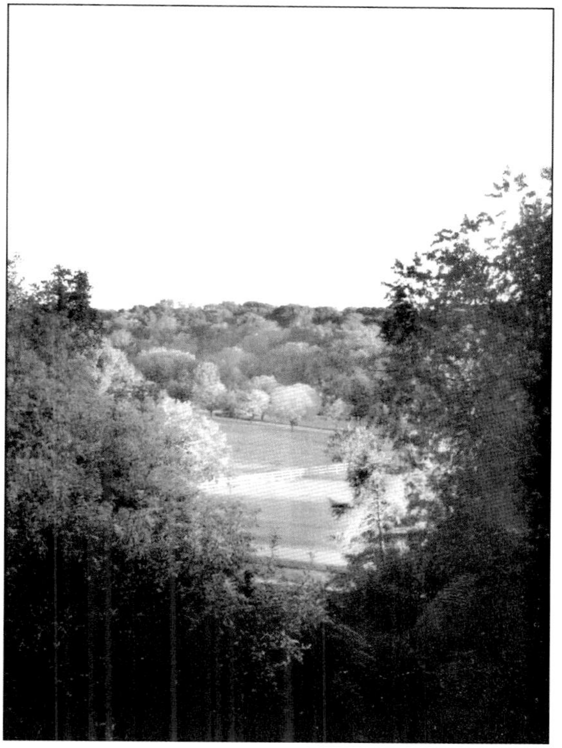

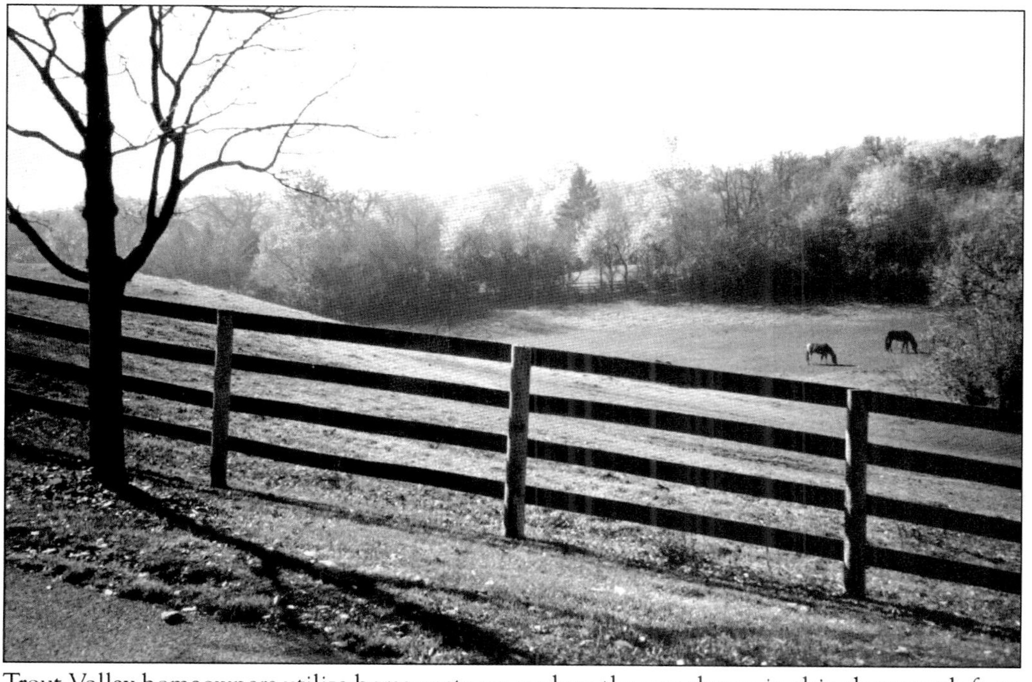

Trout Valley homeowners utilize horse pastures, such as the one shown in this photograph from 2000, to continue the equestrian tradition established by John D. Hertz. There are deeded riding trails located throughout Trout Valley. (Courtesy of Todd Somers.)

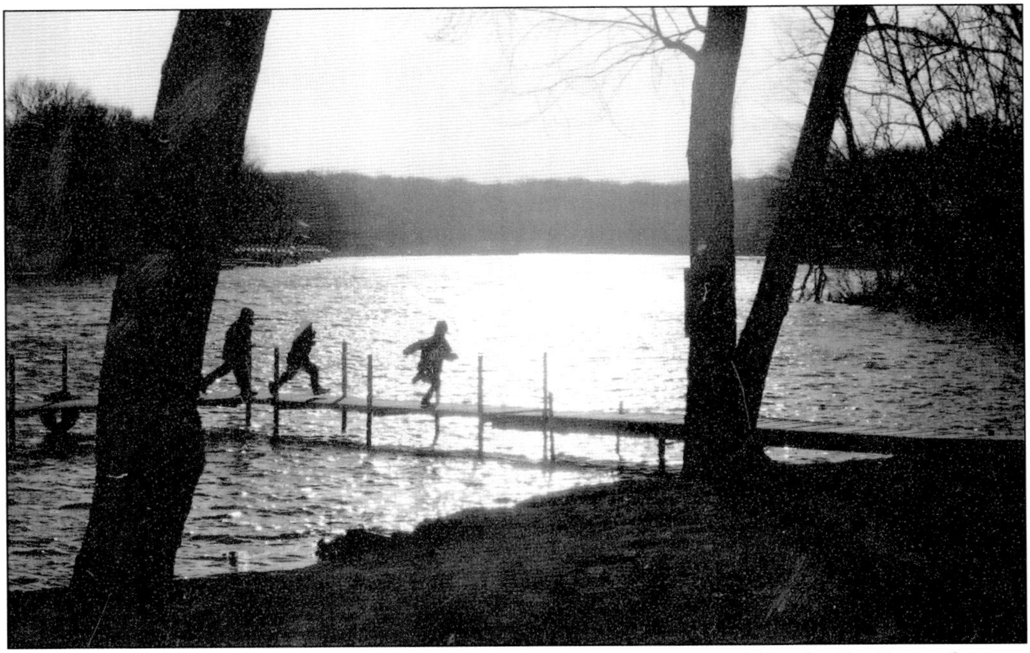

As the sunlight fades, children dash off the Trout Valley pier in late fall. The Fox River flows in the background. (Photograph by Lorette Dodt.)

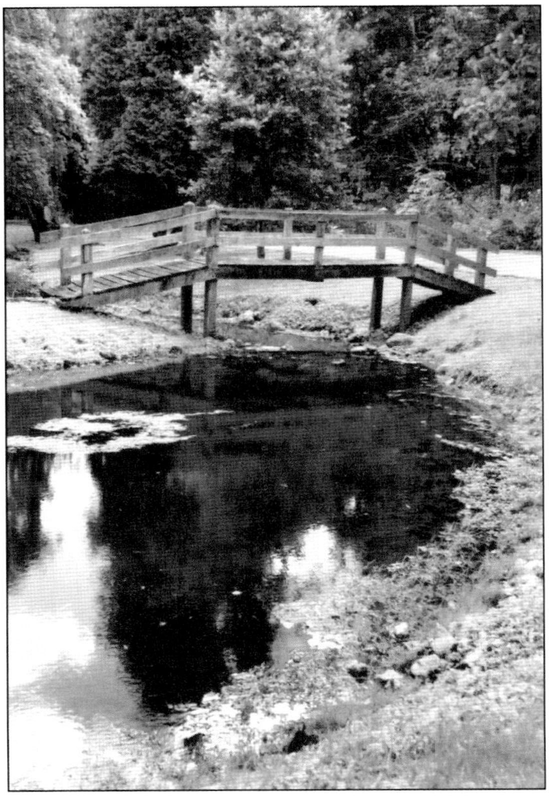

The Rainbow Bridge is a perennial favorite for couples and families seeking a photo opportunity. (Photograph by Lorette Dodt.)

The horse pasture, viewed in this photograph in the early-morning light, was once a Hertz polo field. This open space is now dedicated as parkland and used by both four-legged fence jumpers and two-legged base stealers. (Photograph by Lorette Dodt.)

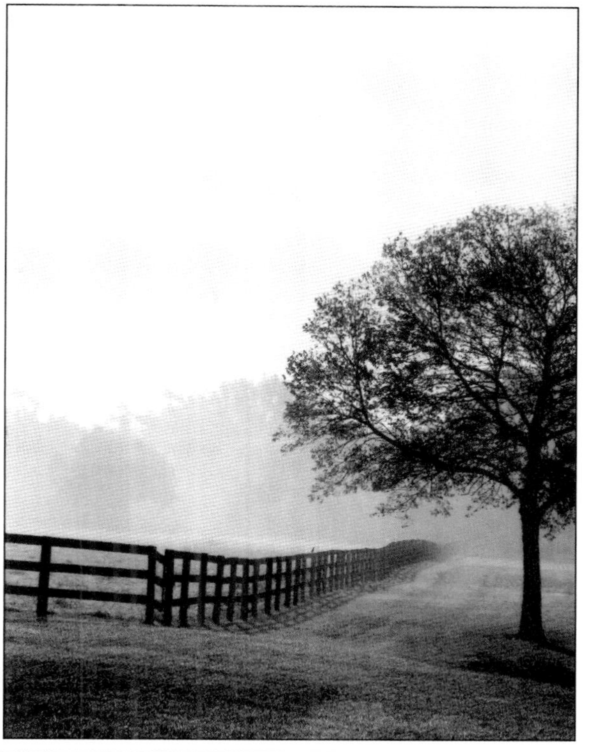

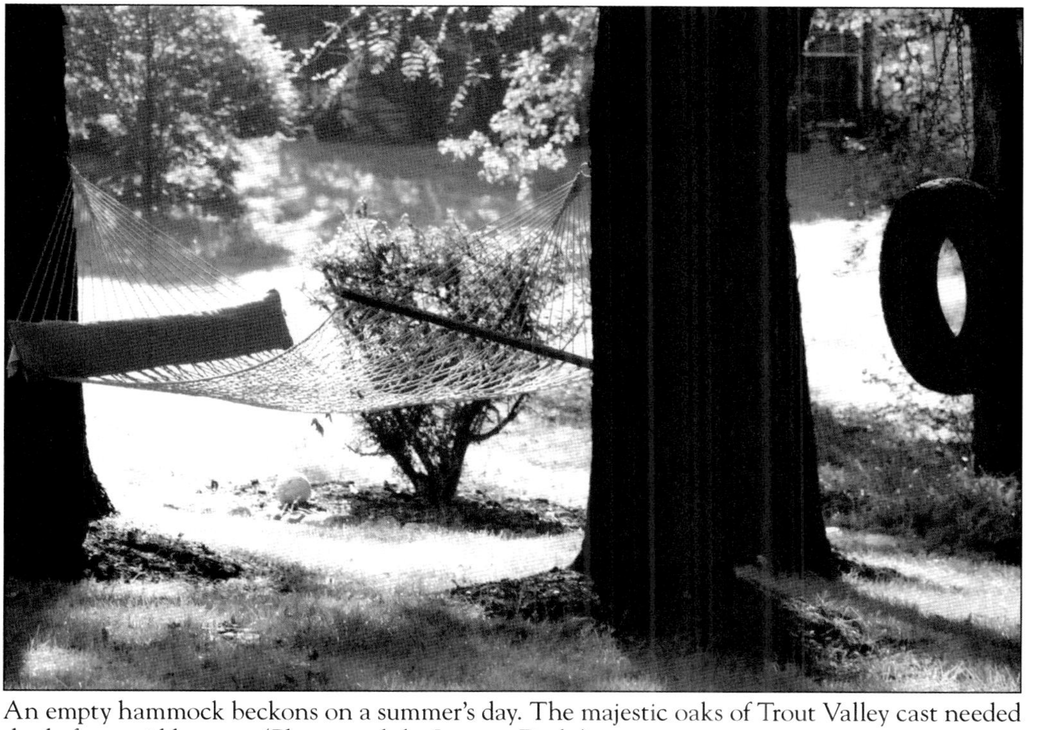

An empty hammock beckons on a summer's day. The majestic oaks of Trout Valley cast needed shade for a midday nap. (Photograph by Lorette Dodt.)

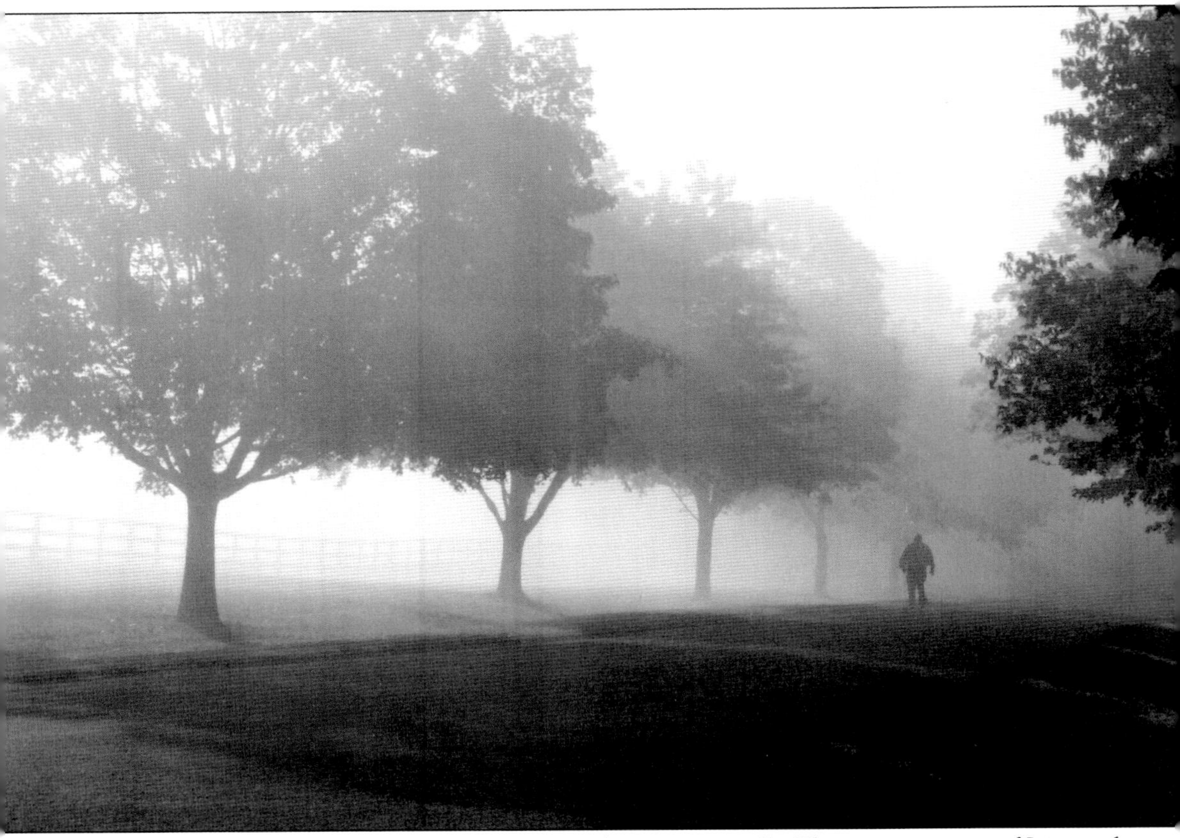

Longtime resident John Liautaud takes an early-morning walk. Three generations of Liautauds have lived in Trout Valley. (Photograph by Lorette Dodt.)

One

The Hertz Era

John D. Hertz was a self-made millionaire who purchased land from several farms in Cary during the 1920s. The Smith Farm, along with those of Seebert, Lowe, and others, were combined by Hertz to become Leona Farms, named after Hertz's eldest daughter. Approximately 500 of these 900 acres make up the village of Trout Valley today.

Hertz lived on this land with his wife, Fanny-Kay, and his two daughters, Leona Jane and Helen Betty. He also had one son, John D. Hertz Jr. (originally named Leonard Hertz at the time of his birth). John hired the famous landscape architect Jens Jensen to survey and design a landscape for the estate.

In 1929, he built a home, just east of the main estate house, for his daughter Leona, her husband Alfred Ettlinger, and their one son, John. Originally referred to as the guest house and later as "the little mansion," it still serves as a private residence on Marryat Drive.

During the Hertz era (approximately 1920–1944), roughly 100 people lived and worked on the Hertz estate whose responsibilities included maintaining the grounds, polo fields, and trout ponds; raising chickens, breeding and training German Shepherd dogs; caring for the extensive flower and vegetable gardens; and furthering the goals of Hertz's various equestrian activities.

Show horses, polo ponies, and racehorses were bred, raised, and/or trained at Leona Farms. Some of Hertz's famous thoroughbreds included Reigh Count, his son Count Fleet, and Fleet's son Count Turf. Reigh Count won the Kentucky Derby in 1928 along with the 1929 Coronation Cup in England, and Count Fleet won the Kentucky Derby in 1943, as well as the Triple Crown. Count Turf was sold as a colt but went on to become a Kentucky Derby winner in 1951.

Hertz hired English horticulturalist George Bainbridge to cut vistas through the old Smith woods and plant a variety of imported trees and shrubs. As a result of Bainbridge's efforts, a wide variety of plants and old growth trees are found throughout Trout Valley, a phenomenon that is arguably unsurpassed throughout the Midwest.

The Hertz estate was also the site of many glamorous Great Gatsby–like galas that attracted politicians, movie stars, and business tycoons alike. Many of Trout Valley's original buildings, as well as the primary roads, polo grounds, swimming pool, and ponds, were built or remodeled under the direction of John D. Hertz. Most of these historic and scenic treasures are still maintained in Trout Valley today.

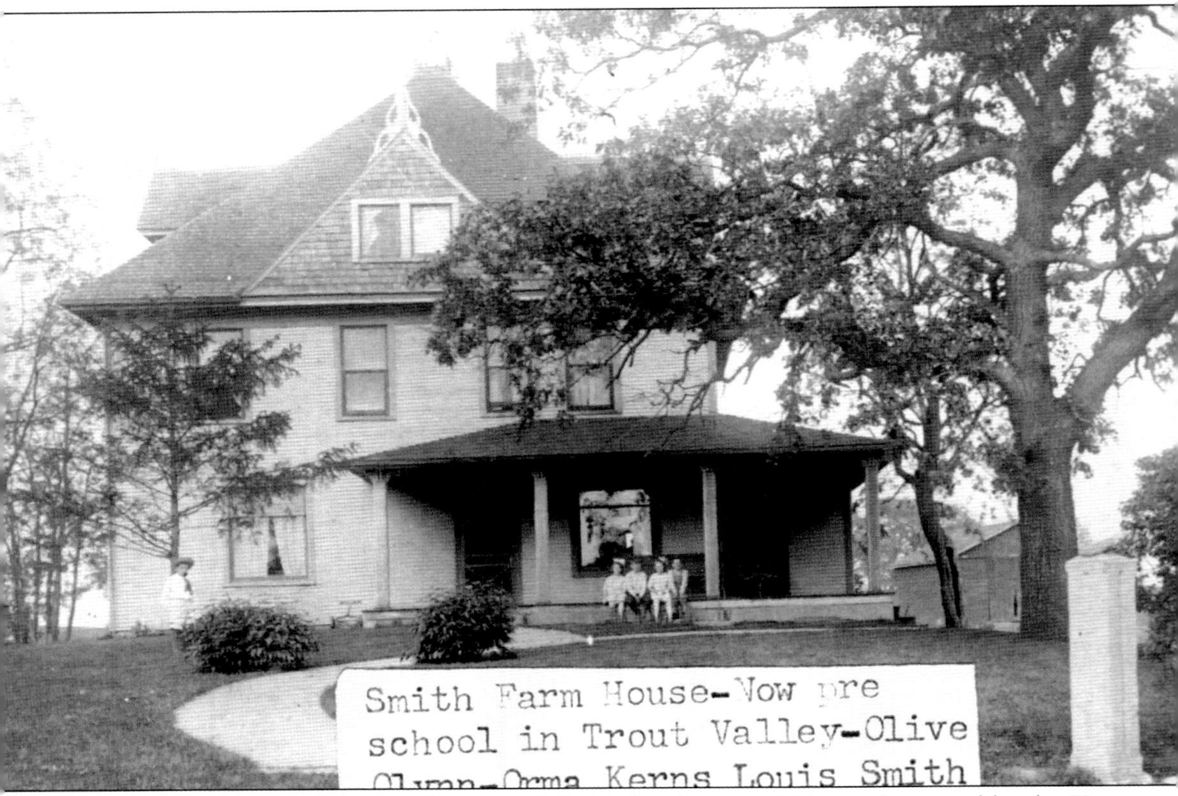

This 1920s postcard depicts the original Smith farmhouse, which was later used by the Hertz estate as a boardinghouse for his various horse groomsmen, polo players, and other male employees and was subsequently used by Curtiss Farms in a similar fashion. In Trout Valley's early history, it served as the location of Chantry's Pantry, a tearoom and antique shop, and in more recent times it has housed a preschool for young children. It is one of the estate's original buildings and remains standing today.

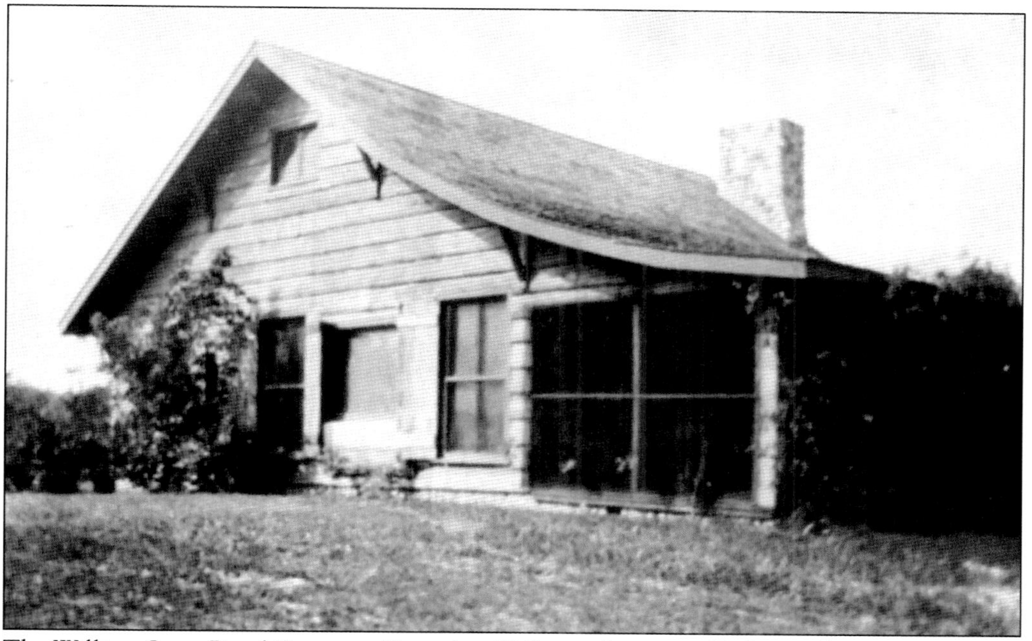

The William Scott Bond House on Horseshoe Hill, now known as Turkey Hill Road, was among the area's original structures, predating the Hertz era. It is seen here in the 1920s.

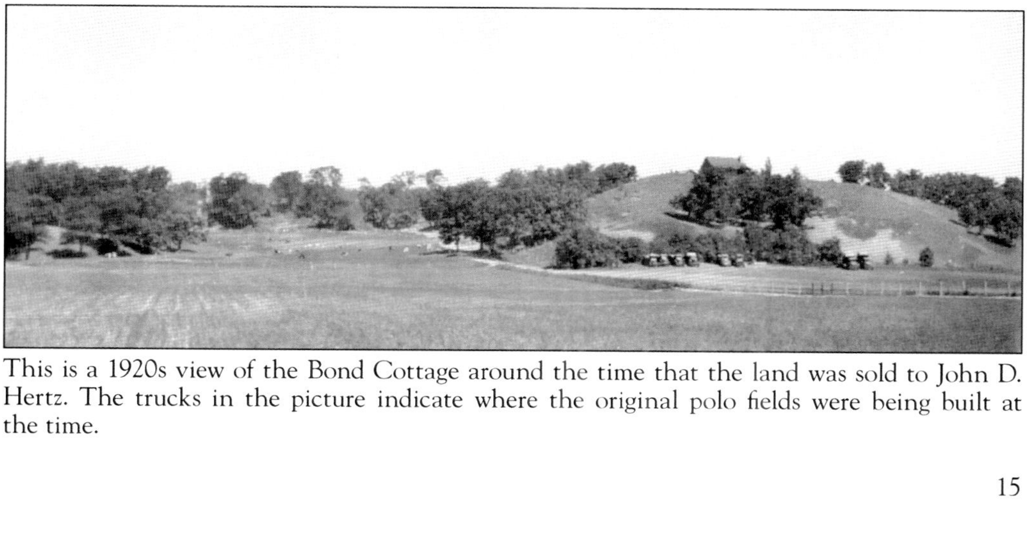

This is a 1920s view of the Bond Cottage around the time that the land was sold to John D. Hertz. The trucks in the picture indicate where the original polo fields were being built at the time.

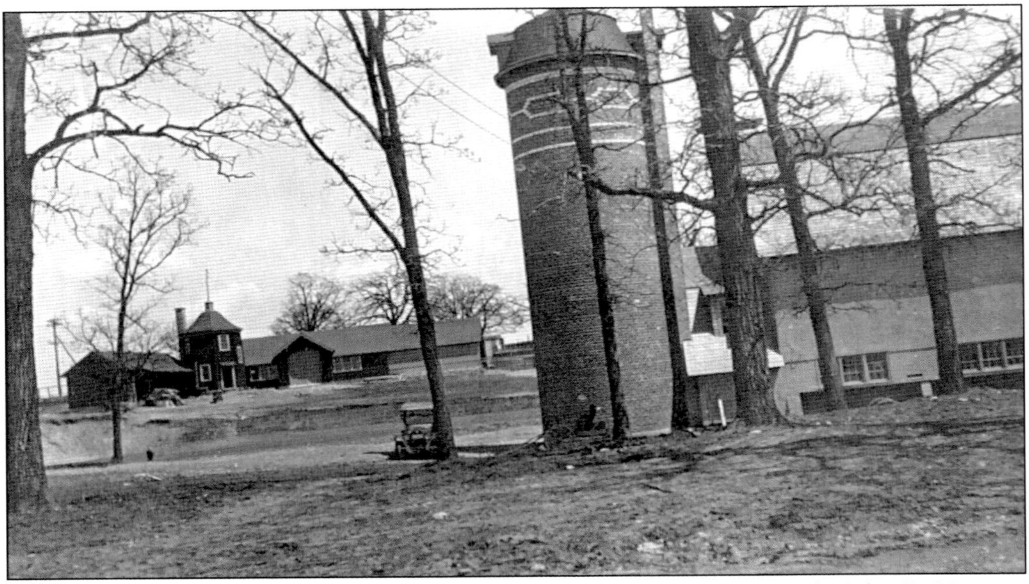

This is a c. 1918 photograph of the Smith Farm, prior to the land purchase by John D. Hertz.

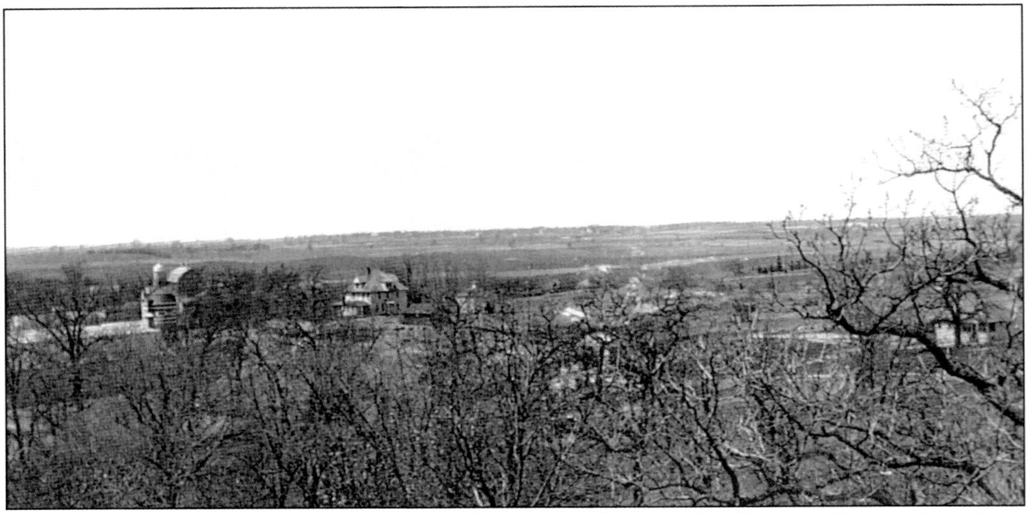

This is a 1920s view of the Smith Farm landscape. Much of this land now makes up the village of Trout Valley.

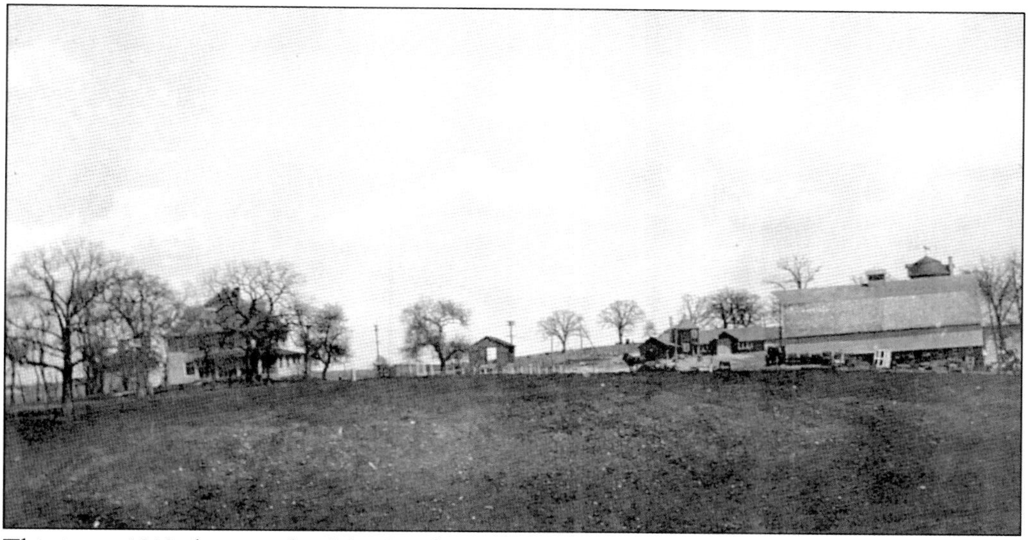

This is a c. 1918 photograph of the Smith Farm estate, predating the Hertz era.

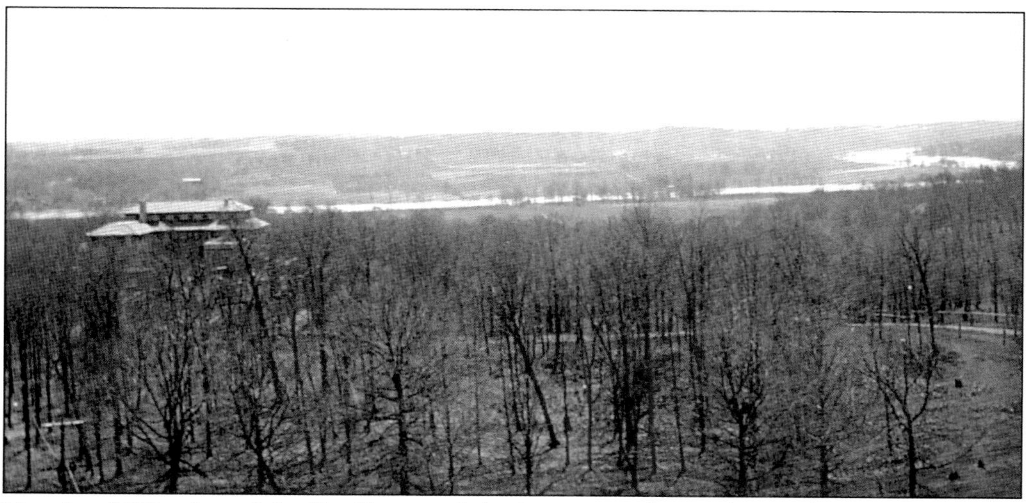

Here is a 1920s view of the Fox River and the large estate house during the Smith Farm era. Trout Valley sits along the Fox River, where many residents still enjoy boating and other water activities.

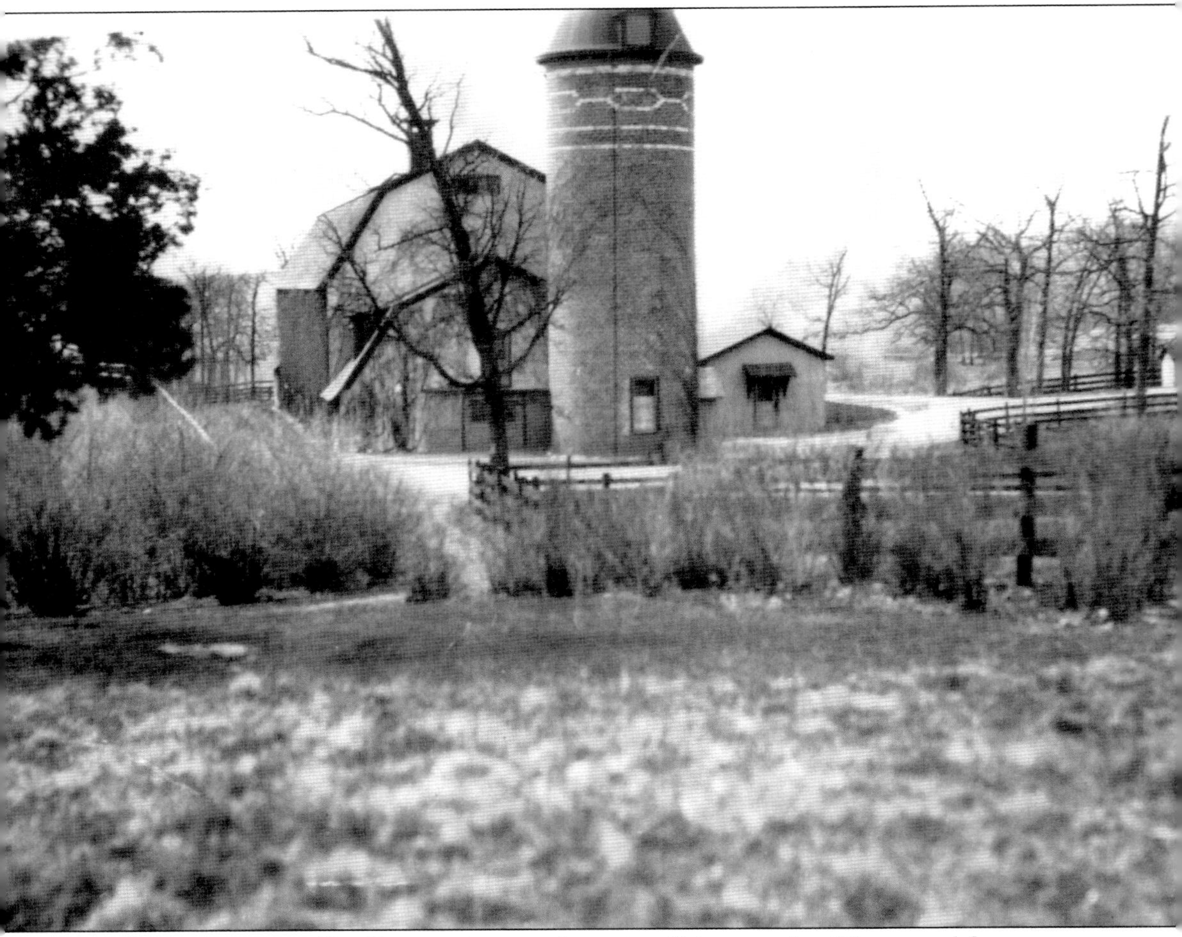

This structure, used by Hertz as the main barn, is still in use today. The second floor serves as a community recreation and meeting area and is the site of numerous holiday parties throughout the year. Horses are still boarded in the stables below. It is seen here in 1918.

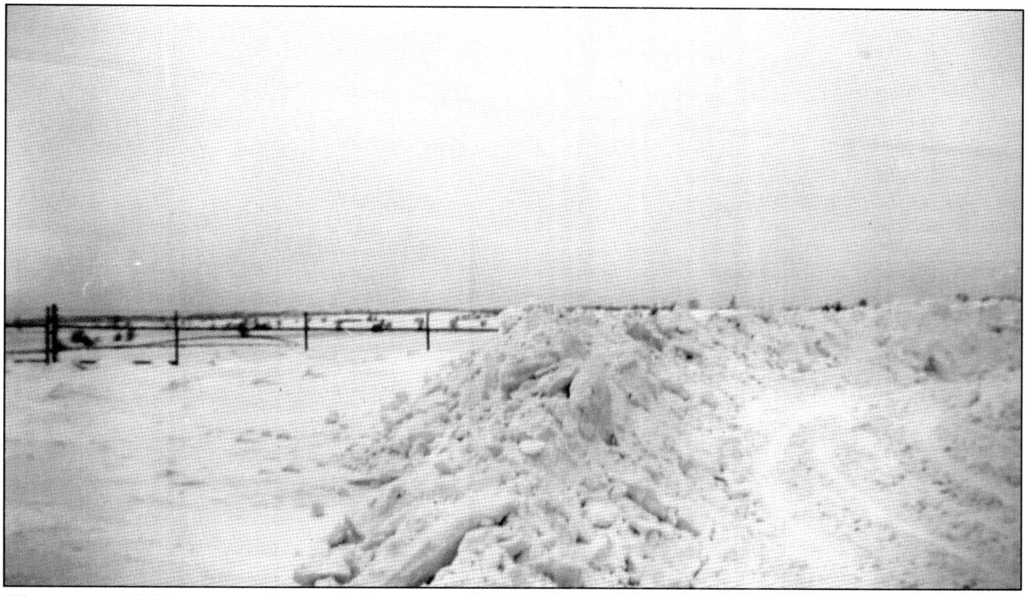

This is a c. 1918 picture of one of the original roads through Trout Valley, built prior to the Hertz era, likely during the time of the Smith Farm. Heavy snows made transportation in and out of Trout Valley difficult, if not altogether impossible, during the early years.

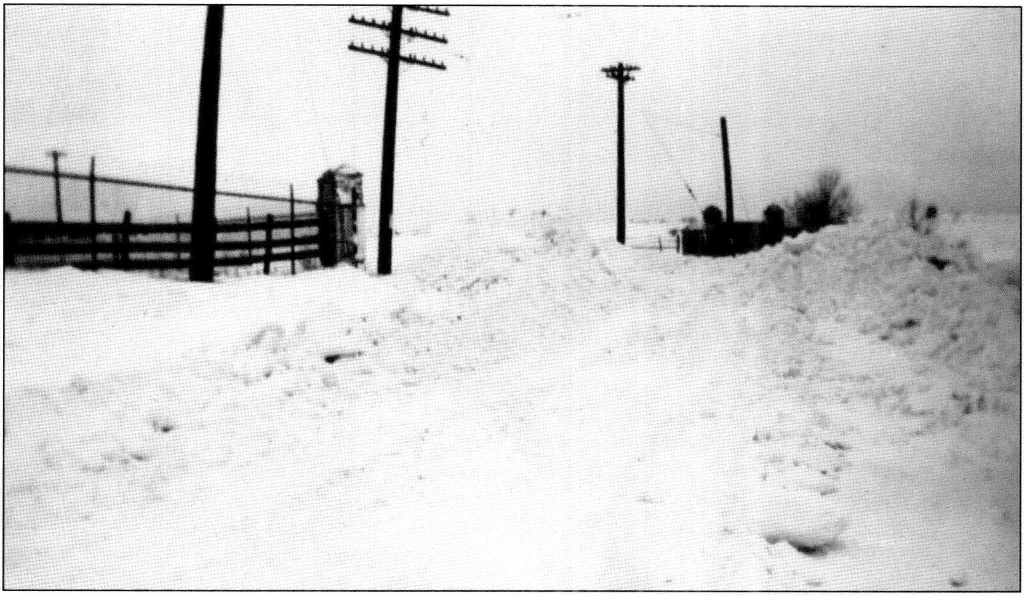

This c. 1918 photograph of the Smith farmland covered in snow predates the Hertz era. The barn can be seen in the distance.

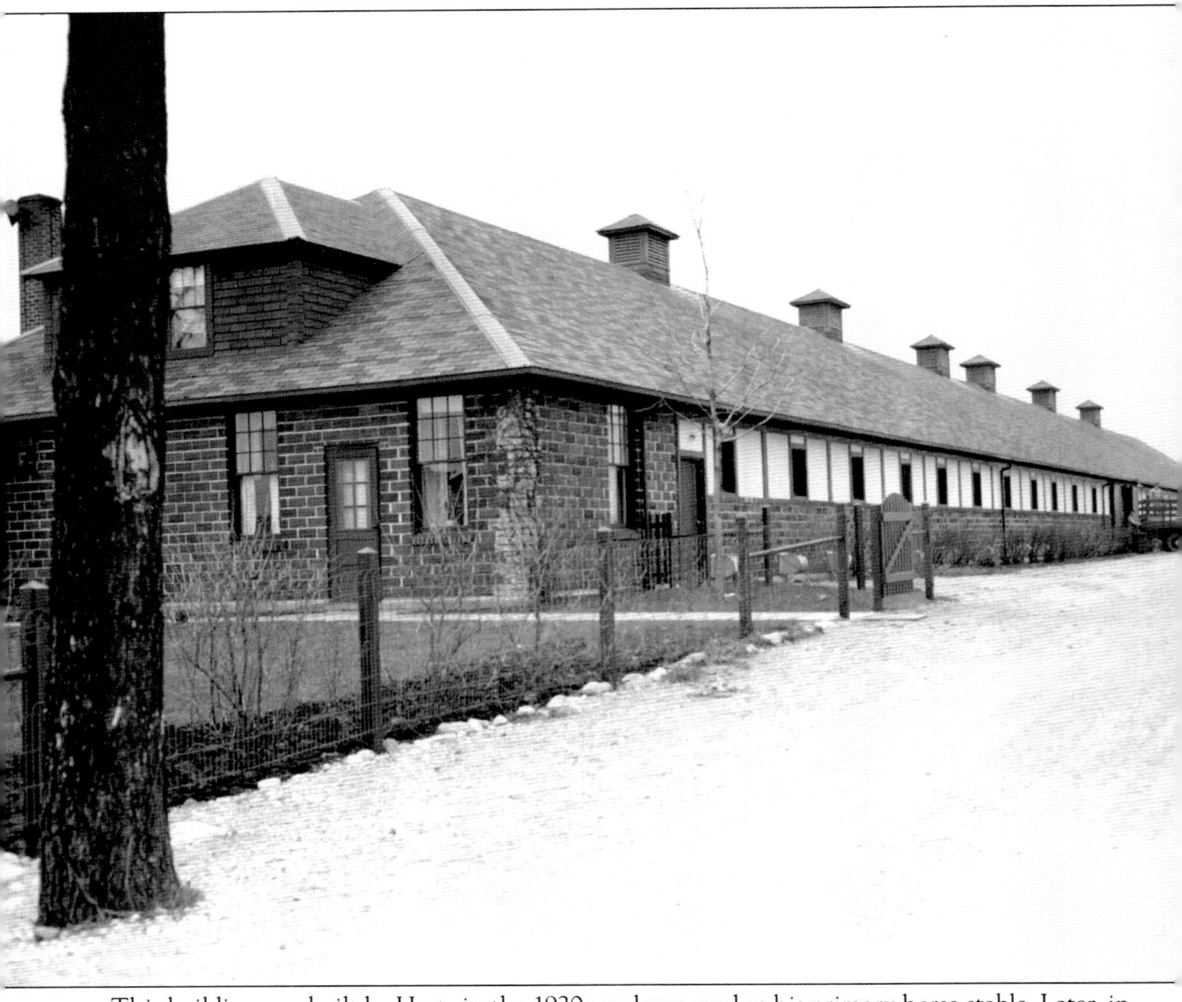

This building was built by Hertz in the 1920s and was used as his primary horse stable. Later, in the Curtiss era, it was used by the Schnerings to house chickens, cows, and families who were employed by Curtiss Farm. It is seen here in the 1930s.

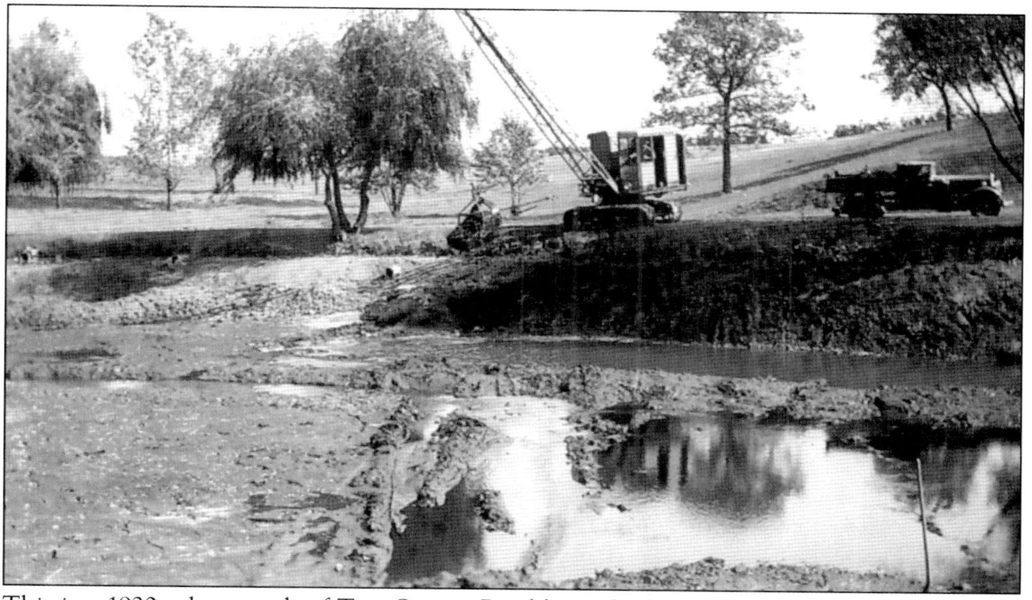

This is a 1920s photograph of Tom Sawyer Pond being built or rebuilt under the guidance of John D. Hertz. This pond is still stocked and used as a private fishing locale by Trout Valley residents today. (Courtesy of Elmer Anderson.)

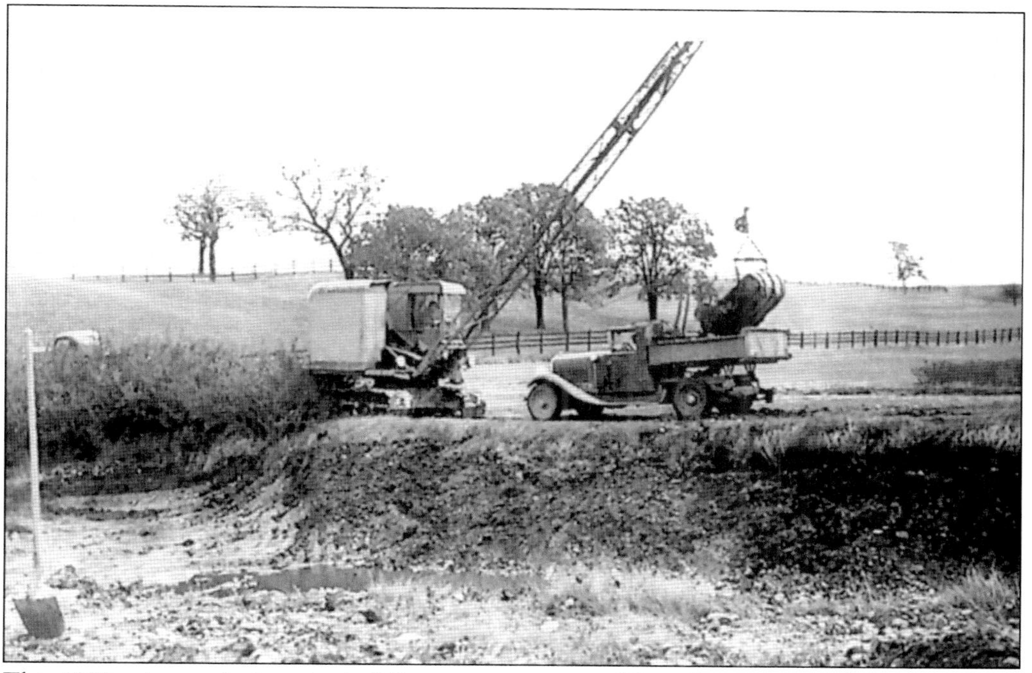

This 1920s picture depicts the building or renovation of Tom Sawyer Pond during the Hertz era. In the spring and summer, Trout Valley residents are still seen fishing and enjoying this historic pond. (Courtesy of Elmer Anderson.)

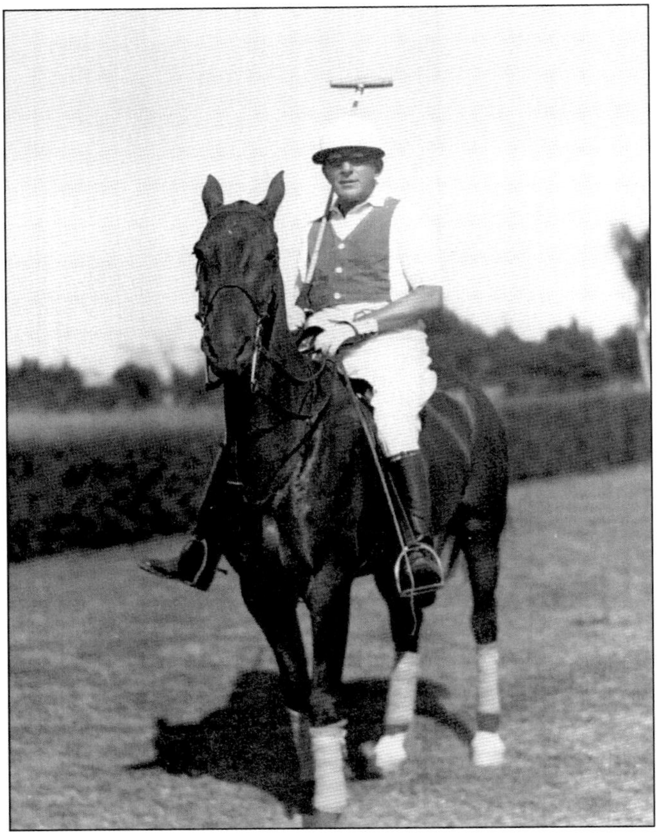

John D. Hertz enjoyed playing polo on his estate, and he often invited famous guests to join him for polo matches. It has been reported that some of the celebrity guests who visited during the Hertz years included Will Rogers, Myrna Loy, and Walt Disney. This image is from the 1920s.

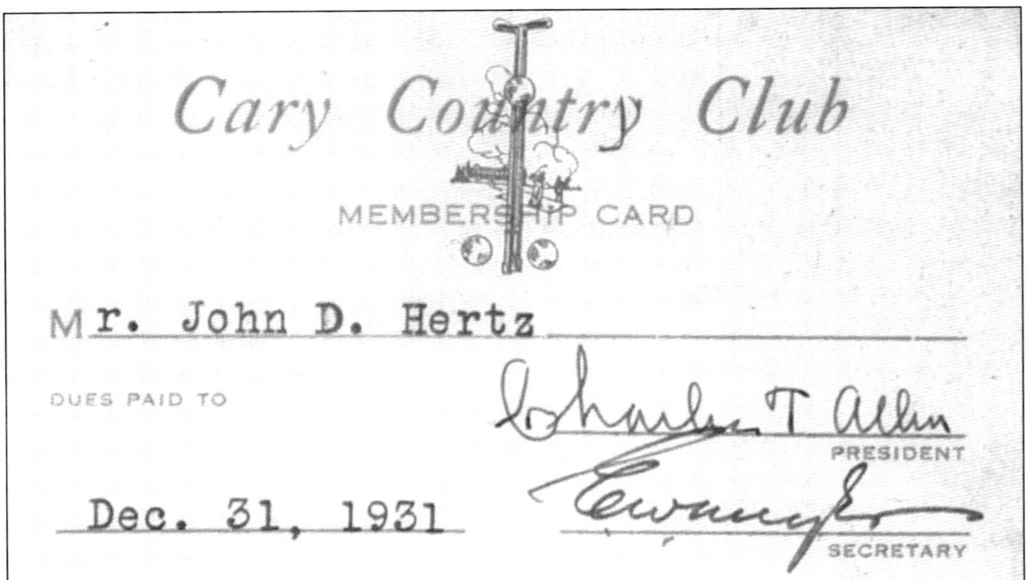

Cary Country Club

MEMBERSHIP CARD

Mr. John D. Hertz

DUES PAID TO

Dec. 31, 1931

Charles T Allen
PRESIDENT

SECRETARY

Hertz's membership card for the Cary Country Club, dated December 31, 1931, is seen here.

Here is a photograph of Frances (Fannie) Kesner Hertz.

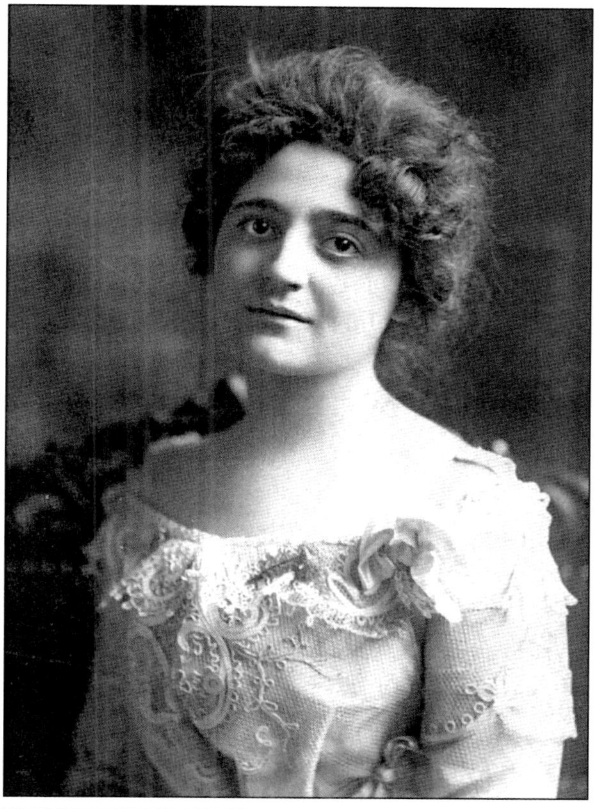

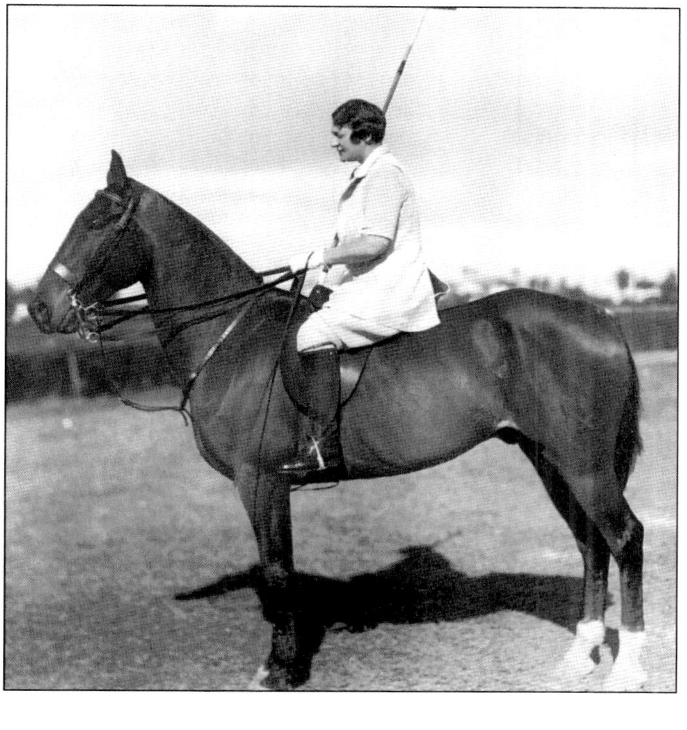

This 1920s picture shows Fannie playing polo. The Hertz family oversaw the building of the original polo fields on this land.

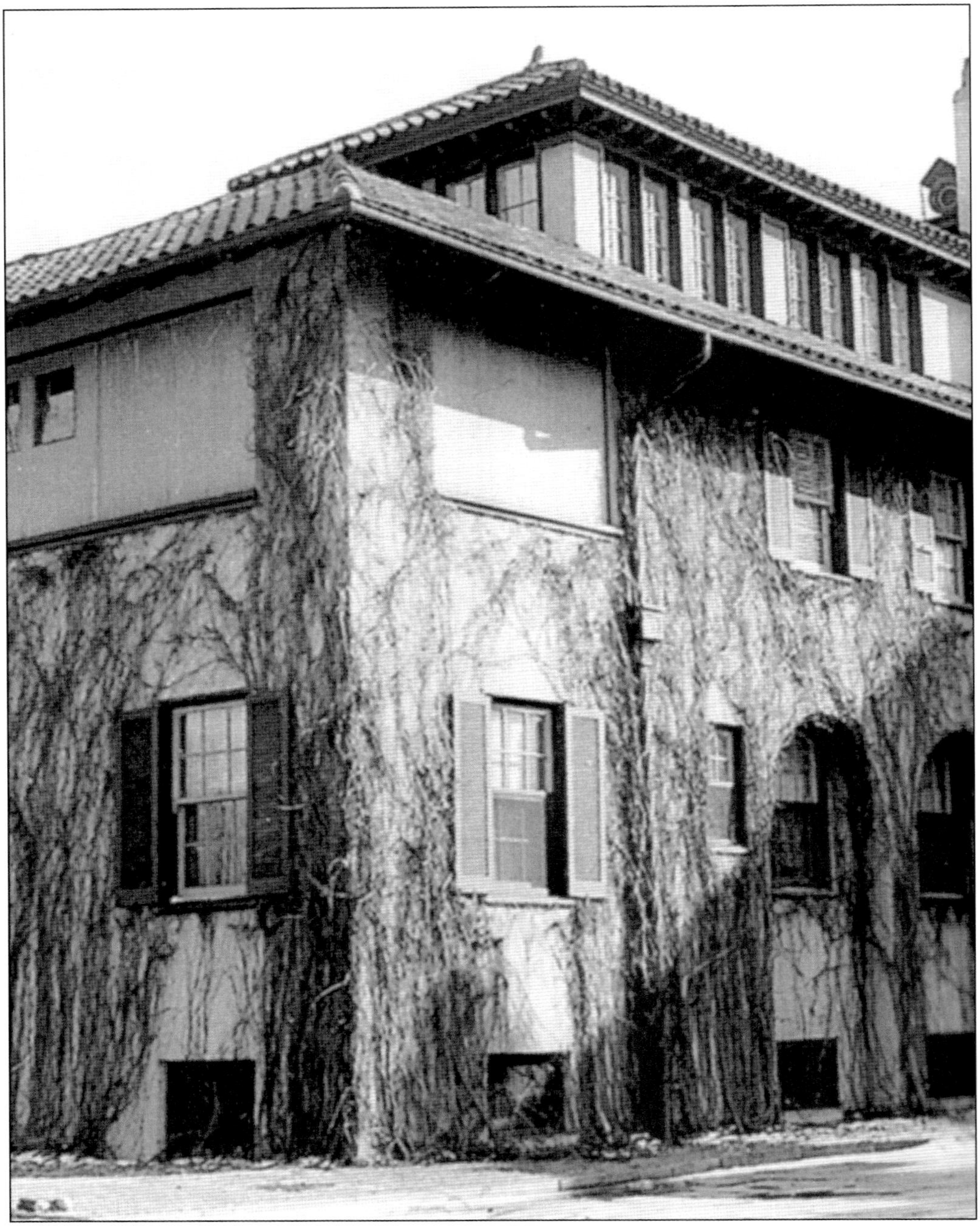

This c. 1929 photograph shows the large estate home, taken during the Hertz era.

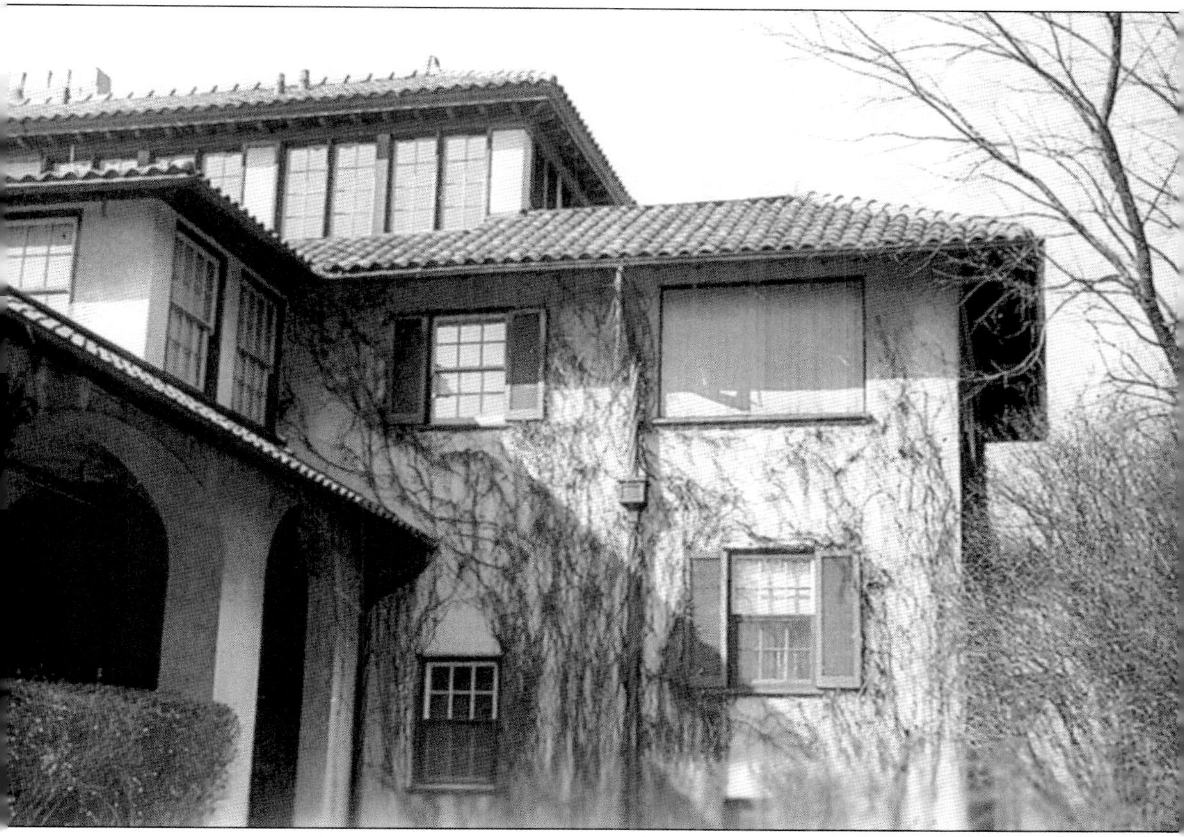

Here is another view of the estate home, taken during the Hertz years. Cars entered through the archway. The maids' quarters were on the left side of the house. It is seen here around 1929.

CURTISS FLYING SERVICE

NATIONAL COMMERCIAL FLYING, SCHOOLS, SALES & SERVICE

SALES AGENTS FOR
:URTISS AEROPLANE & MOTOR CO., INC.
:URTISS-ROBERTSON AIRPLANE MFG. CO.
COMMAND-AIRE, INC.
SIKORSKY AVIATION CORPORATION
IRELAND AIRCRAFT, INC.
CESSNA AIRCRAFT CO.

NEW YORK OFFICE
27-29 WEST 57TH STREET
PHONE WICKERSHAM 9600

DUPLICATE INVOICE

Invoice No. 8-164

Mr. John Hertz,
231 South LaSalle Street,
Chicago, Ill.

1 Sikorsky Amphibion, Mfg. No. 214-5 with two Wasps Engines Nos. 1712 & 1713, Department of Commerce No. NC 74-K	$56,800.00

Extras

Install 2 Eclipse Electric Starters with Exide Storage Battery 6 TX-13-1 Eclipse Generator and Generator Control Box.	$813.00
1 Pioneer Earth Inductor Compass	810.00
1 Pioneer Altimeter in Cabin	70.00
1 Pioneer Air Speed Indicator in Cabin	65.00
1 Pioneer Rate of Climb Indicator	150.00
1 Vanity Case with Swiss 8 Day Clock	35.00
2 Pressure Fire Extinguishers with fitting tubing etc.	131.00
8 Life Preserver Jackets	28.00
2 Drinking Glasses	4.00
1 Thermos Carafe	32.50
Engines and Magnetos Shielded for Radio	240.00
Cabin lined with Celotex	26.28
2 Special Swivel Chairs	345.00
2 Special Stationery Chairs	345.00
1 R.H. Rear Seat and Back, Toilet Seat, Pilot's Seats and backs - special leather	154.12
1 Carpet Rug	60.50
Curtains in Cabin	57.60
Painting License Number-	16.67
	3,383.59

Total	$60,183.59
Less Deposit	50,500.00
Balance Due	9,683.59

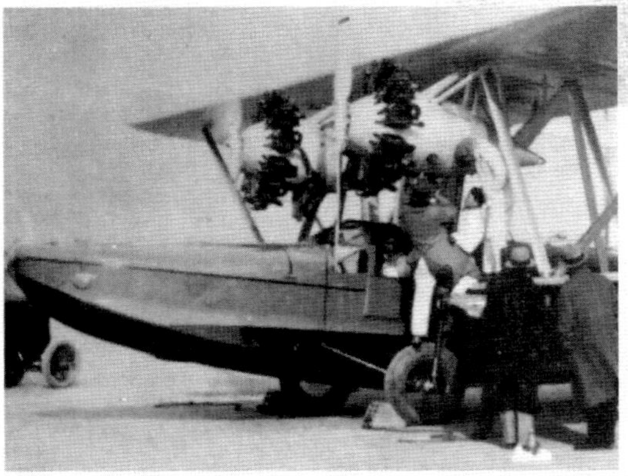

016. The private airplane of John D. Hertz was referred to as the "Three Johns." His daily flight between Cary, IL and Chicago, IL was estimated to take approximately ten minutes. (1924)

017. The invoice for John D. Hertz's airplane, purchased in August of 1929, shows a final purchase price of $60,183.59. Hertz was known to land his amphibious plane on Lake Michigan, where he would have a special modified version of one of his Yellow Cab cars waiting to pick him up and chauffeur him to his office in downtown Chicago, IL. (1929)

The private airplane of John D. Hertz was referred to as the *Three Johns*. His daily flight between Cary and Chicago was estimated to take approximately 10 to 15 minutes. The invoice for Hertz's airplane, purchased in August 1929, shows a final purchase price of $60,183.59. Hertz was known to land his amphibious plane on Lake Michigan, where he would have a specially modified version of one of his Yellow Cabs waiting to chauffeur him to his office in downtown Chicago.

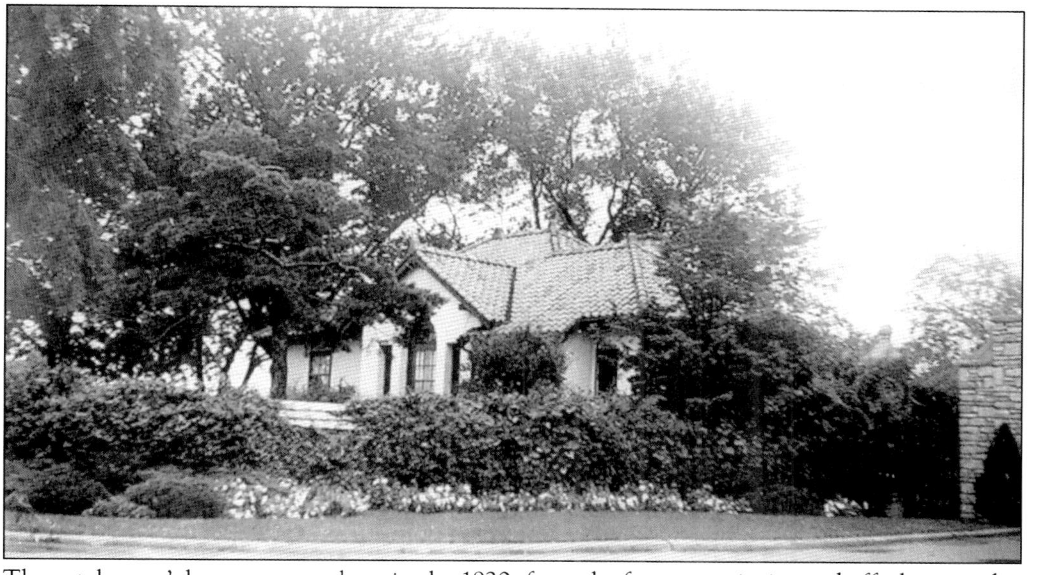

The gatekeeper's house, as seen here in the 1920s from the front gate, is situated off what is today known as Stonegate Road. During the Hertz era, the gates at both Stonegate Road and Country Commons Road were kept locked at all times. When Hertz's chauffeur would approach the gate, he would flash the car's headlights, and the gate keeper, Edvin Anderson, would come out to unlock the gate at the Stonegate Road entrance. State police were often present, patrolling and serving as armed guards throughout the area when John D. Hertz was in residence. (Courtesy of Elmer Anderson.)

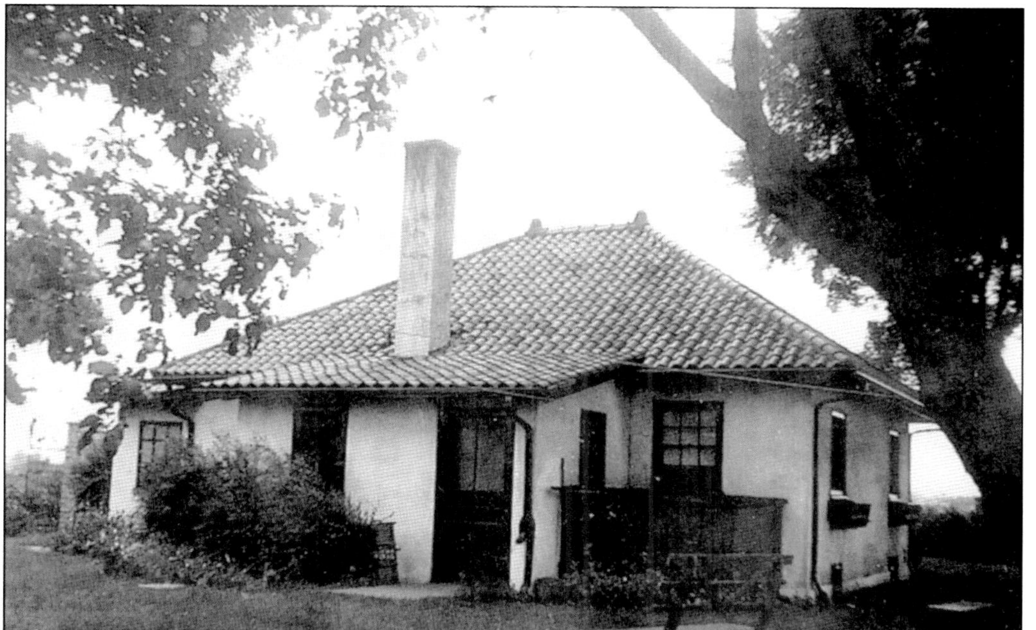

A side view of the gatekeeper's bungalow during the Hertz era, as seen from the front gate, is seen here in the 1930s. In 1934, Joe Tichy was hired by Hertz to serve as the superintendent of Leona Farms, and he moved into the gatehouse. (Courtesy of Elmer Anderson.)

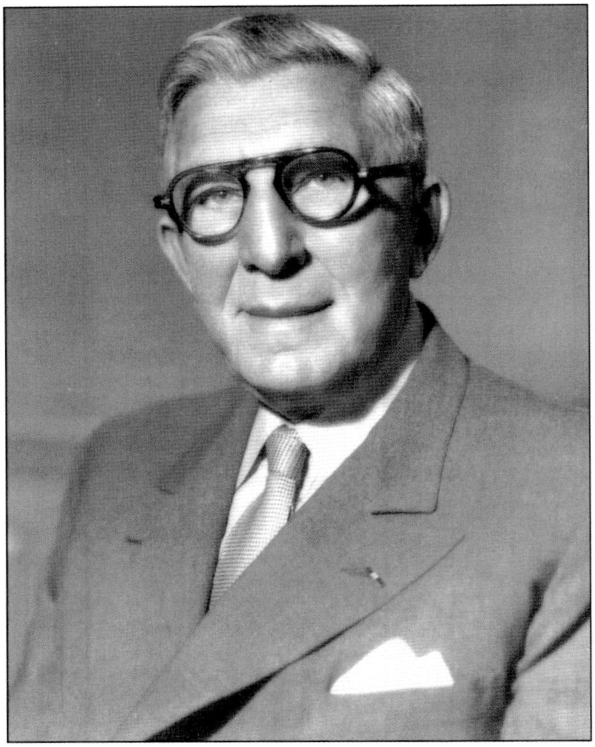

Here is a portrait of John D. Hertz. Hertz founded Yellow Cab and Coach Company in 1915, Hertz Drive-Ur-Self Corporation (the first rental car business in the United States) in 1924, and was a partner in the firm of Lehman Brothers Financiers.

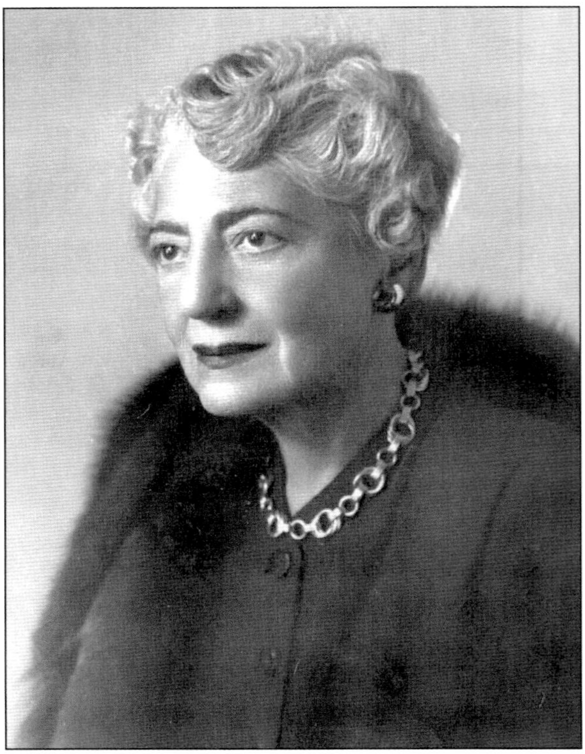

Here is a portrait of Fannie Hertz.

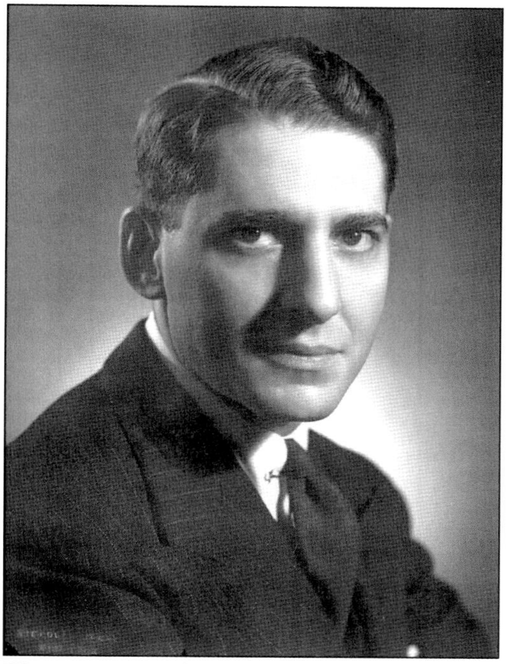 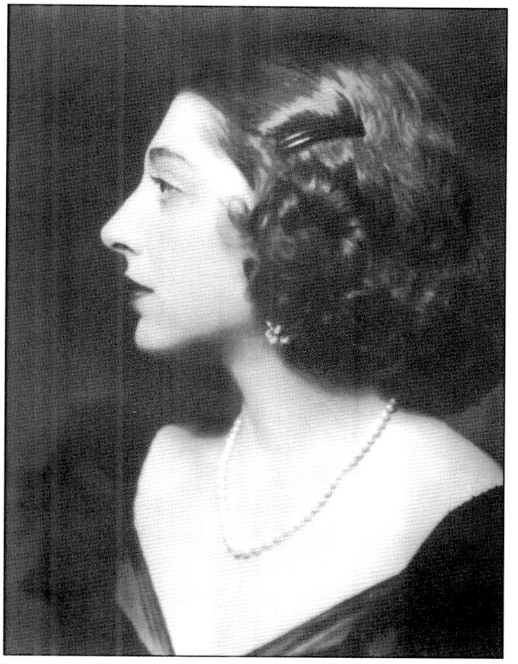

These portraits show John Hertz Jr. and Leona Hertz, children of John D. and Fannie Hertz.

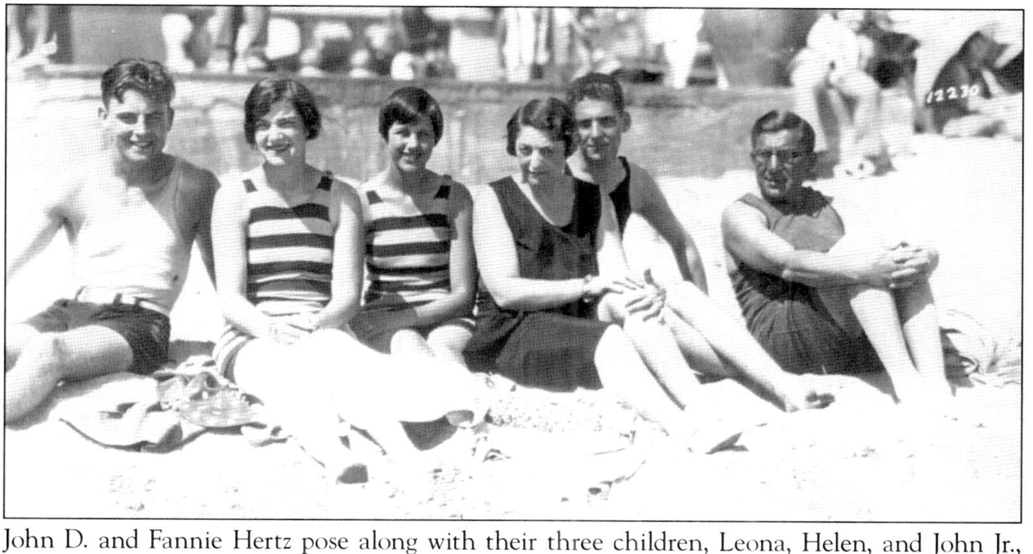

John D. and Fannie Hertz pose along with their three children, Leona, Helen, and John Jr., enjoying a day at the beach.

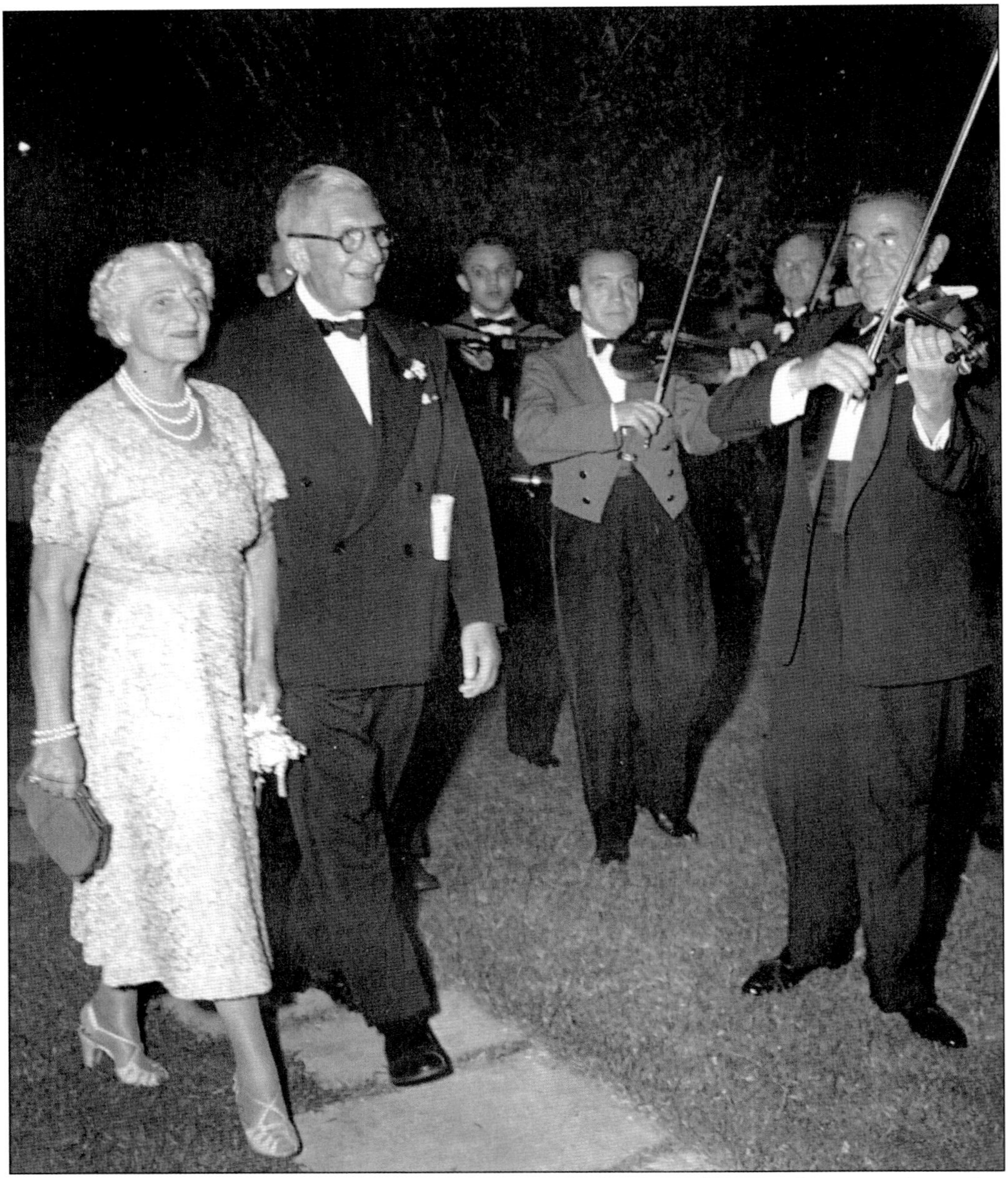

The c. 1930 50th wedding anniversary celebration of John D. and Fannie Hertz was hosted at the Hertz estate pool. This pool was built by Hertz in 1923. It presently serves as the Trout Valley community pool, and frequent parties are still hosted here during the summer season.

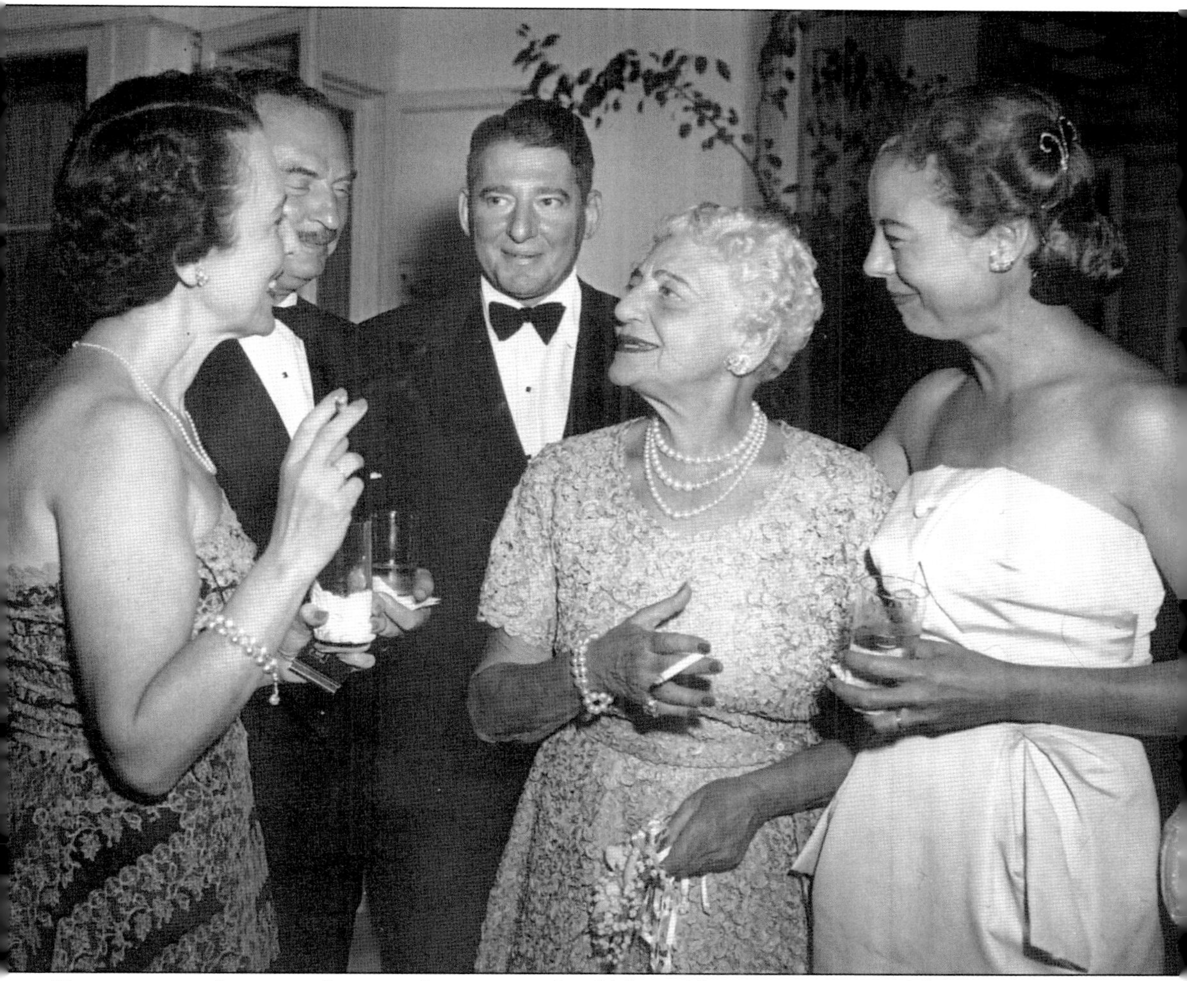

Fannie is seen here socializing with guests at the 50th wedding anniversary celebration of her and her husband around 1930.

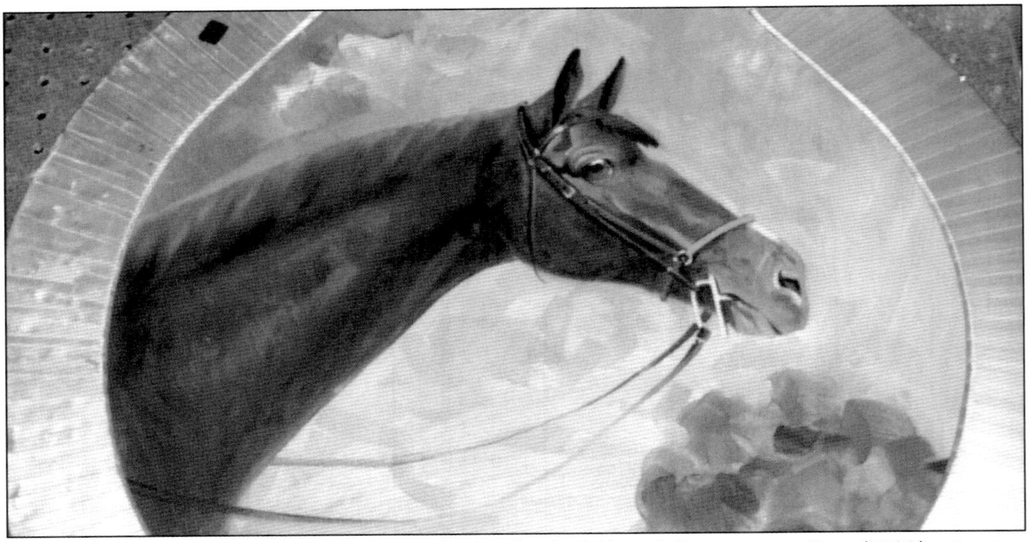

This is a painting of the famous Kentucky Derby (1928) and Coronation Cup (1929) winning racehorse Reigh Count, owned by Fannie and John D. Hertz. Reigh Count was ridden by Chick Lang, the only Canadian jockey in history to win the most prestigious races in both the United States and Canada.

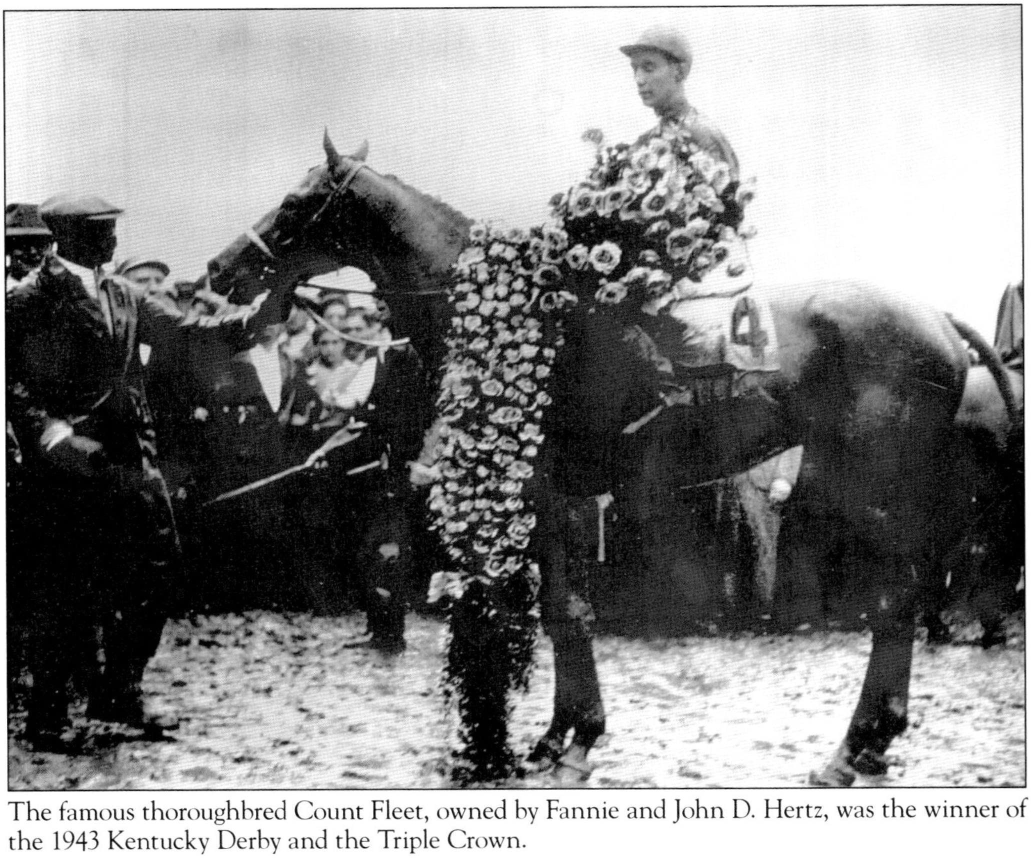

The famous thoroughbred Count Fleet, owned by Fannie and John D. Hertz, was the winner of the 1943 Kentucky Derby and the Triple Crown.

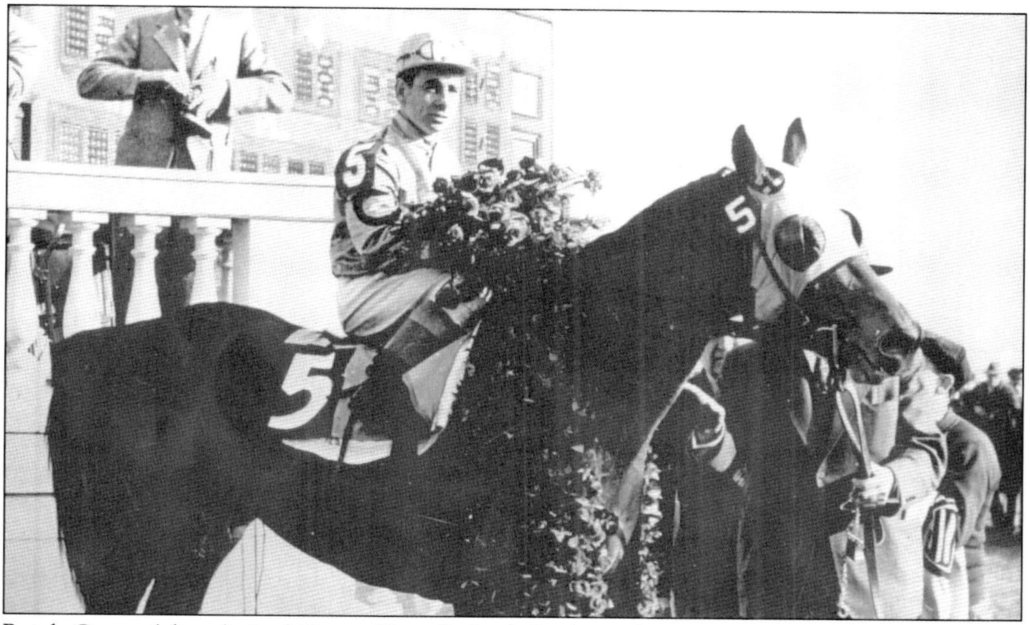

Reigh Count (above) sired Count Fleet (below). Both racehorses were owned by Fannie Hertz and went on to become Kentucky Derby winners. Trading cards were printed for Kentucky Derby winners. This one, depicting Count Fleet, is autographed by jockey John Longden. The caption on the back of the trading card reads: "John D. Hertz, in whose wife's colors COUNT FLEET raced, had offered to sell the colt for $4,500 as a yearling, but there were no takers. COUNT FLEET also was available at that price in the spring of his 2-year-old season, but jockey John Longden said he talked Hertz into keeping the colt, who went on to earn $250,300. COUNT FLEET came out of the Wood Memorial with an injury, but he made it to the 1943 Kentucky Derby anyway and, so much the best, he won easily. This great runner later won the Belmont by 25 lengths." (Below, courtesy of Linda Stelle.)

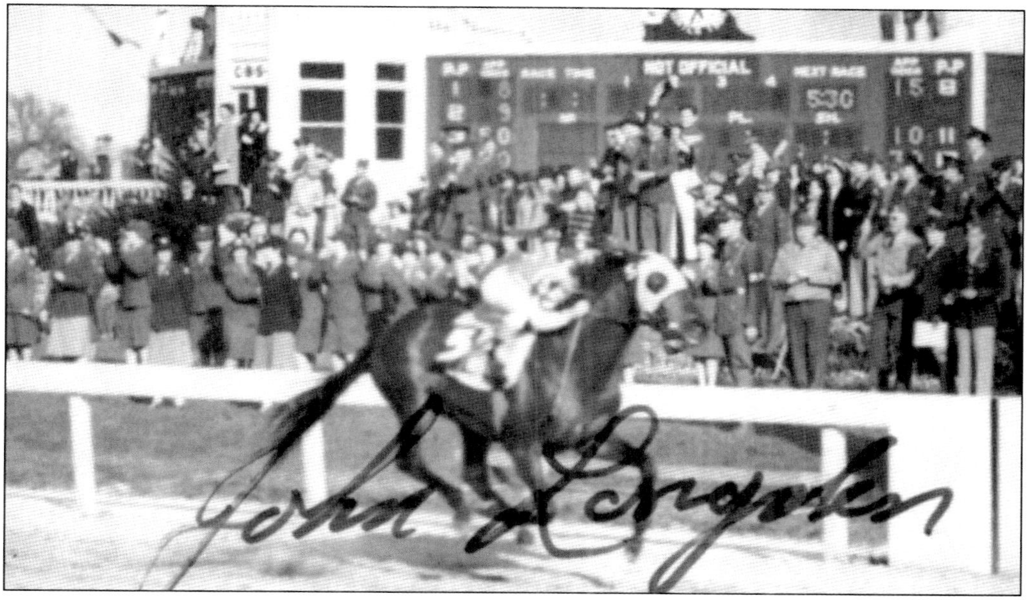

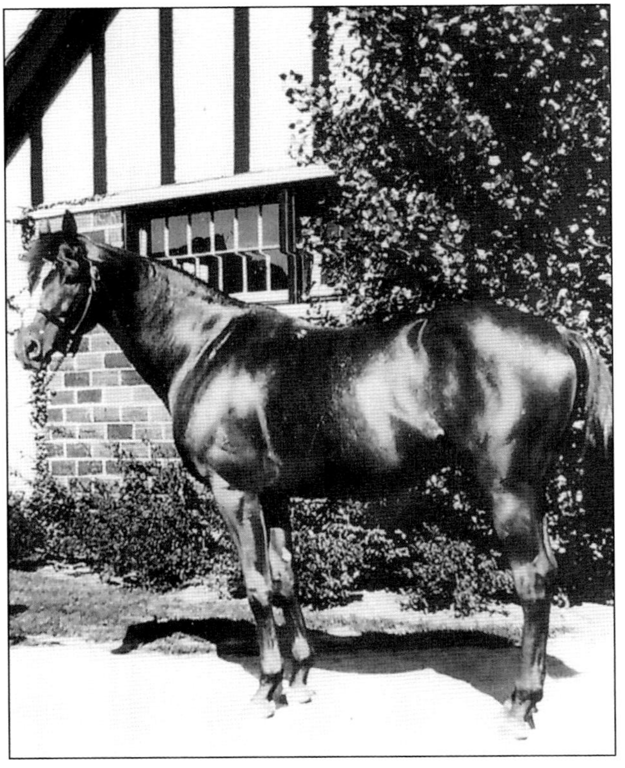

This photograph, again exhibiting John D. Hertz's passion for racehorses, was taken in the 1920s on the grounds of what would later become Trout Valley.

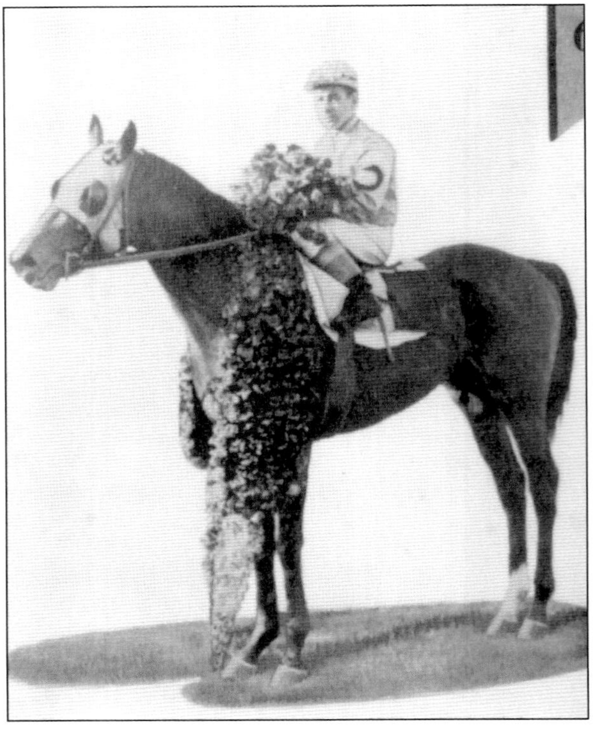

Trained during his younger years by G. D. Cameron, Count Fleet lived to the ripe old age of 33. According to the Count Fleet Kentucky Derby winner trading card, after visiting the aging Count Fleet, *Eclipse* award-winning writer Billy Reed wrote of the encounter: Count Fleet was "just standing there in his stall, looking tired and infirm. His back was swayed and his ribs stuck out and he couldn't hear very well . . . Even so, he seemed to have something regal about him. Maybe it was the way he held his head or the look he got sometimes in his eye. He seemed to know that he was something special—that one day, long ago, he had won this phenomenon called the Kentucky Derby."

Two

Otto Schnering and the Curtiss Candy Company

In 1943, Otto and Dorothy Schnering purchased 650 acres of land from John D. and Fannie Hertz. A portion of this, which was to become the first of several farms started by the Schnerings, makes up present-day Trout Valley.

Schnering was the founder of the Curtiss Candy Company, maker of Baby Ruth and Butterfinger candy bars. When he began his candy company in 1916 at the age of 24, Schnering opted to use his mother's maiden name rather than his own German name for the candy company, in light of anti-German sentiments of the day.

His entrepreneurial spirit led Schnering to succeed after starting the candy company with four friends and nothing more than a single stove and a five-gallon kettle. He struggled to keep the company in business during the Great Depression and difficult economic market of the 1920s. On more than one occasion, it was the partnership, dedication, and keen business sense of his wife Dorothy that helped hold the company together during hard times. This was particularly true after his untimely death, when Dorothy continued furthering the goals of her late husband's business interests.

Driven to start a farm of his own in order to provide high quality ingredients for his candy company, Otto also fostered the land to serve as a farming showcase, where he raised cattle, chickens, turkey, sheep, hogs, mink, and fish. Otto and Dorothy Schnering were responsible for many advances in the field of livestock farming.

By the late 1940s, Curtiss Farm chickens produced more than 2.5 million eggs annually. Otto was able to cut the growing time for broilers from 12 weeks to 11 weeks through his livestock diet program. He raised animals whose diets and needs were compatible with each other, and made the most of the land used.

It is likely that the Schnerings were indirectly responsible for the name Trout Valley. In addition to their many other entrepreneurial endeavors, they chose to develop the area's natural spring-fed ponds into trout hatcheries, raising fish that were later sold in large quantities to hotels and restaurants.

Some of the families, such as the Johnsons and the Tegels, who worked on Curtiss Farm remained in Trout Valley, developing a love and appreciation for this unique land. One of those individuals, Nancy Johnson Helmer, has dedicated much of her adult life to preserving the rich history of Curtiss Farms, and many of her photographs, documents, and memories are featured within the Curtiss era chapters.

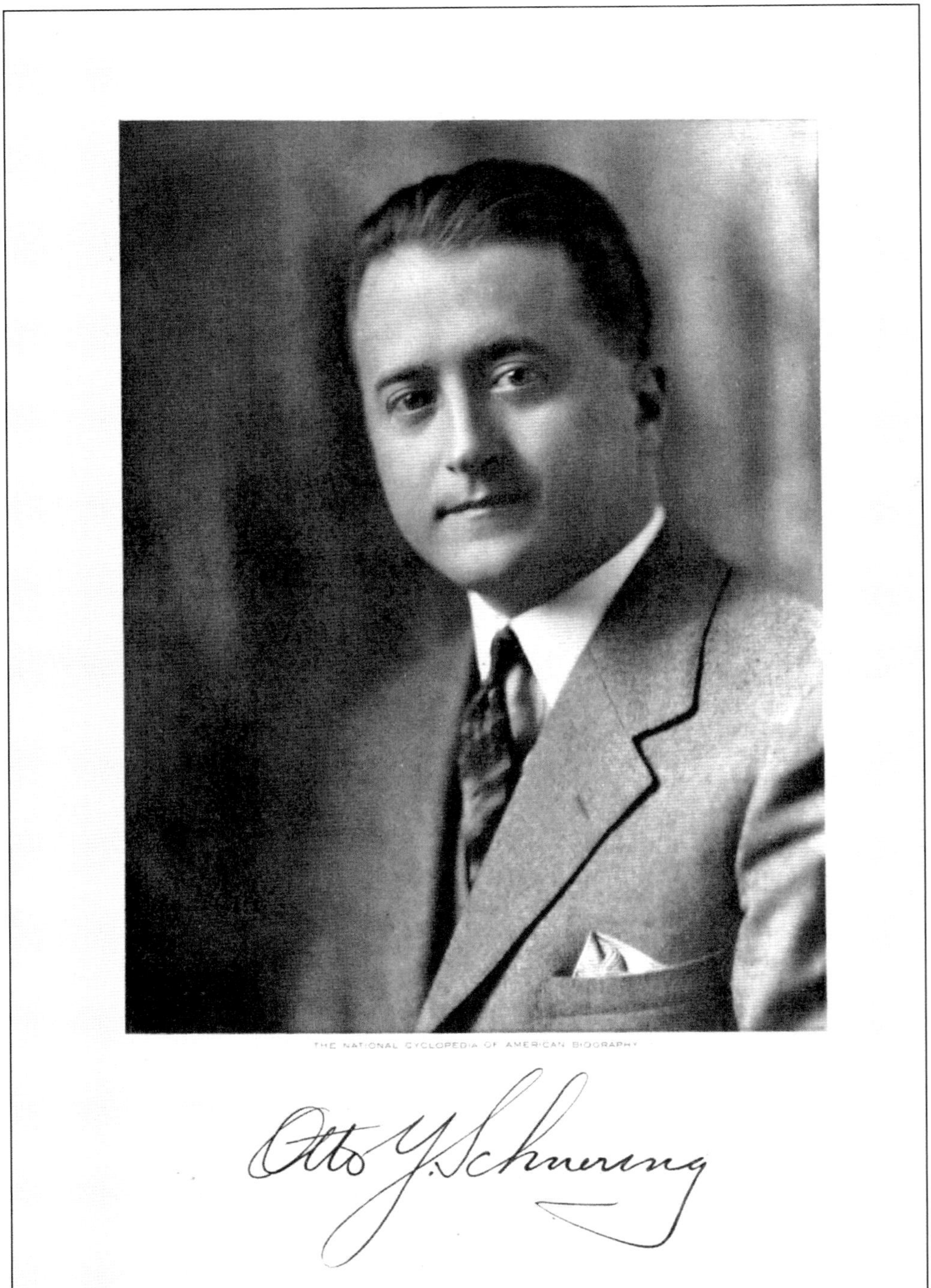

This portrait of Otto Schnering features his signature. Owner of Curtiss Candy Company, Schnering was a self-made millionaire who has been credited with inventing the individually-wrapped candy bar. Additionally he and his wife Dorothy are acknowledged as having made many innovations in the process of breeding livestock.

Well-known for associating with America's most prominent individuals, the Schnerings attended many exclusive events. This is an invitation to the inaugural ceremonies for Pres. Franklin D. Roosevelt in 1933.

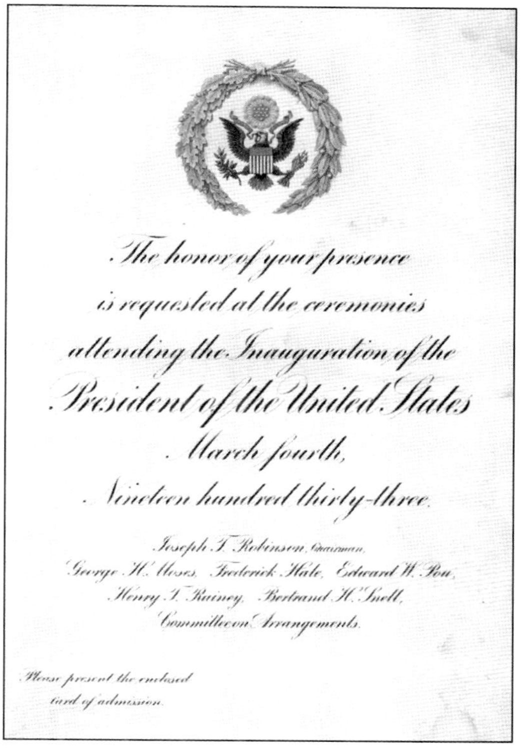

The honor of your presence
is requested at the ceremonies
attending the Inauguration of the
President of the United States
March fourth,
Nineteen hundred thirty-three.

Joseph T. Robinson, Chairman,
George H. Moses, Frederick Hale, Edward W. Pou,
Henry T. Rainey, Bertrand H. Snell,
Committee on Arrangements.

Please present the enclosed
card of admission.

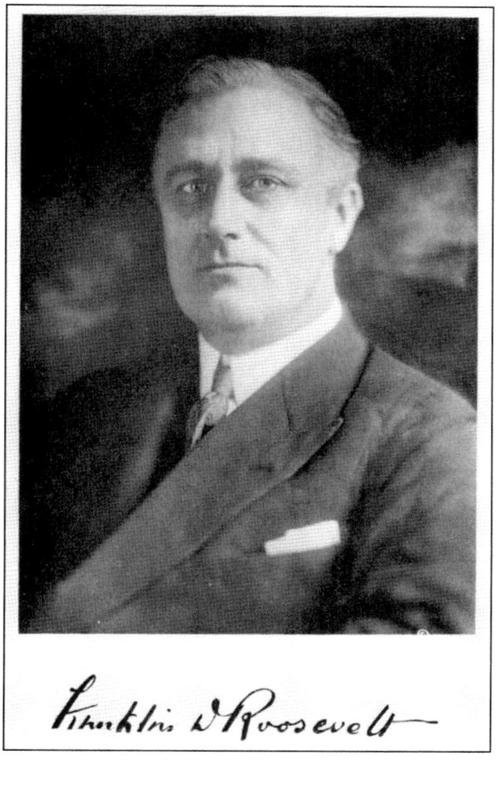

This photograph of Pres. Franklin D. Roosevelt with his signature was included as an insert in the inauguration invitation.

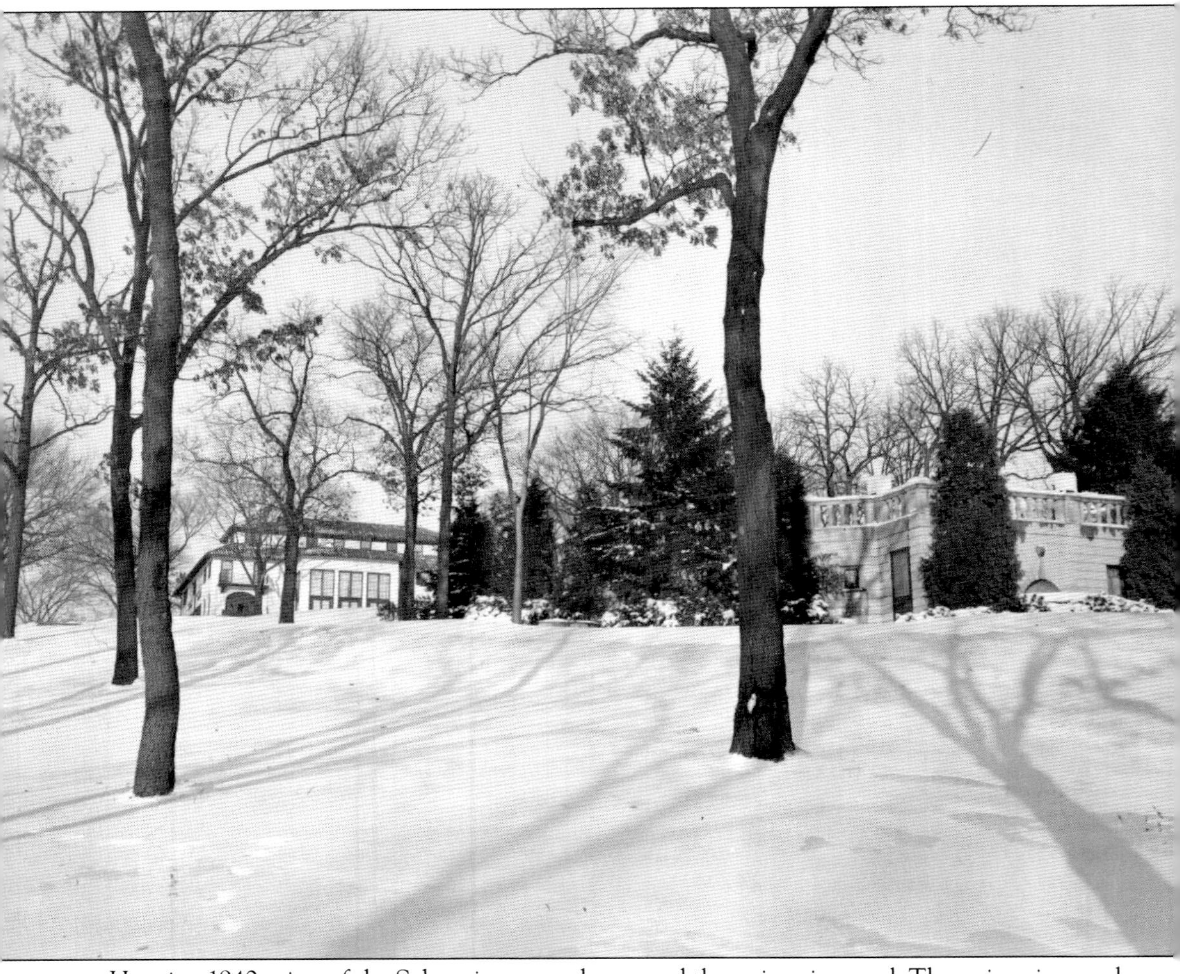

Here is a 1940s view of the Schnering estate home and the swimming pool. The swimming pool, built in 1923, is one of the original structures still used by the Trout Valley community.

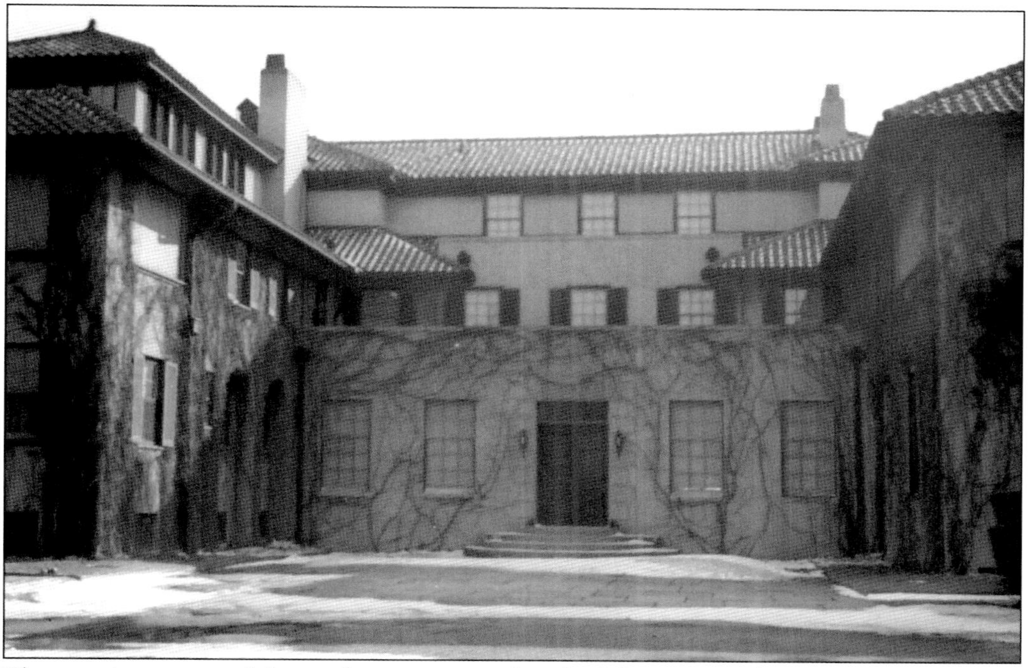

The mansion courtyard during the time it served as the Schnering residence is seen here around the 1940s.

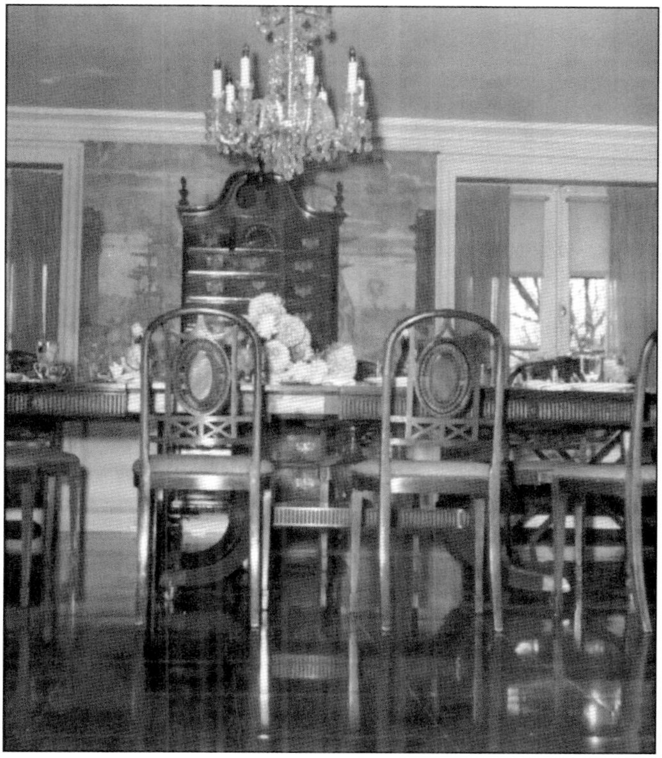

This 1940s photograph shows the dining room in the large estate home during the Curtiss Farm era.

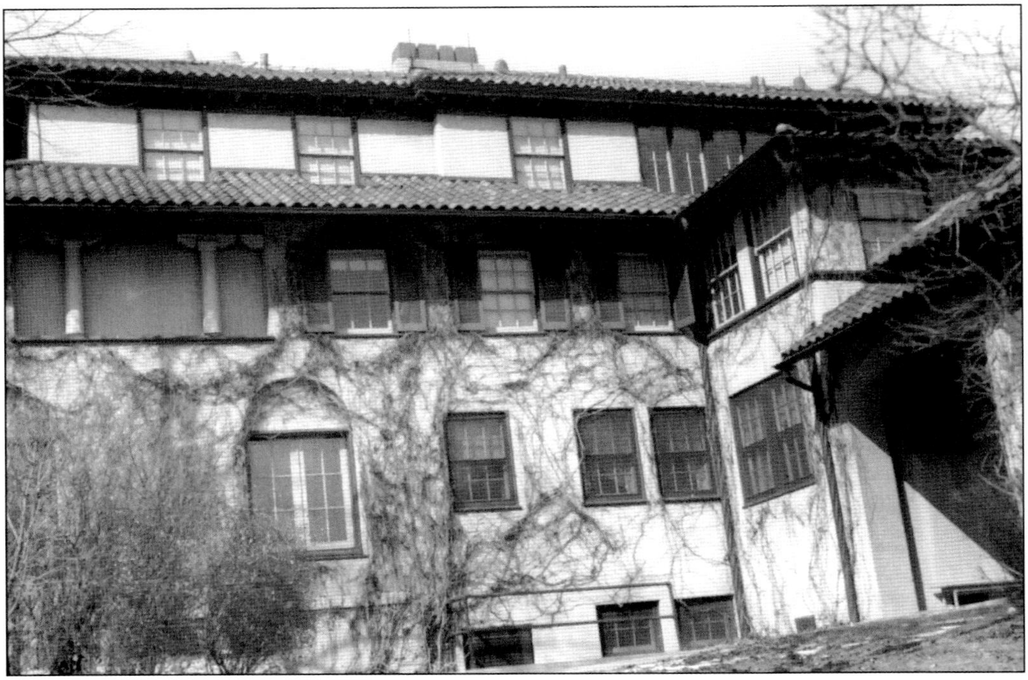

This estate home was occupied year-round as the Schnering's main family residence during the Curtiss Farm era, seen here around the 1940s. It is said that Otto and Dorothy Schnering first met on a blind date.

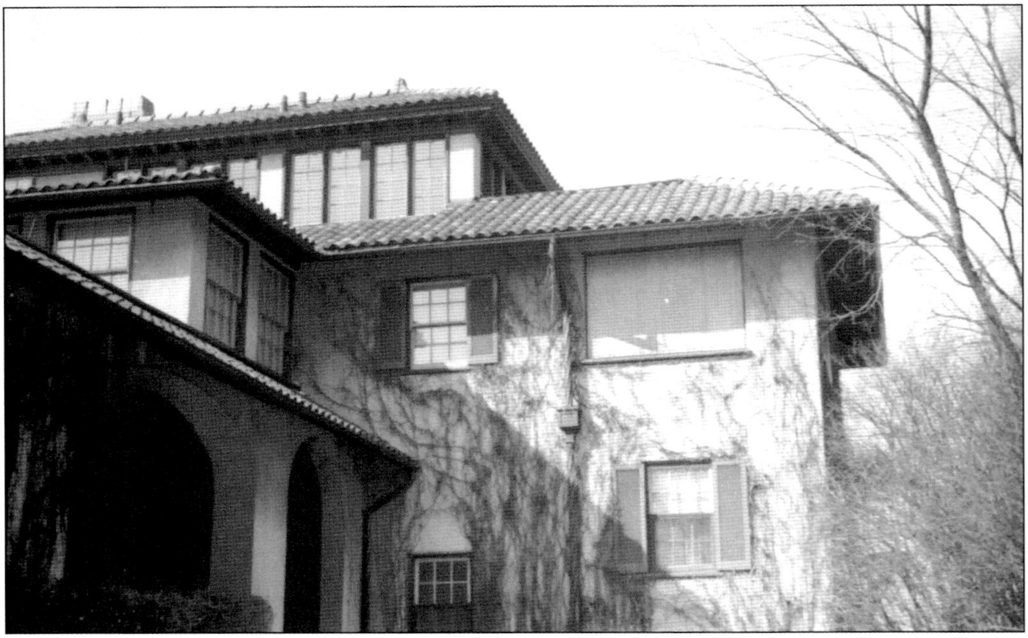

It was commonly noted that when visitors came to call at the Schnering residence, they were likely greeted first not by a staff member, but by Dorothy Schnering herself, who would often answer her own door and welcome guests to the Curtiss Farm. This image is from the 1940s.

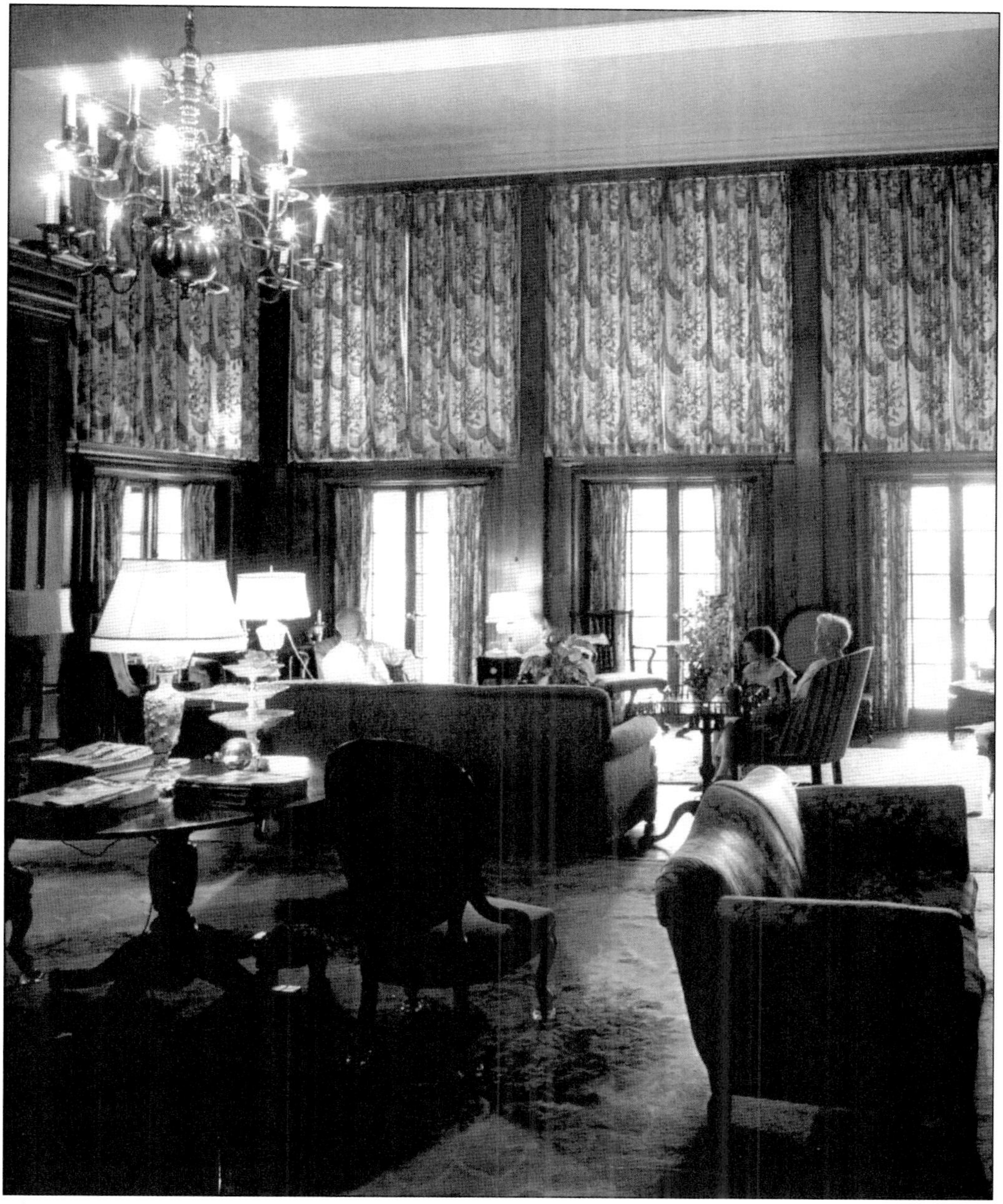

This is a 1940s photograph of Otto and Dorothy Schnering visiting with their granddaughter in the living room in the main residence estate. They had room set aside on the third floor of the main house for their grandchildren to stay. Even though it was expansive, this large estate home maintained the feel of a family residence. One story is told of the Schnerings' granddaughter Barb McFarland inspiring Otto to invent the Curtiss Saf-T-Pop with the soft fiber loop handle after her lollipop got stuck in her throat while rough housing in the Schnering home.

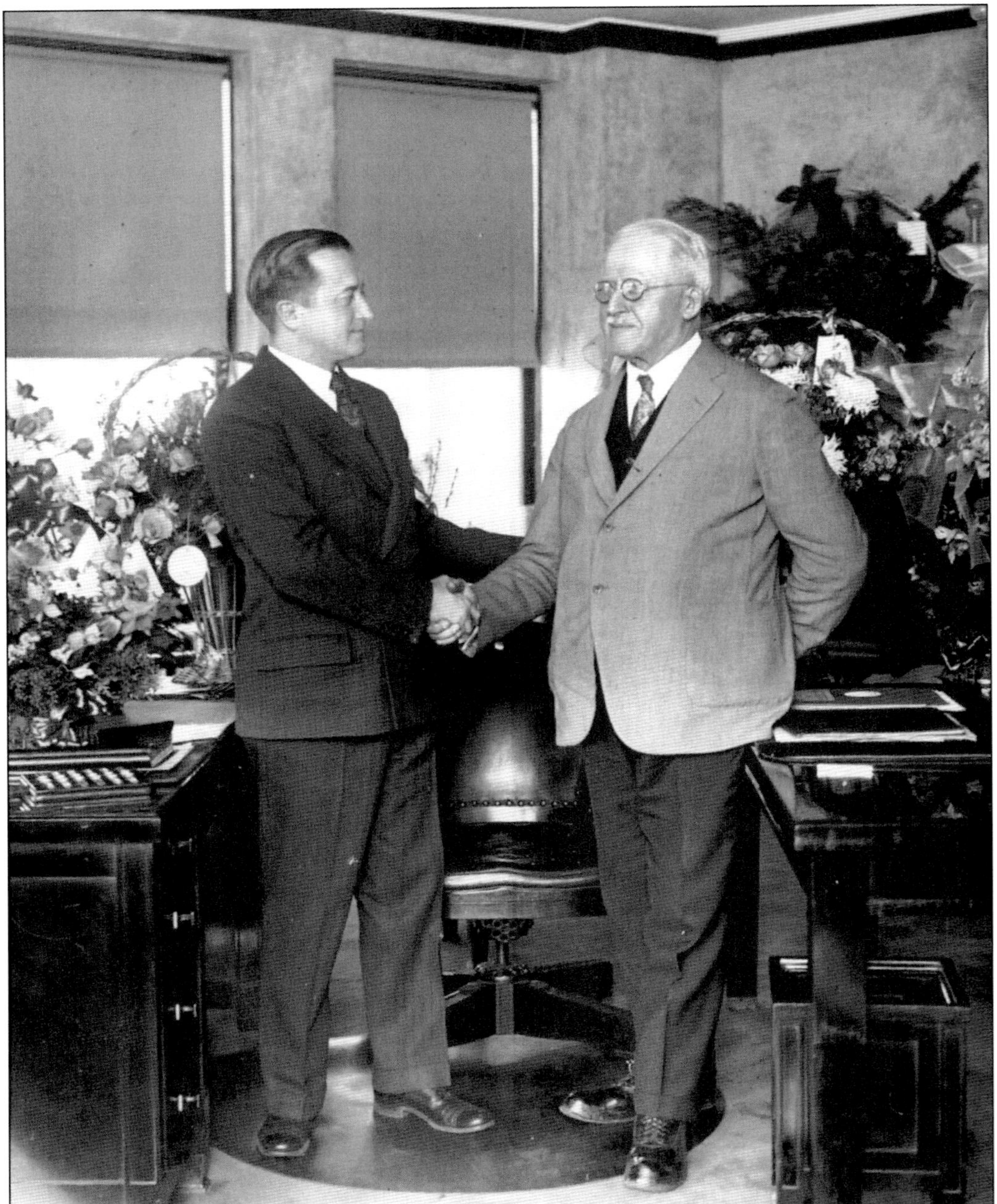

Otto Schnering poses with his father.

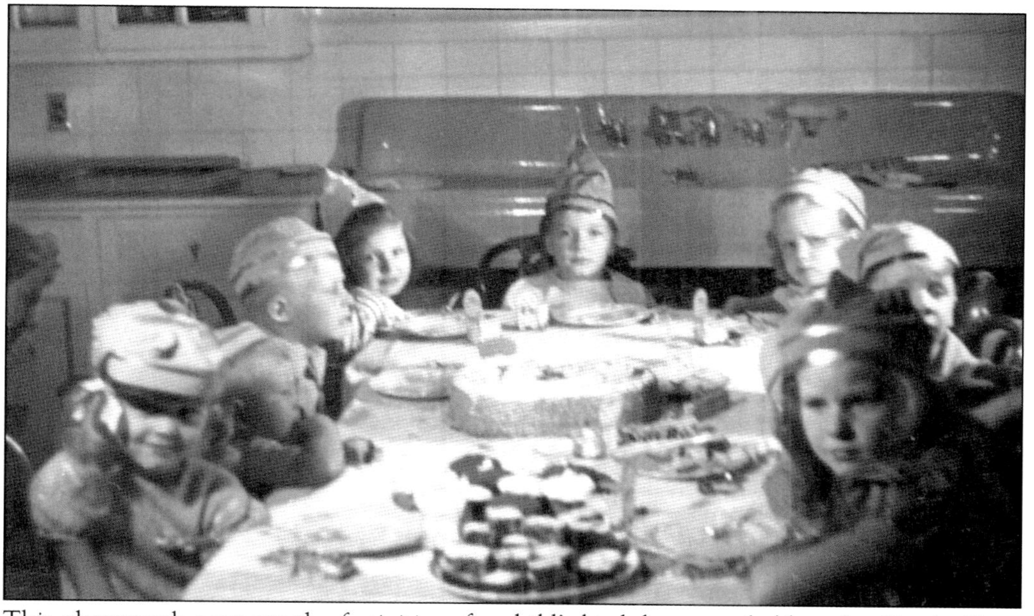

This photograph captures the festivities of a child's birthday party held at the Curtiss Farm Guest House, where the Vogel family lived. Children were always made to feel welcome on the Curtiss Farm estate. When Schnering's secretary Erna Vogel occasionally brought her daughter Barbie Vogel along with her to Schnering's library in the main residence, he was known to move a picture aside in order to open his office safe, where he stored a puzzle for the young girl to enjoy while her mother took dictation.

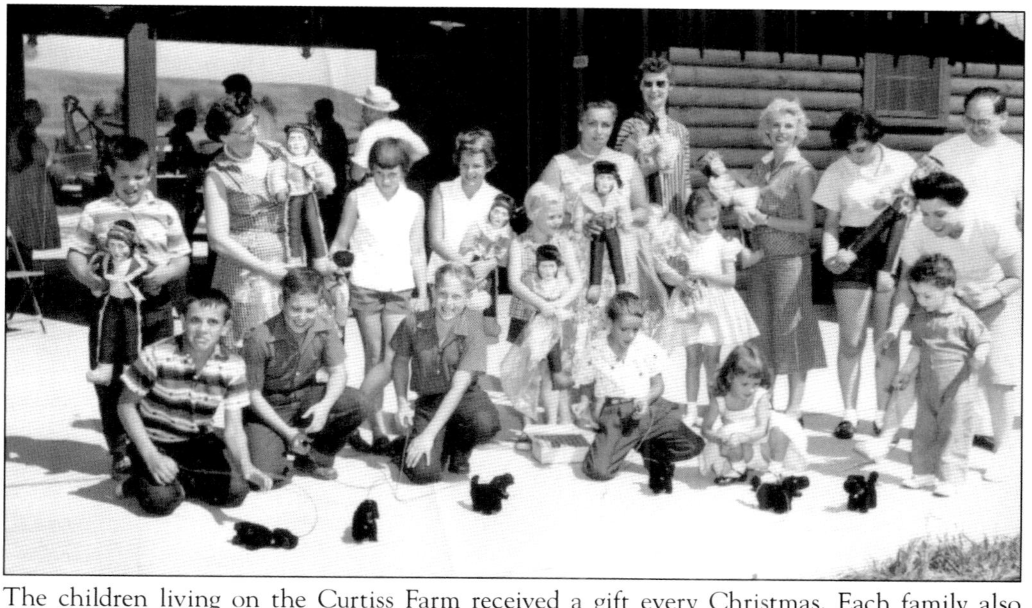

The children living on the Curtiss Farm received a gift every Christmas. Each family also received a turkey and a box filled with every variety of candy made by Curtiss Candy Company. The Curtiss Candy Company was one of the first businesses in the country to offer employment plans that included pensions and profit sharing, as well as health, accident, and life insurance programs for employees. His employees never appeared to show an interest in unionism.

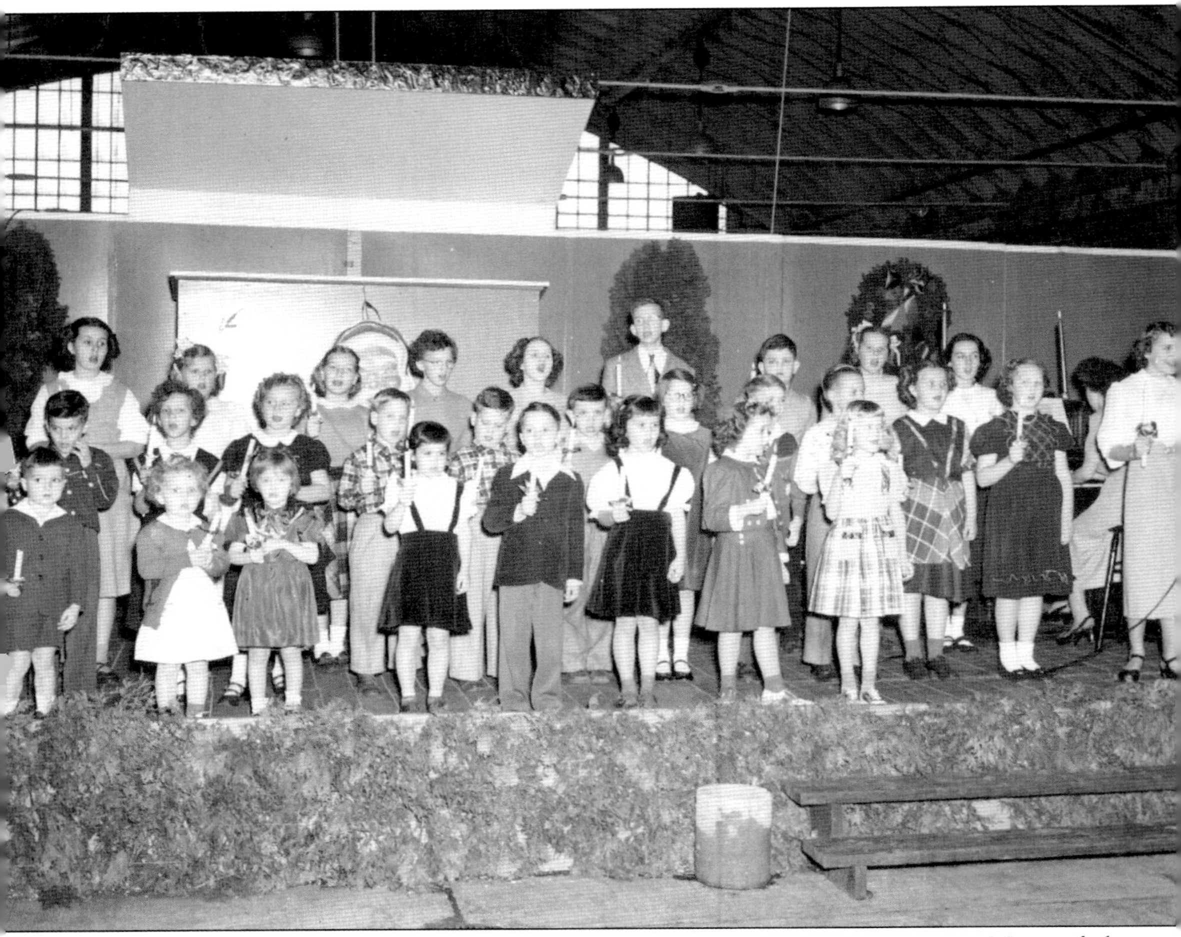

Children sang during the Christmas celebration at the Curtiss Farm estate. Many of the family-oriented holiday parties that were established by Otto Schnering still continue in Trout Valley every year.

This is a picture of one of Otto Schnering's granddaughters, taken during a Christmas party. The tradition of an annual children's Christmas party has continued in Trout Valley, and Santa still arrives each year to deliver gifts to the children. The Cary-Grove High School Swing Choir has often performed for this special event.

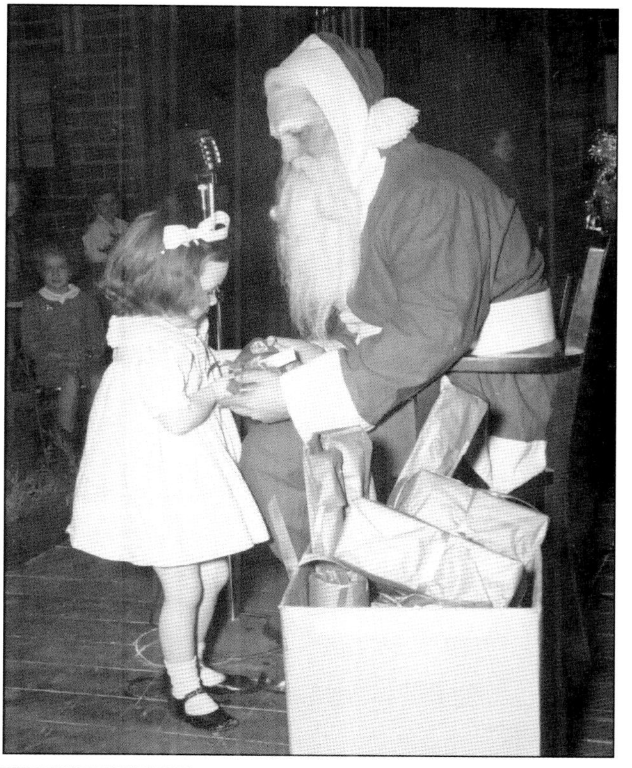

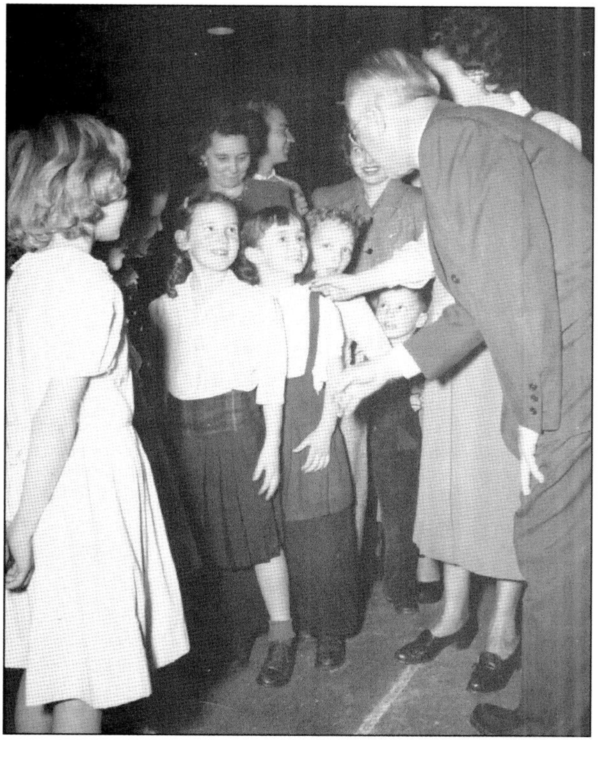

This photograph shows Otto Schnering greeting Mary Saer, Suzie Clark, Darryl Forrest, Tommy Kingston, and others at a Christmas party in 1948.

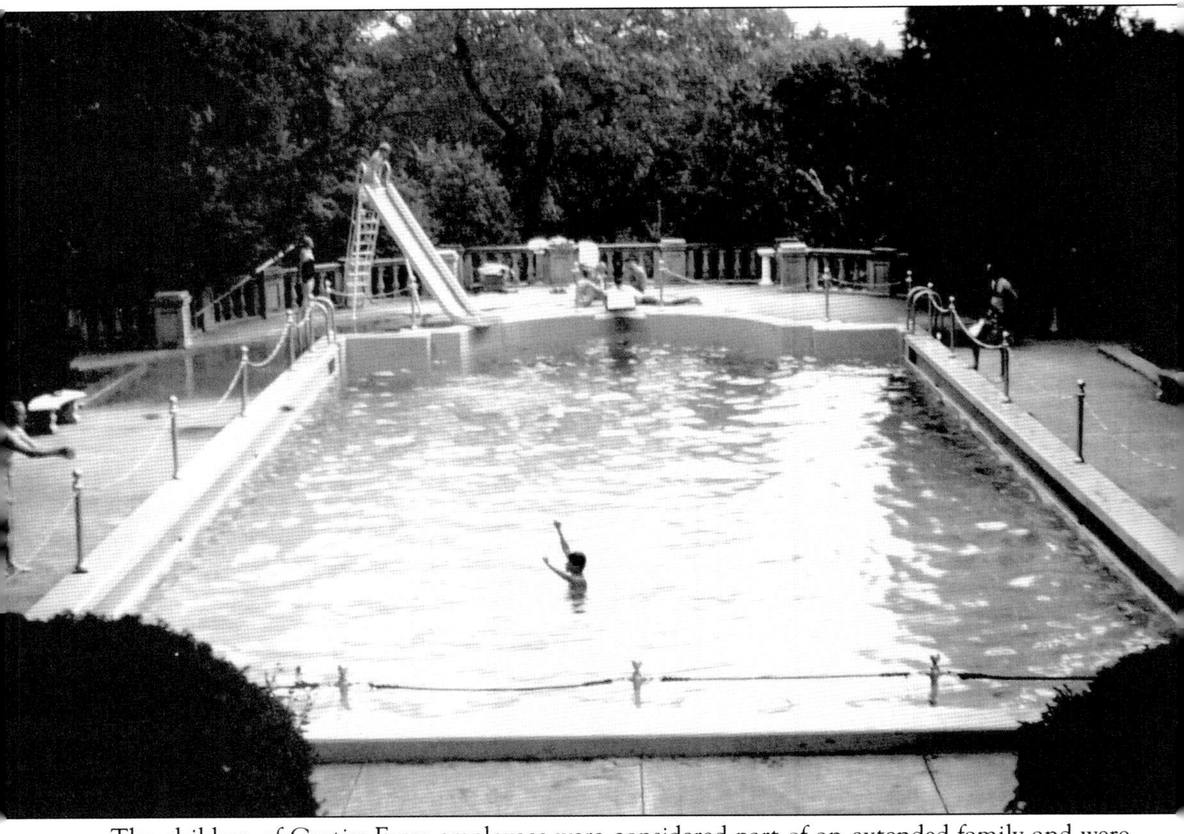

The children of Curtiss Farm employees were considered part of an extended family and were regularly allowed to enjoy the Curtiss Farm swimming pool. They were provided with swim lessons by an instructor at Otto Schnering's expense. Children were also seen playing year-round throughout the Curtiss Farm estate—riding bikes, playing badminton and baseball, enjoying complimentary horseback lessons, picking apples from the fruit orchard, sledding, ice-skating, and enjoying the occasional sleigh ride provided on the farm during winter. Families were also allowed to partake of the vast vegetable garden on the farm and received fresh eggs, milk, and chicken from the farm's stock.

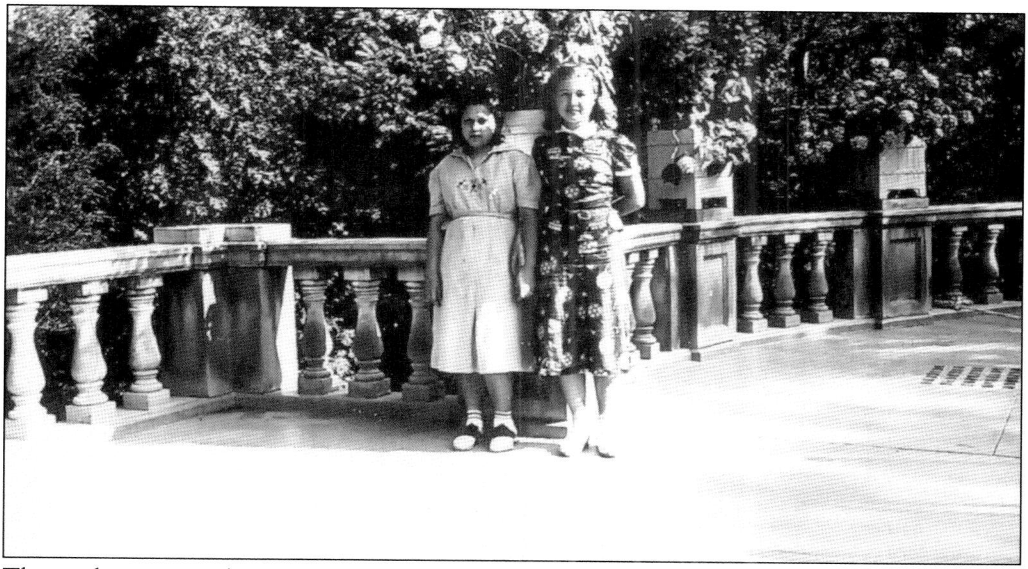

The pool was a popular recreational area for Curtiss Farm families.

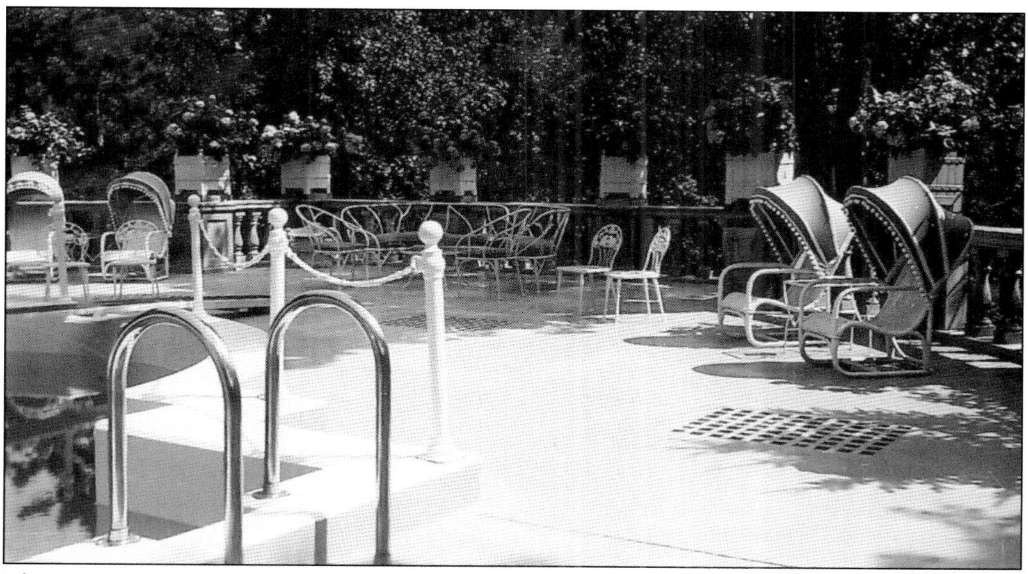

The estate swimming pool was the site of numerous parties during both the Hertz era and the Curtiss era. To this day it remains a recreational facility maintained and widely enjoyed by Trout Valley residents.

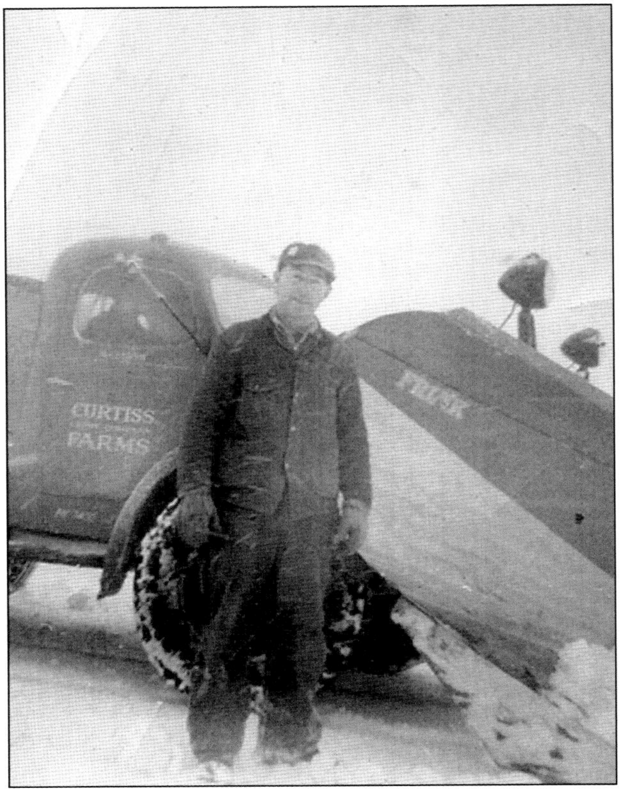

This is a photograph of Pat Fitzgerald in the large snow storm between Christmas and New Year's in 1951. Fitzgerald used the Curtiss Farm truck to plow the public Cary-Algonquin Road, as well as to rescue Otto Schnering who was snowbound on Route 62 at the time.

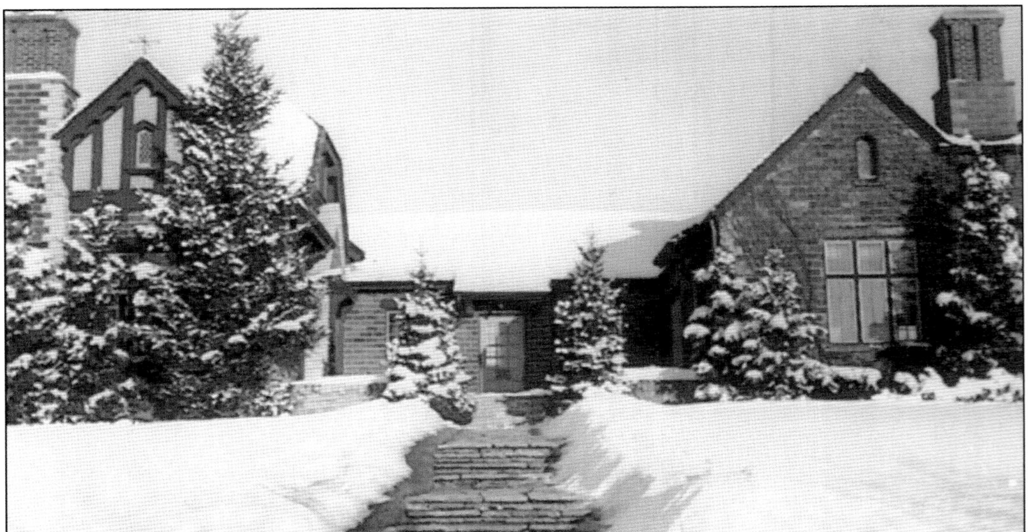

The structure that served as the Curtiss Farm main office now serves as the location of the administration building for the village of Cary.

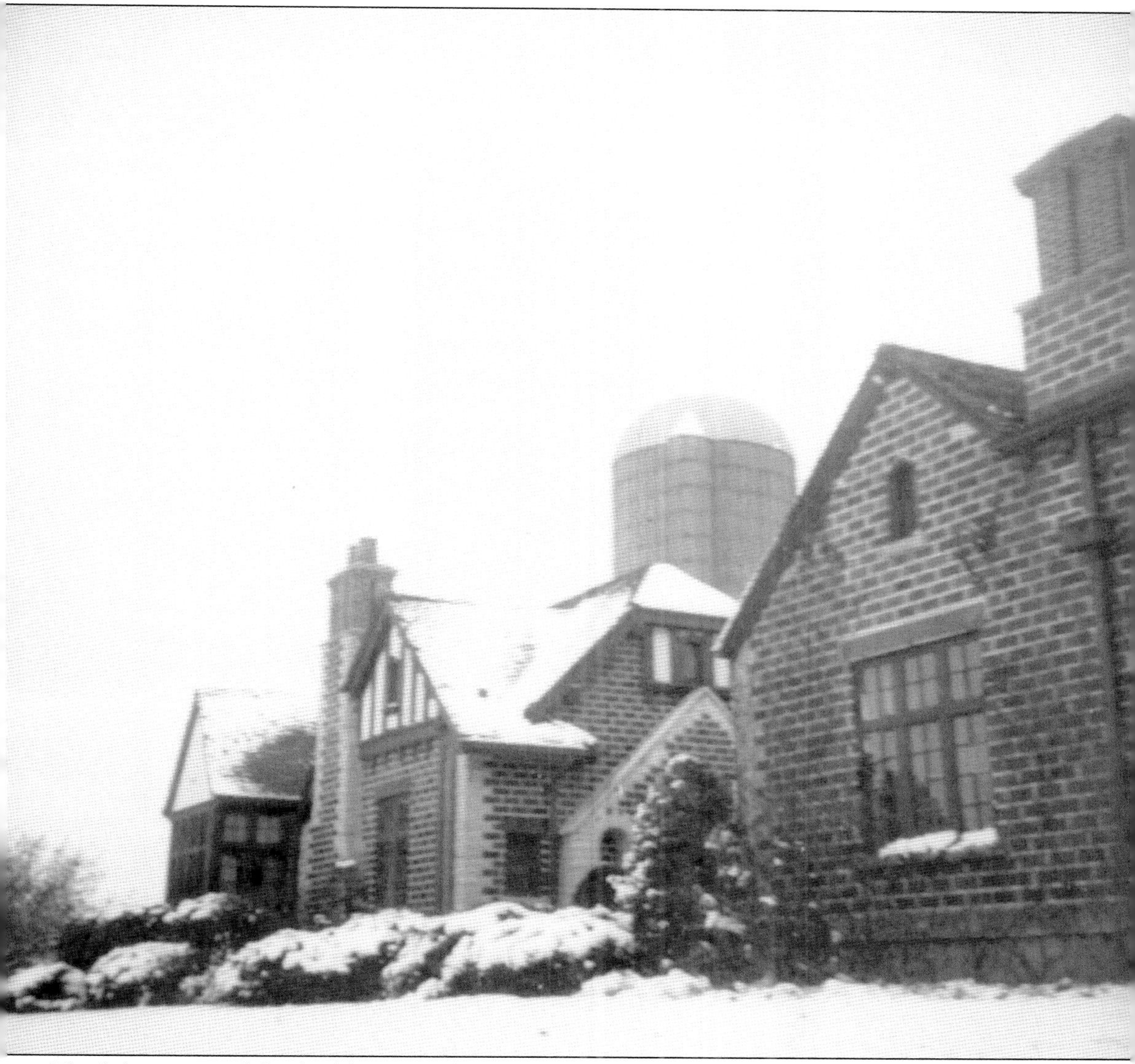

The left portion of this building served as the Curtiss Trophy Room where numerous trophies and blue ribbons won by Curtiss Farm livestock were on display. The center section was the Curtiss Farm main office, and the right portion of the building housed some of the employees who lived in residence on Curtiss Farm.

From the desk of

OTTO SCHNERING

One half of the 20th Century has now passed. What will the second half hold for us? That seems to be the big question. More mechanical and scientific progress has been made these last 50 years than in any similar period in history. Will we continue with that rate of progress?

But the big question is in regard to human relationships. Will the peoples of the world learn to live together better, to settle their difference peacefully, etc.?

I, as one individual in this big world, feel that we have made real progress these last 50 years. We still have lots of problems, but not as many as before. We are now willing to talk about our problems--that is real progress. So, there is plenty of hope for the years to come. We are getting ahead.

Otto Schnering updated employees regularly with a newsletter about what was happening in the company. This memo from Schnering was printed inside the front cover of the January 1950 bimonthly newsletter publication for employees of the Curtiss Candy Company.

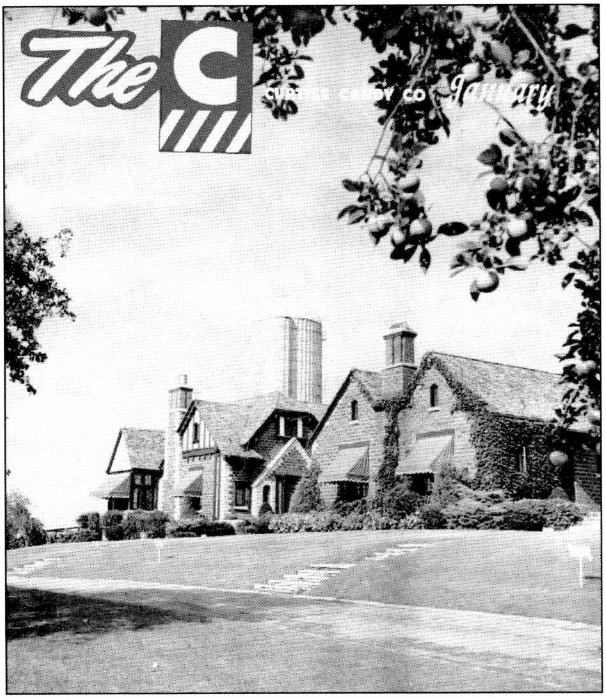

This is the cover photograph for the January 1950 employee newsletter publication for the Curtiss Candy Company.

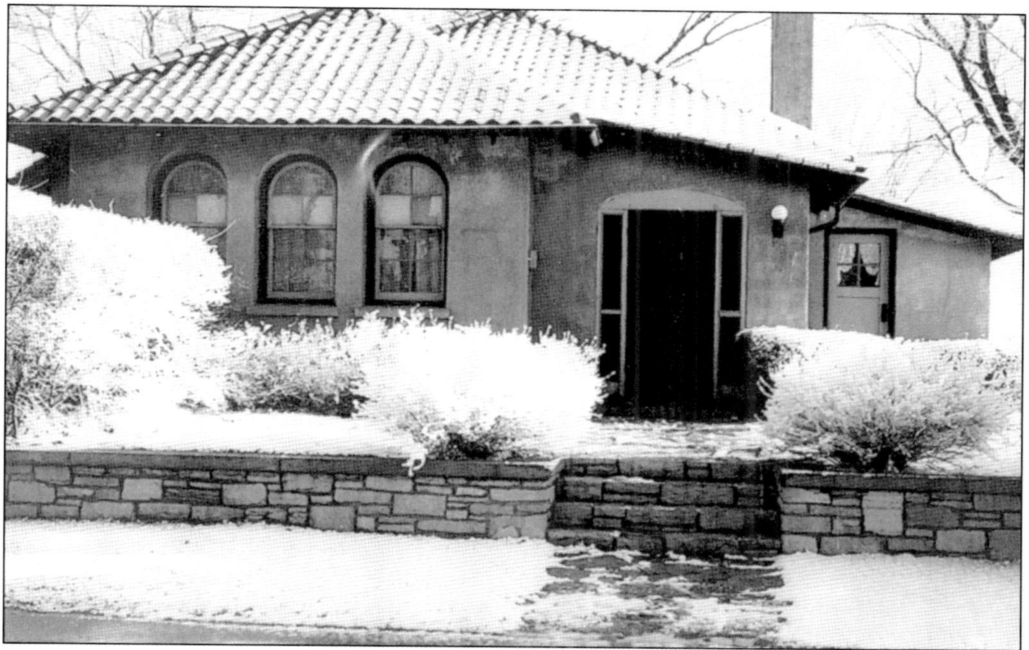

The gatehouse was the home of Edwin Anderson during the Hertz era. Later Hertz hired Edwin's son Arthur Anderson, who worked for Hertz for 12 years and then later for Schnering for 33 years. Arthur and Grace Anderson had twin boys, Elmer and George, while living on the Curtiss Farm estate. A pair of twin bulls born on the farm was later named after Elmer and George. One of the other gatehouses of Curtiss Farms served as the home of Schnering employees Hilding and Jenny Johnson and their two daughters, Nancy and Jeanette.

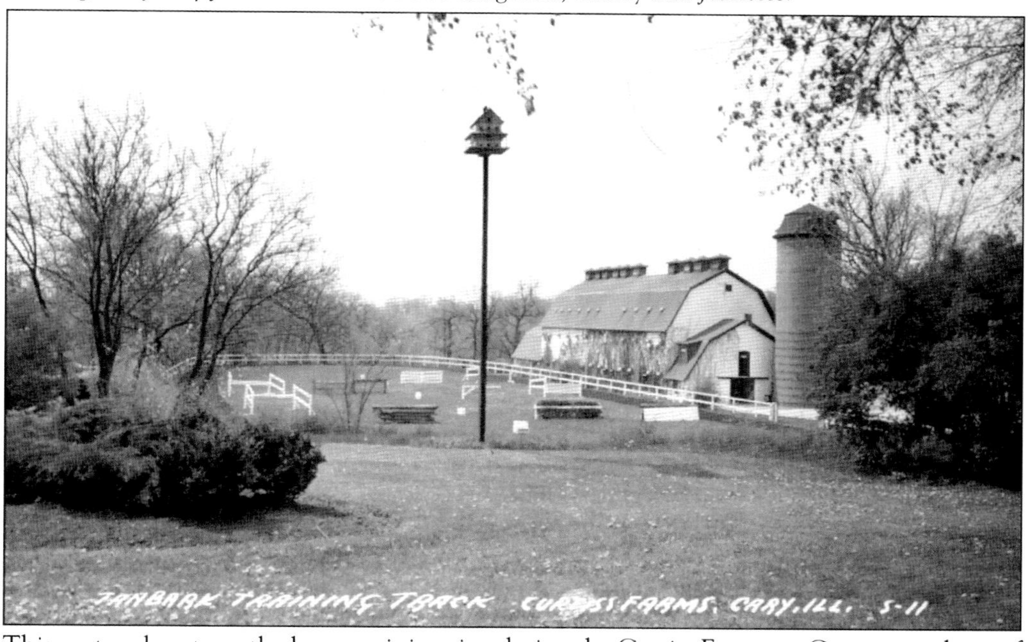

This postcard portrays the horse training ring during the Curtiss Farm era. Current residents of Trout Valley still use this area for the same purpose.

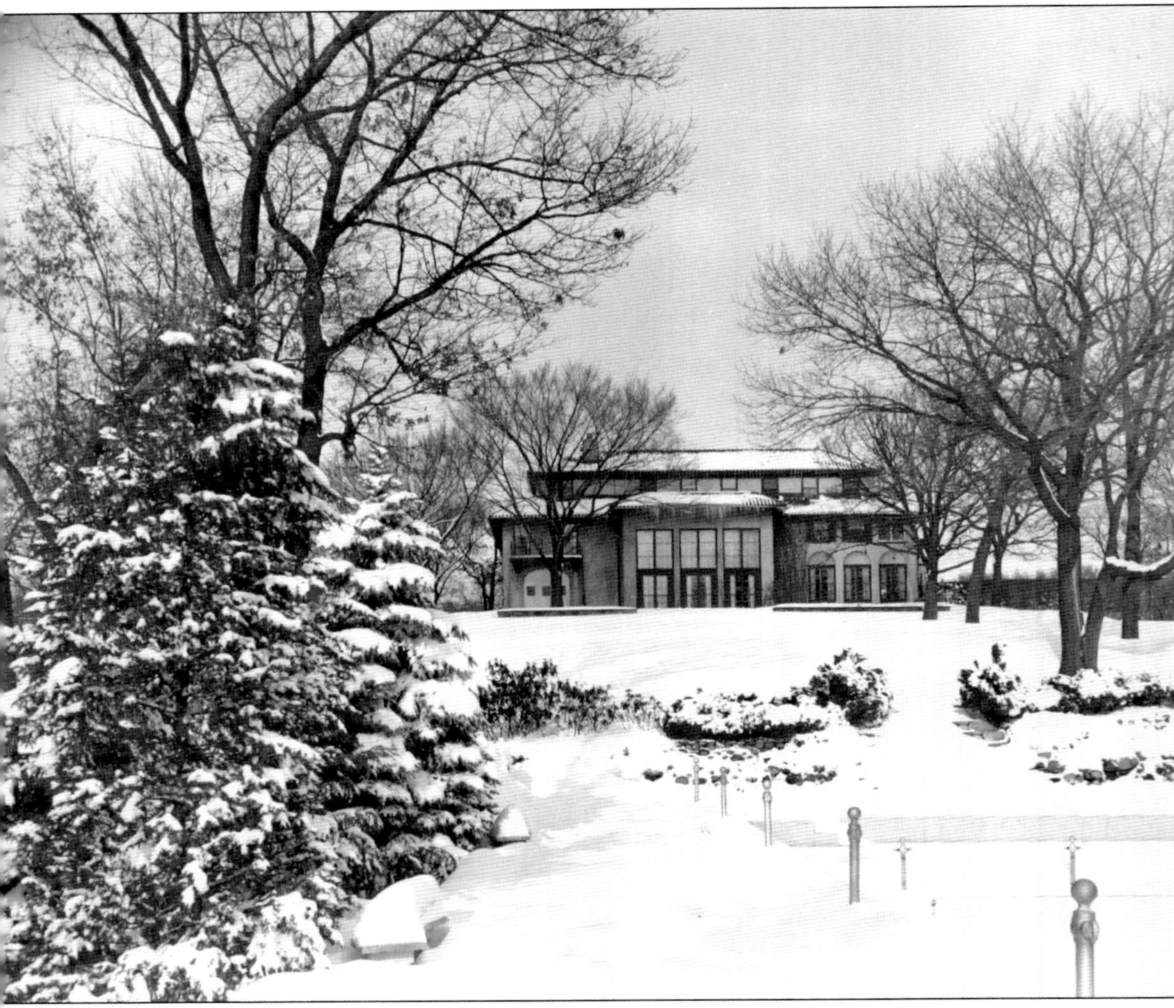

The estate is shown here covered in snow during a frosty Midwestern winter.

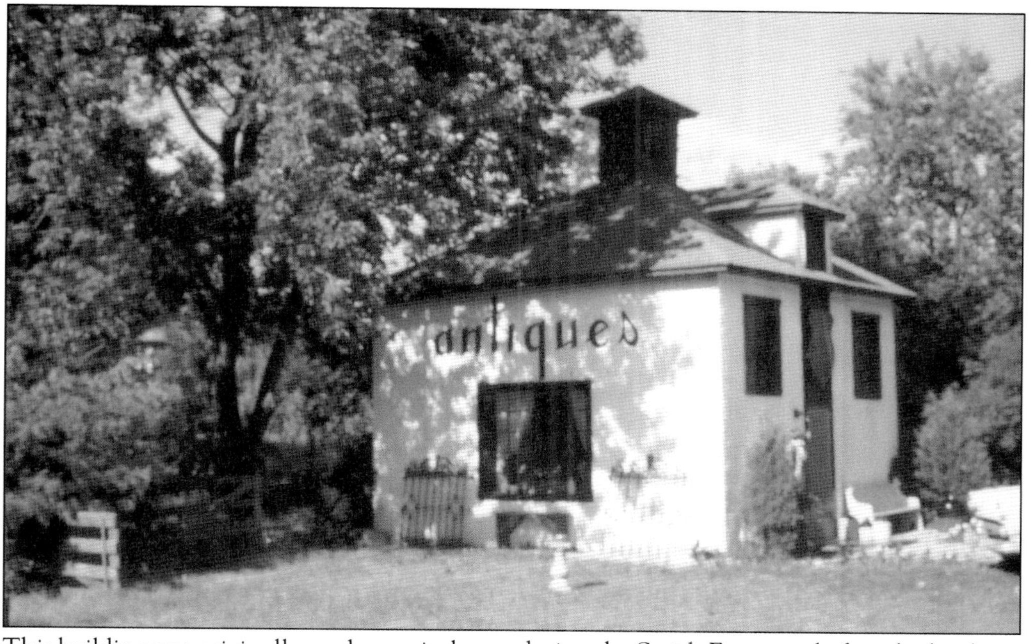

This building was originally used as an icehouse during the Smith Farm era, before the land was purchased by John D. Hertz or Otto Schnering. After the land was sold to private developers, it served as an antique store during the late 1950s. It is seen here around 1960.

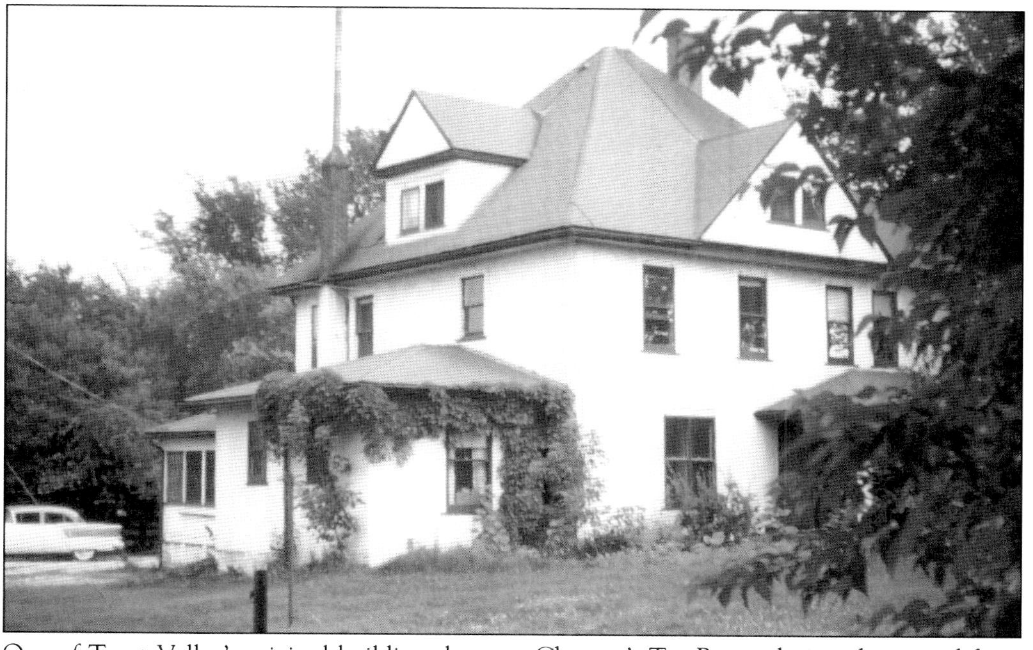

One of Trout Valley's original buildings became Chantry's Tea Room during the period from 1958 to 1961, after Schnering sold the land. This building still stands, and in more recent years, it has served as the site of Cary Country Preschool and headquarters for the charitable organization Giving Real Opportunities to Women, otherwise known as GROW. It is seen here around 1960.

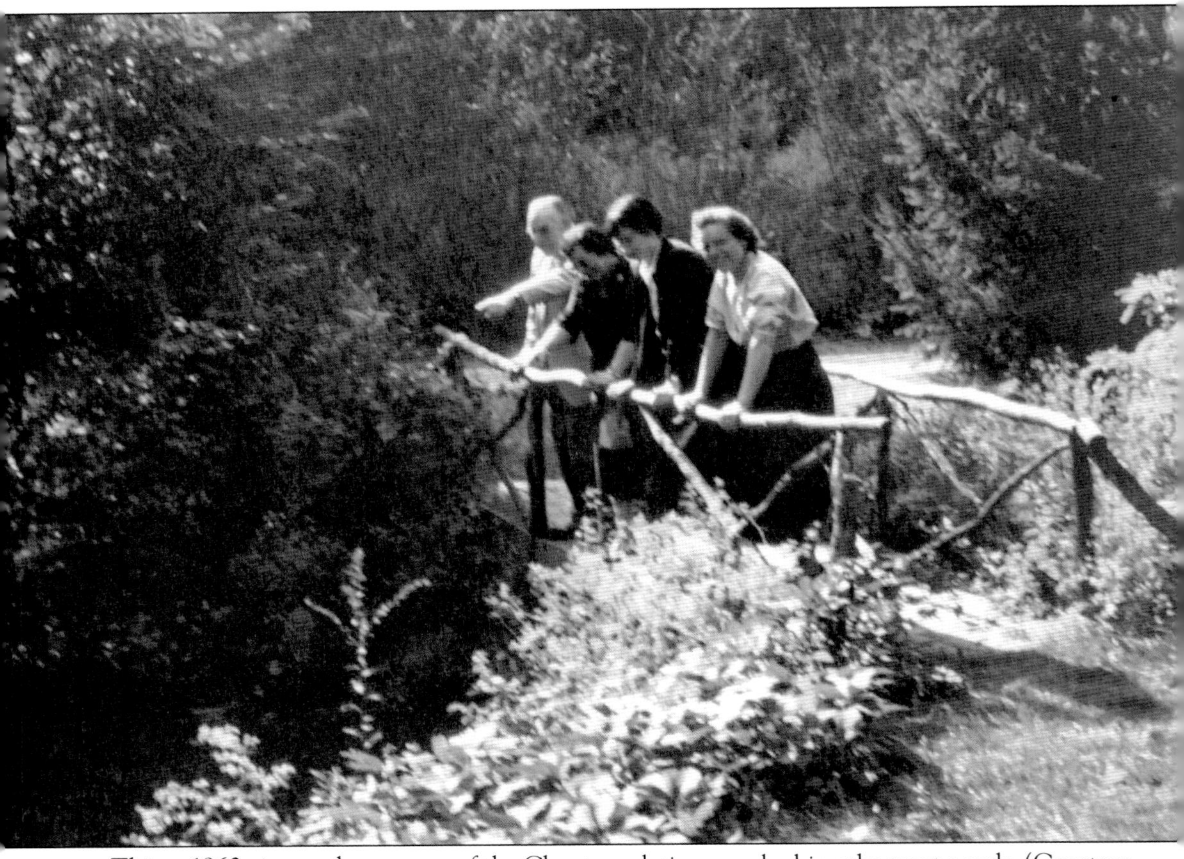

This c. 1960 picture shows some of the Chantry relatives overlooking the trout ponds. (Courtesy of David Chantry.)

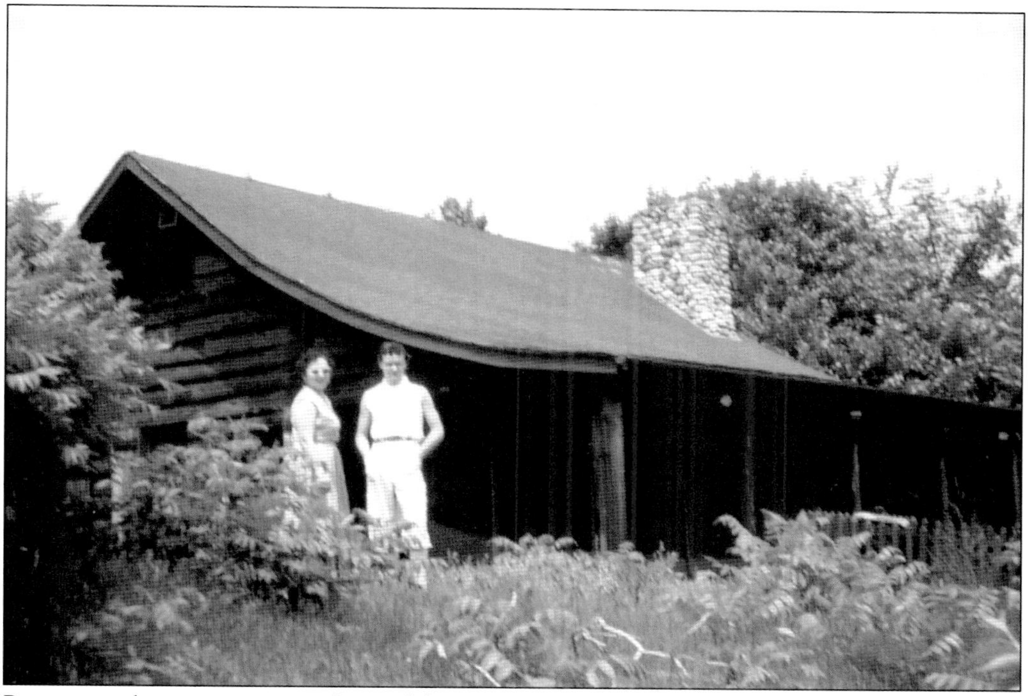

Prospective buyers are seen in front of the Bond Cottage, shortly after Curtiss Farm was sold.

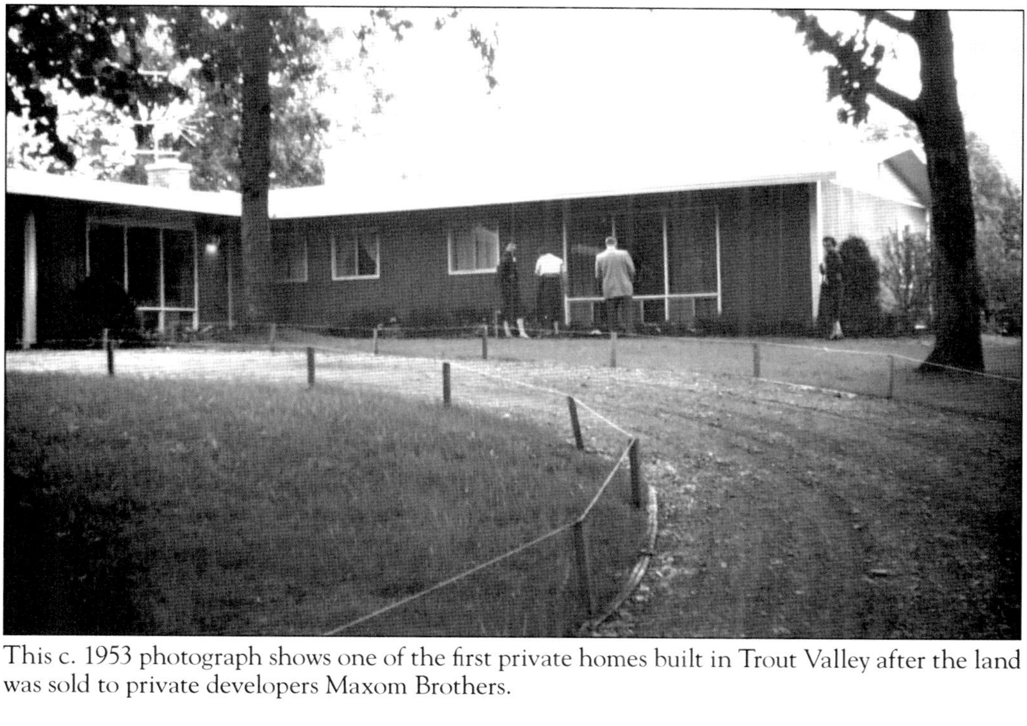

This c. 1953 photograph shows one of the first private homes built in Trout Valley after the land was sold to private developers Maxom Brothers.

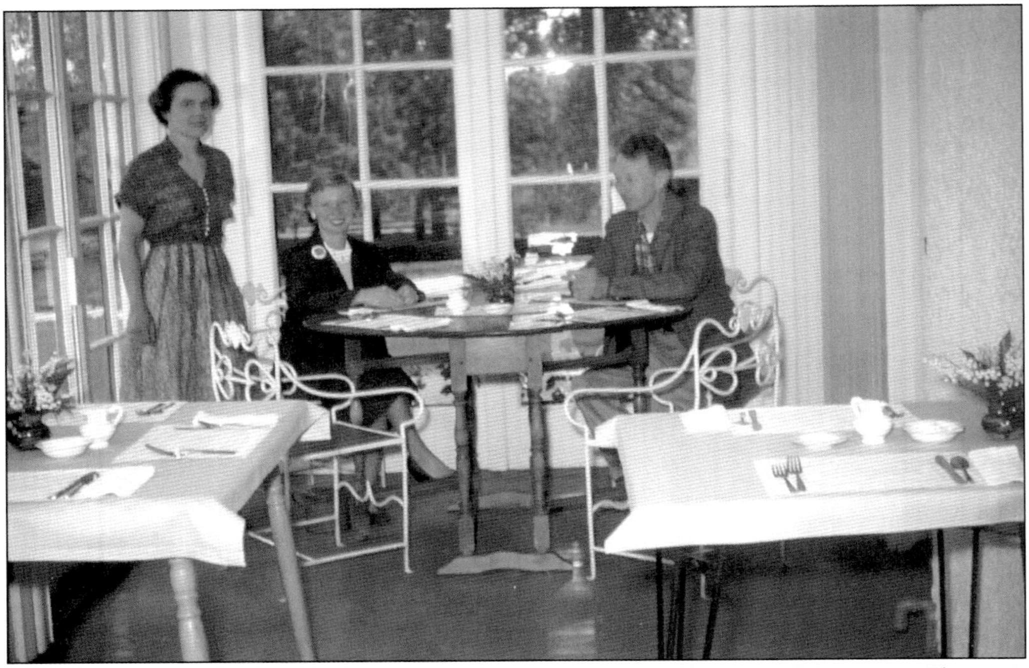

Phyllis Chantry is seen here around 1960 with Robert and Louise Sinnett in Chantry's Tea Room.

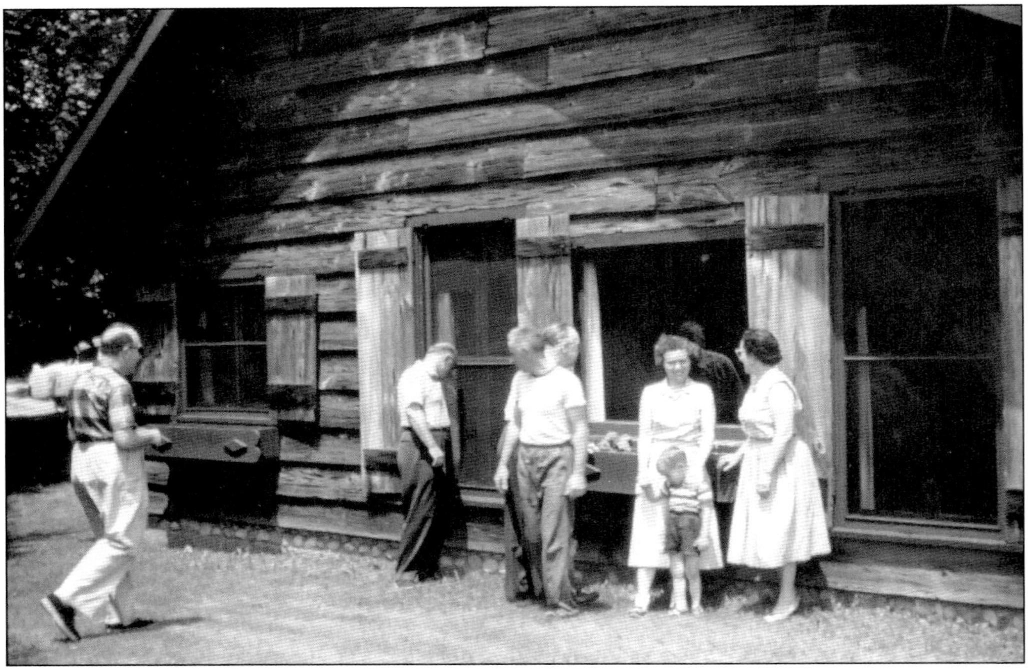

Relatives of Phyllis Chantry are shown here around 1960 at the Bond Cottage, another of the original buildings. The Sinnett family resided at the cottage after the Curtiss Farm era.

This is a c. 1960 picture of Doris Fonda in the antique shop that earlier served as the Smith Farm icehouse.

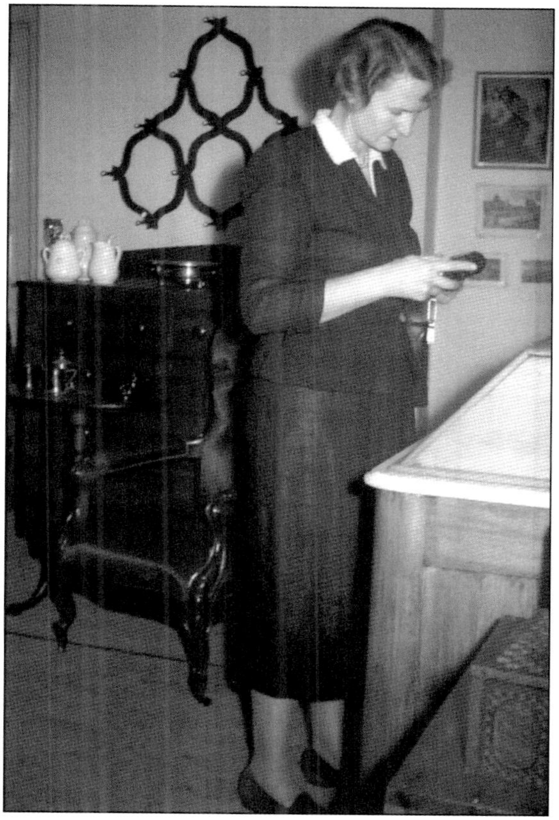

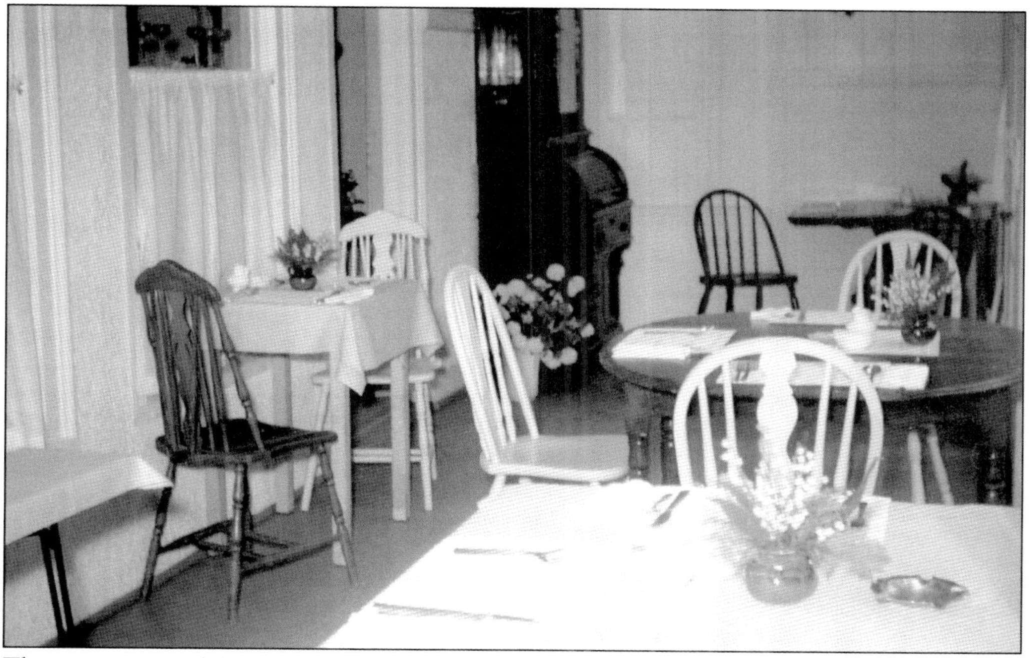

This is a picture of the interior of Chantry's Tea Room.

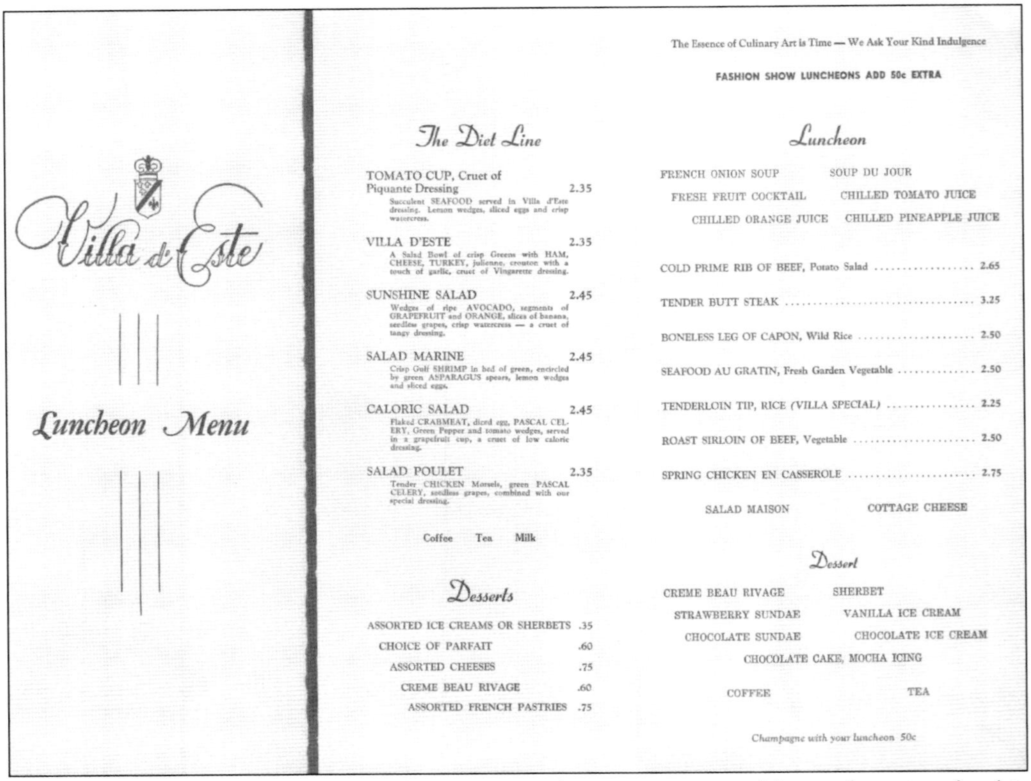

Villa d'Este

Luncheon Menu

The Essence of Culinary Art is Time — We Ask Your Kind Indulgence

FASHION SHOW LUNCHEONS ADD 50c EXTRA

The Diet Line

TOMATO CUP, Cruet of Piquante Dressing 2.35
Succulent SEAFOOD served in Villa d'Este dressing. Lemon wedges, sliced eggs and crisp watercress.

VILLA D'ESTE 2.35
A Salad Bowl of crisp Greens with HAM, CHEESE, TURKEY, julienne, crouton with a touch of garlic, cruet of Vingarette dressing.

SUNSHINE SALAD 2.45
Wedges of ripe AVOCADO, segments of GRAPEFRUIT and ORANGE, slices of banana, seedless grapes, crisp watercress — a cruet of tangy dressing.

SALAD MARINE 2.45
Crisp Gulf SHRIMP in bed of green, encircled by green ASPARAGUS spears, lemon wedges and sliced eggs.

CALORIC SALAD 2.45
Flaked CRABMEAT, diced egg, PASCAL CELERY, Green Pepper and tomato wedges, served in a grapefruit cup, a cruet of low calorie dressing.

SALAD POULET 2.35
Tender CHICKEN Morsels, green PASCAL CELERY, seedless grapes, combined with our special dressing.

Coffee Tea Milk

Desserts

ASSORTED ICE CREAMS OR SHERBETS .35
CHOICE OF PARFAIT .60
ASSORTED CHEESES .75
CREME BEAU RIVAGE .60
ASSORTED FRENCH PASTRIES .75

Luncheon

FRENCH ONION SOUP SOUP DU JOUR
FRESH FRUIT COCKTAIL CHILLED TOMATO JUICE
CHILLED ORANGE JUICE CHILLED PINEAPPLE JUICE

COLD PRIME RIB OF BEEF, Potato Salad 2.65
TENDER BUTT STEAK 3.25
BONELESS LEG OF CAPON, Wild Rice 2.50
SEAFOOD AU GRATIN, Fresh Garden Vegetable 2.50
TENDERLOIN TIP, RICE (VILLA SPECIAL) 2.25
ROAST SIRLOIN OF BEEF, Vegetable 2.50
SPRING CHICKEN EN CASSEROLE 2.75

SALAD MAISON COTTAGE CHEESE

Dessert

CREME BEAU RIVAGE SHERBET
STRAWBERRY SUNDAE VANILLA ICE CREAM
CHOCOLATE SUNDAE CHOCOLATE ICE CREAM
CHOCOLATE CAKE, MOCHA ICING

COFFEE TEA

Champagne with your luncheon 50c

This is a sample of the c. 1963 Villa d'Este's original restaurant menu. Notice the prices for this elegant fine dining restaurant during this time period. (Courtesy of Sue Sheetz.)

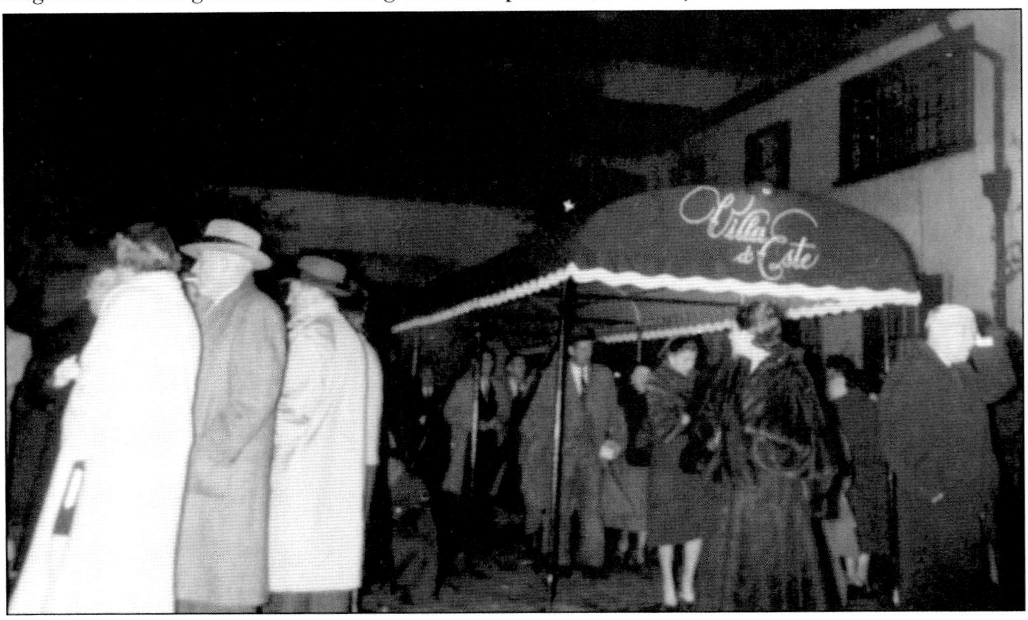

This c. 1968 picture shows guests arriving to dine at the upscale Villa d'Este restaurant. During the Hertz era and the Curtiss era, this building served as the main residence house.

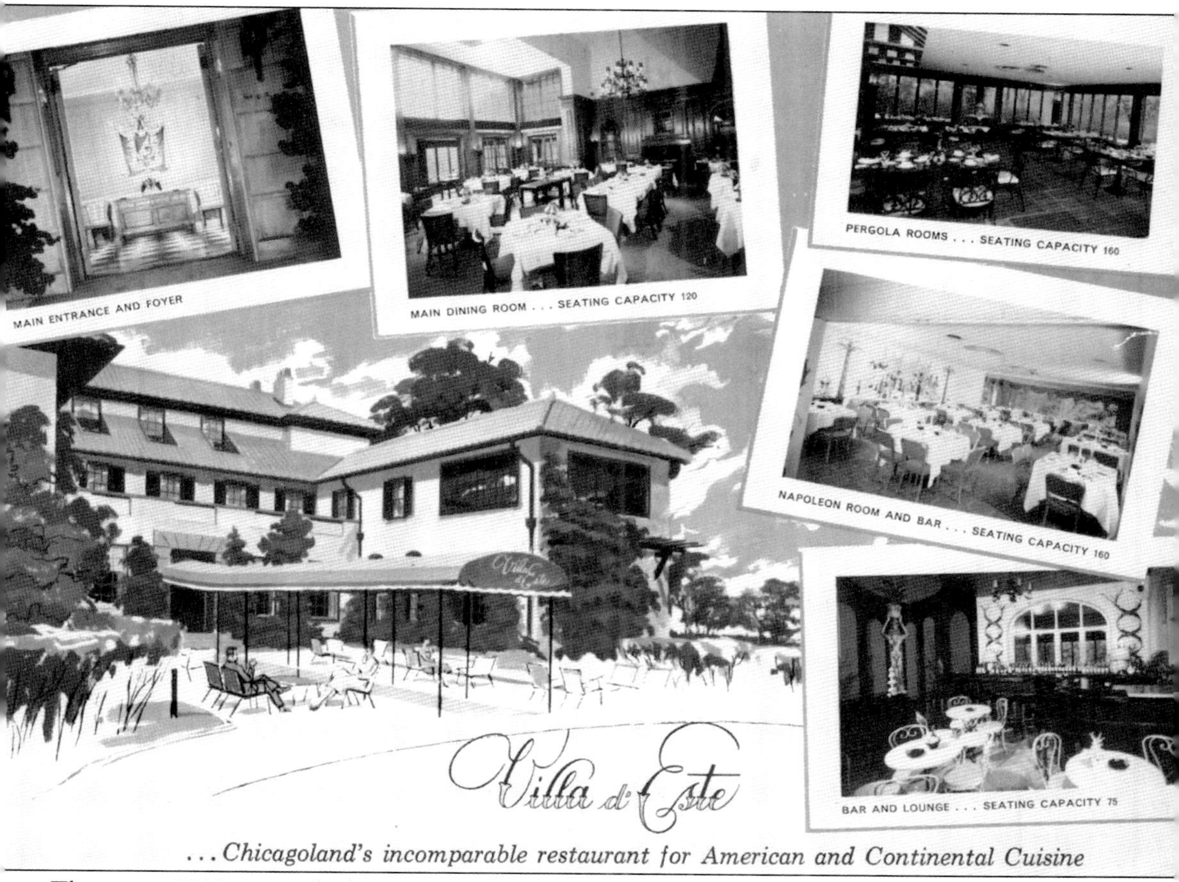

This is a c. 1968 postcard advertisement for the Villa d'Este restaurant.

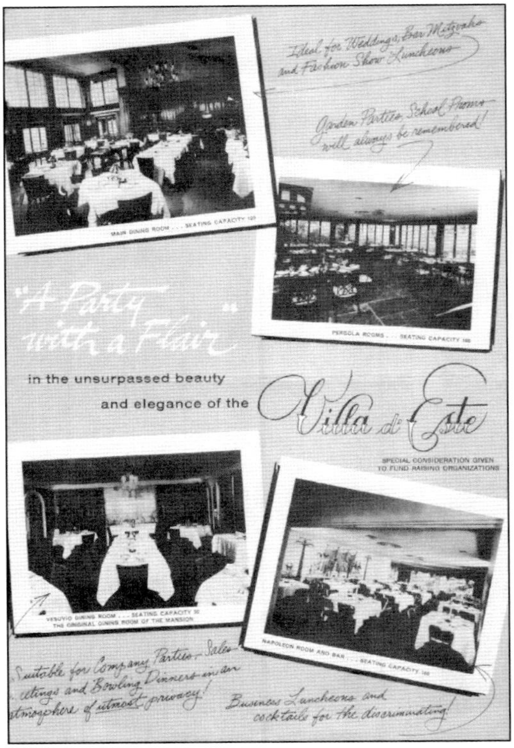

This is a c. 1968 advertisement for the Villa d'Este restaurant, which featured luxury dining in an elegant country setting along the Fox River. The restaurant featured fashion show luncheons.

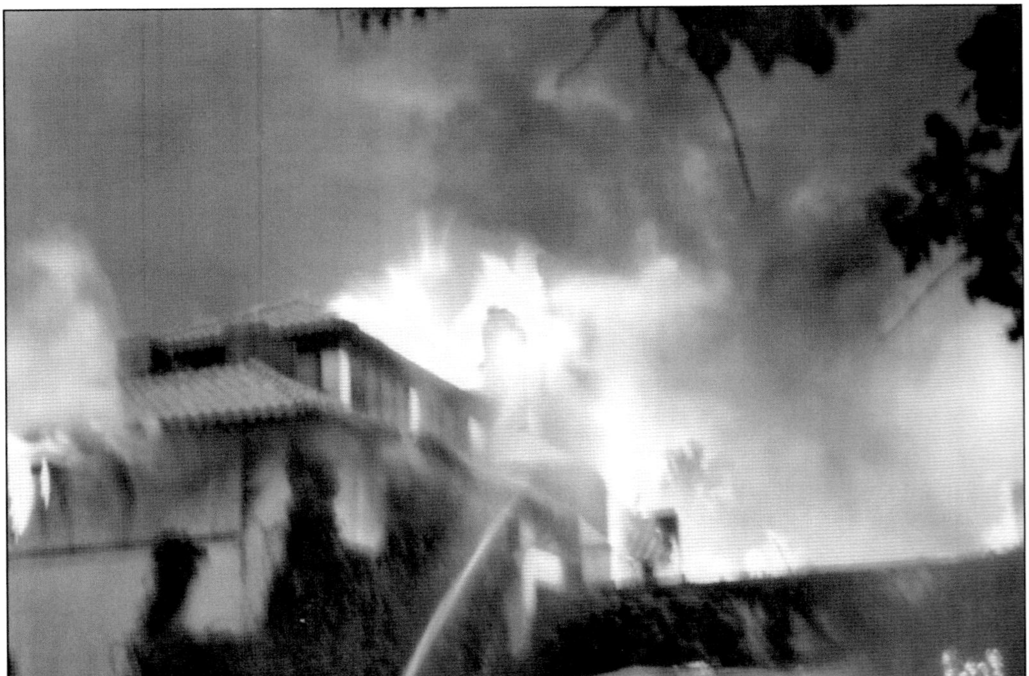

In September 1973, the Villa d'Este restaurant mysteriously burnt to the ground the night before it was to be sold to a new owner. (Courtesy of Keith and Ken Wolters.)

Three

Curtiss Farm Breeding Service

In addition to being the nation's "Candy King," Otto Schnering was also a noted farmer and breeder of prize livestock. He displayed a true passion for livestock farming and was the owner of prized bulls Netherhall Swanky Dan and St. James Philosophers Barbee, among others.

Schnering kept Curtiss Farm immaculately clean, and he produced many innovations in the practice of raising livestock. While other farms at the time had calf mortality rates ranging from 25 to 40 percent, mortality rates for young cows at Curtiss Farm were near zero.

As an example of both his humor and his personal attention to the care of his animals, Schnering was known for displaying a sign in the cow barn that read: "Every cow on this farm is a lady, and should be treated as such."

Schnering launched the first large-scale system of breeding cattle by means of artificial insemination. He sold this service nationwide, and results were guaranteed. Prices ranged from $7 (for "pool" semen from an unspecified bull) up to $150 (produced by a specified sire). Special salesmen were employed to deliver products anywhere in the United States within 24 hours by way of special refrigeration units.

In 1949, Schnering made this statement: "Except for television, artificial breeding is the fastest growing business in the U.S."

After the death of her husband in 1953, Dorothy Schnering persuaded the candy company board of directors to leave the breeding service portion of the business in her capable hands. Under her direction, this portion of the business was renamed Curtiss Breeding Service, Inc., and became a separate entity from the candy company. Dorothy held the controlling interest of the breeding service, and she invited company employees to purchase shares of her personally owned stocks, resulting in employees becoming part owners of the company.

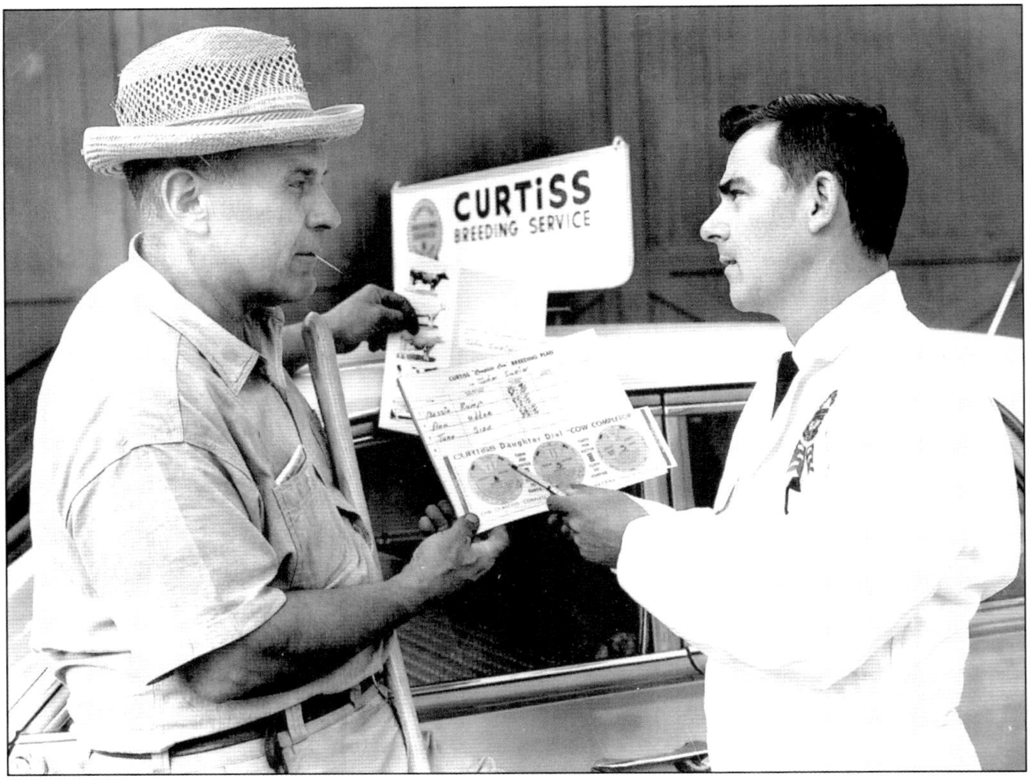

This picture shows Art Anderson (left) and Dick Haegele discussing the Curtiss Breeding Service cows. (Courtesy of Elmer Anderson.)

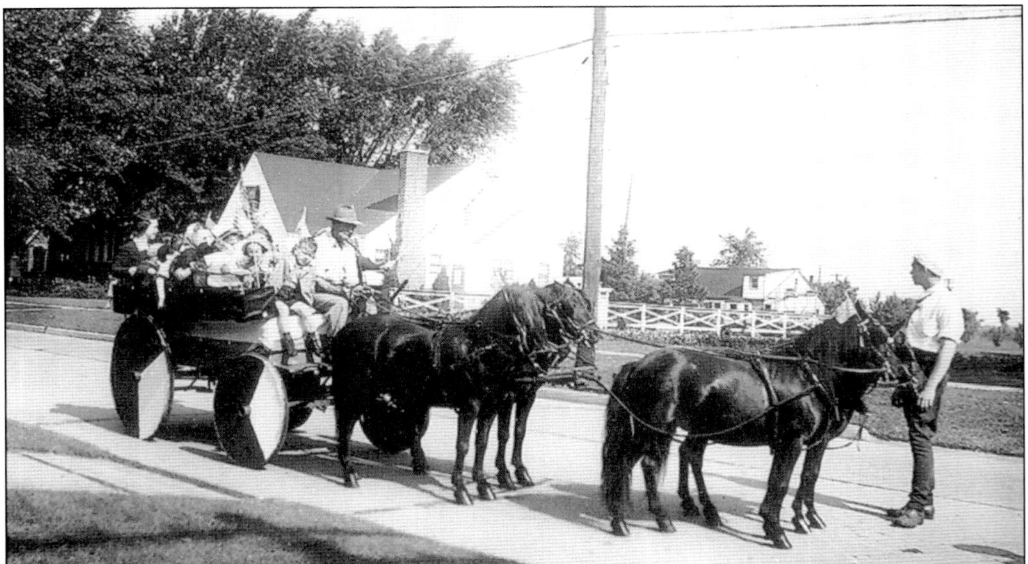

The Curtiss Farm wagon and six-pony hitch marched in many parades, including this one held in Cary.

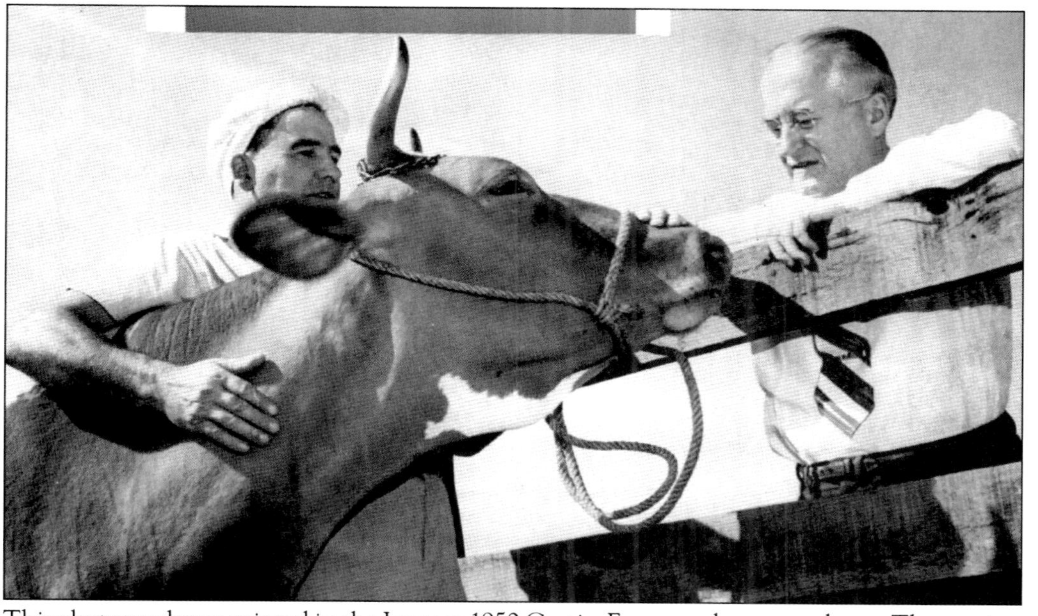

This photograph was printed in the January 1950 Curtiss Farm employee newsletter. The caption below the picture stated: "Founder of the Curtiss Farm system is soft-spoken, quick-stepping Otto Schnering, founder and president of the Curtiss Candy Company. His companion here: Herdsman Jack Morgan and Afton's Golden Marie, twelve times a grand champion, including National Dairyman's Congress, 1948."

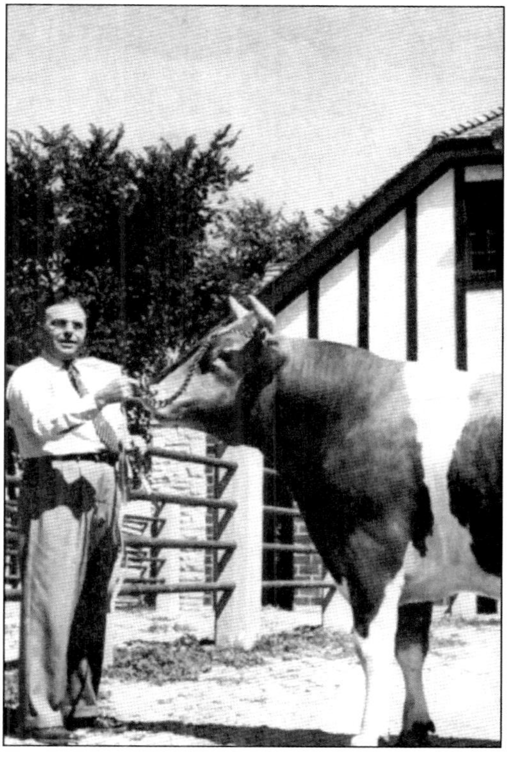

Originally printed in the January 1950 issue of the Curtiss Farm newsletter, the caption below this picture read, "The man behind the livestock program, Delbert H. Kingston, shows his prize Guernsey bull, Curtiss Candy Noble Curtiss. The farm's artificial breeding service makes outstanding sires available to farmers all over the country at minimal cost."

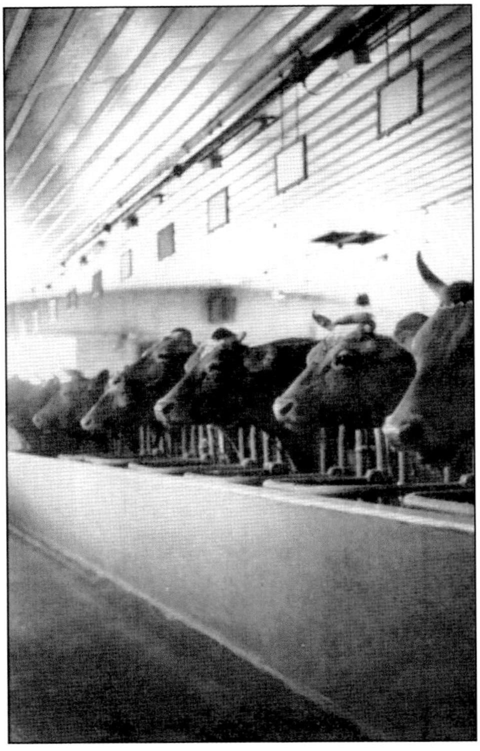

This photograph was taken from the Curtiss Farm employee newsletter's January 1950 issue. The caption below the picture stated: "Beautiful exteriors, spotless interiors are Curtiss trademarks. 'In dairy barns and candy factories, it pays to be clean,' says Otto Schnering, who knows much about both."

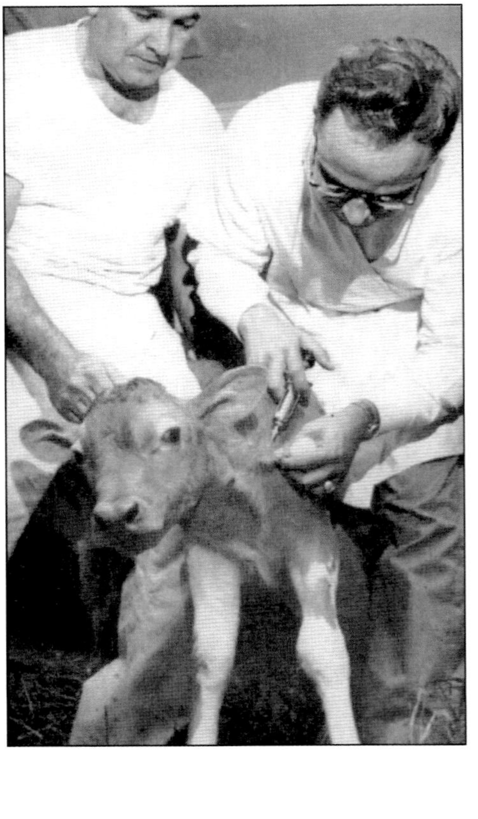

This is another photograph from the January 1950 issue of the Curtiss Farm employee newsletter. The caption below this picture stated: "Calf's eyes bulge as Dr. Joseph Heger prepares to inject his needle. Two full time veterinarians look after animal health and conduct research."

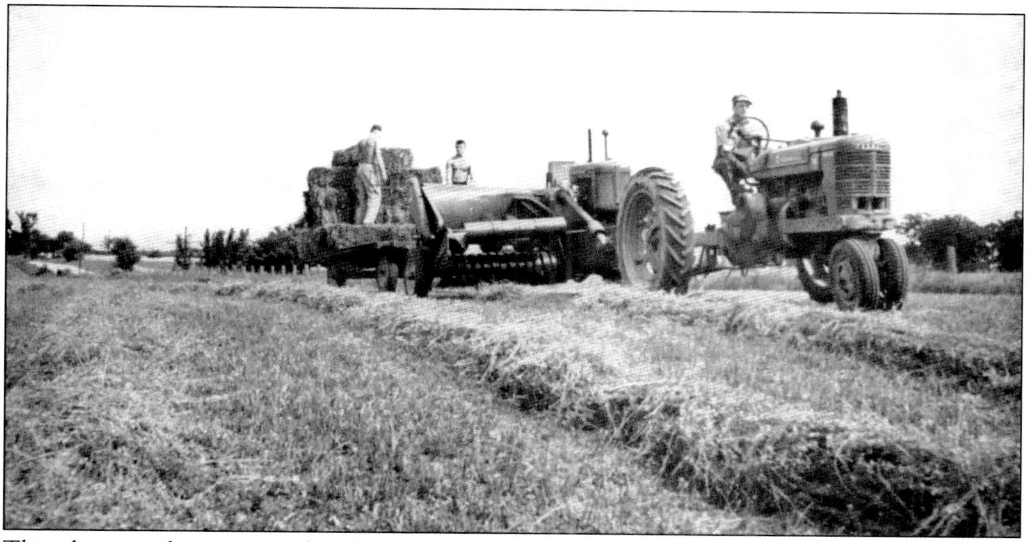

This photograph was printed in the January 1950 issue of the Curtiss Farm employee newsletter. The caption below the picture read: "The 6,772 acres under cultivation produce corn, oats, hay, straw, silage, soybeans, potatoes, and popcorn. Large acreages mean plenty of work for equipment like the Farmall M tractor and the McCormick 50-T hay baler."

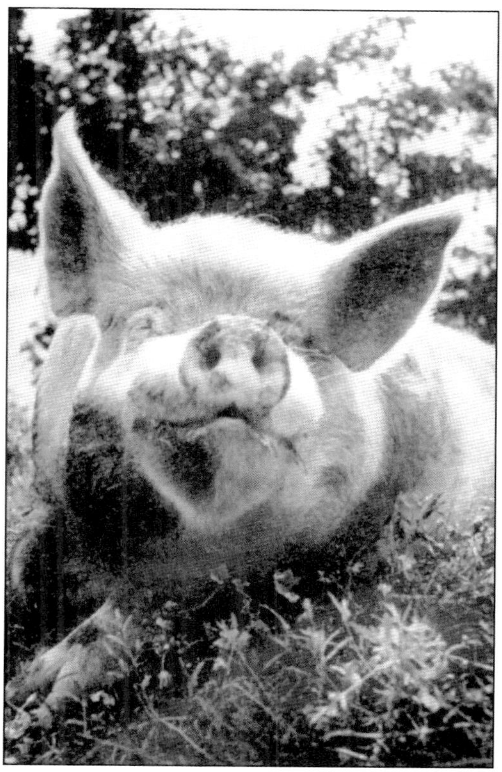

Originally printed in the January 1950 issue of the Curtiss Farm newsletter, the caption below this picture read: "Solihull Dainty Boy 8th, three-year-old Yorkshire boar who was imported from England, is regarded as the top boar of the Yorkshire breed. To some experts this nine-hundred-pounder is the only boar in the breed."

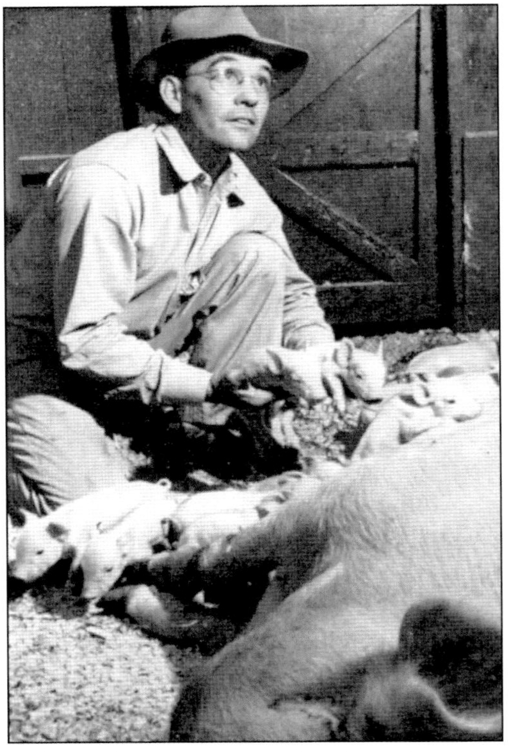

This photograph was printed in the January 1950 issue of the Curtiss Farm employee newsletter. The caption below read: "The 15 Yorkshires shown here with Eric Dennis, are two hours old. The Yorkshire produces large litters and the Curtiss Herd raises one to two pigs per litter over the national average."

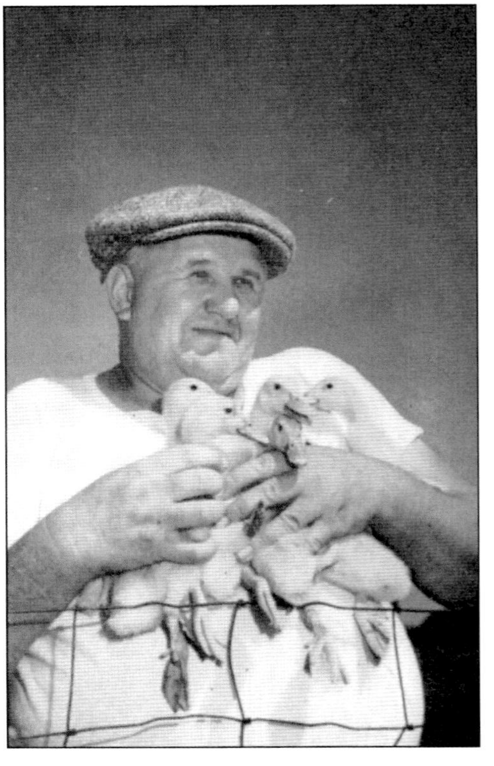

This is another photograph taken from the January 1950 Curtiss Farm employee newsletter. The caption below the picture stated: "Hilding Johnson, the 'duck man,' and friends. These ducks are two weeks old, will go to market at the age of nine weeks. There'll be 28,000 this year plus 5,000 turkeys."

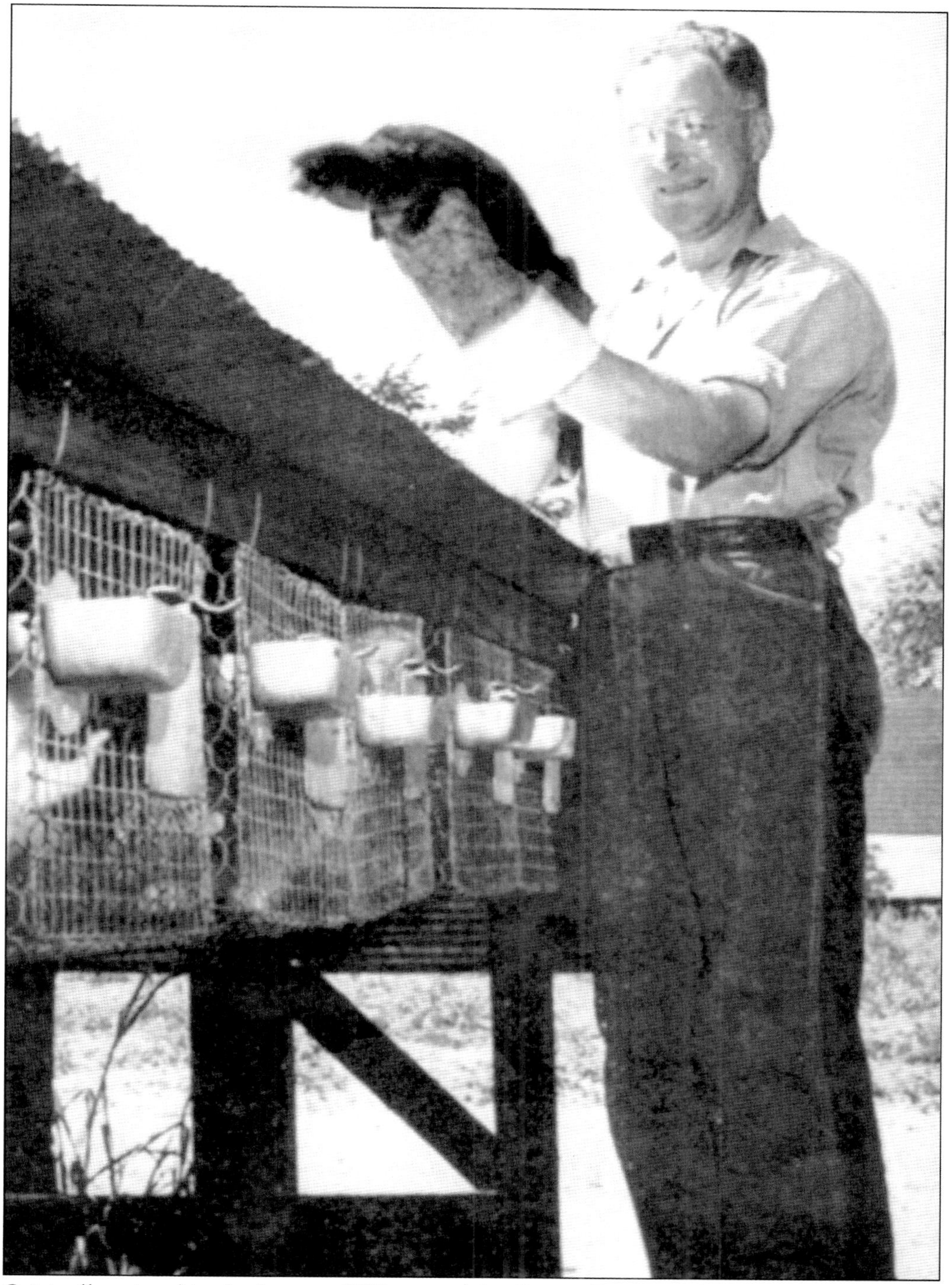

Originally printed in the January 1950 issue of the Curtiss Farm newsletter, the caption below this picture read: "Because slaughter of chickens leaves feet, heads, and entrails, the Curtiss people brought in mink, which thrive on chicken waste. Clarence Vogel examines a Kobuck male, a dark mink with light-blue underfur. The mink population is slightly over 1100."

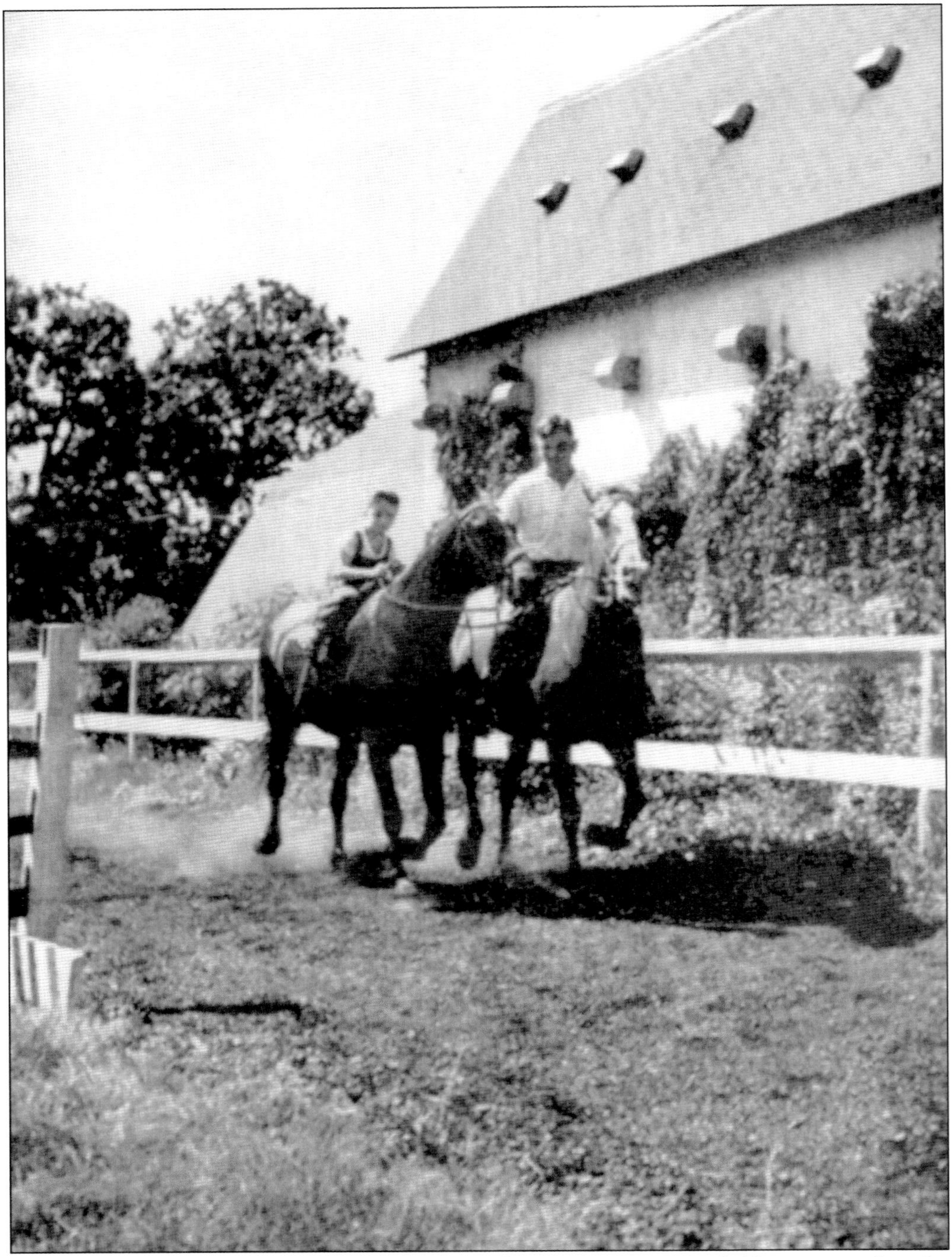

This photograph of Earl "Tuffy" Wilson giving riding instruction to a child was printed in the January 1950 issue of the Curtiss Farm employee newsletter. The caption below the picture read: "Children of farm employees get a six-year riding course from Earl Wilson, operator of the riding stable, take weekly swimming instructions in the Curtiss pool. Along the picturesque farm lanes, 'Children Playing' signs caution motorists to be careful."

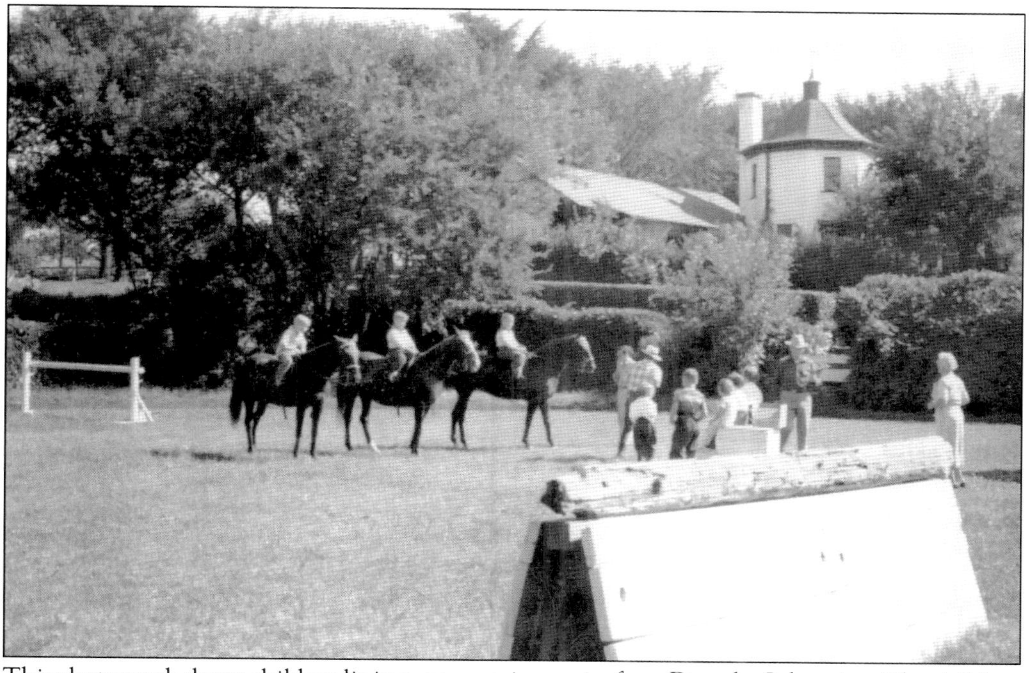

This photograph shows children lining up to receive a prize from Dorothy Schnering. The children of employees who lived on the farm all received complimentary horseback riding lessons.

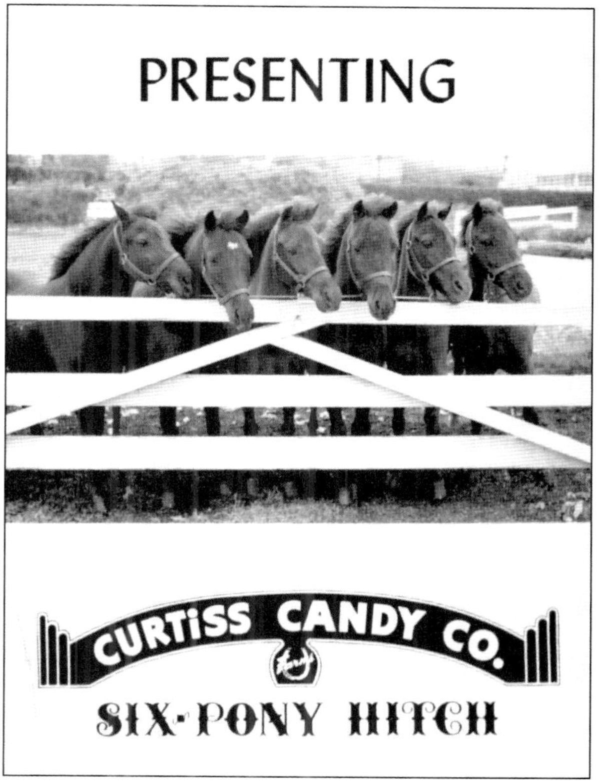

This postcard features the Curtiss Candy Company's famous six-pony hitch.

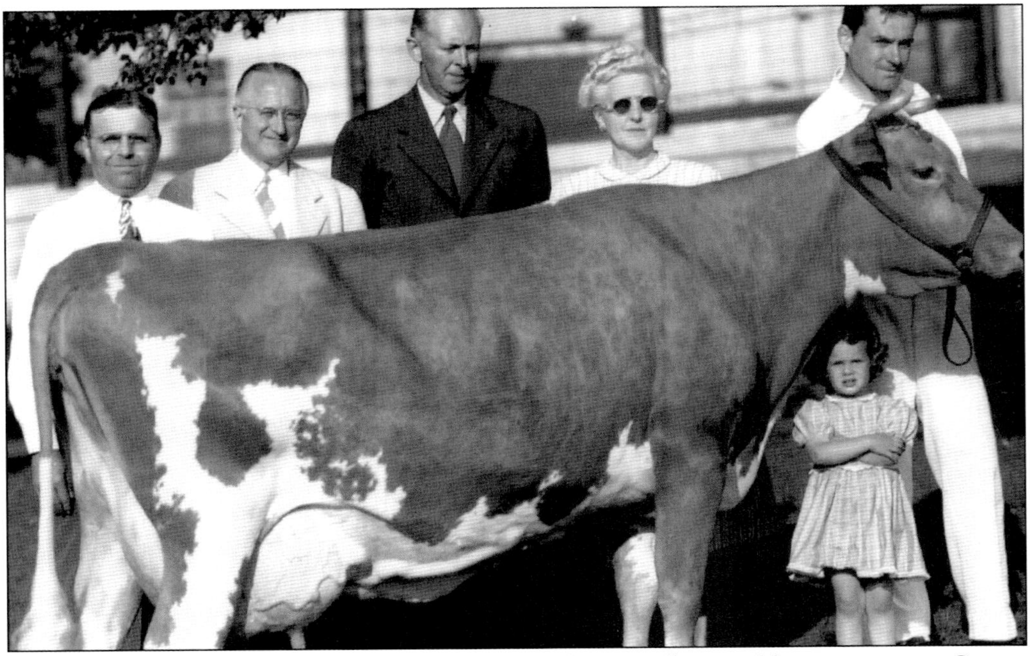

Otto and Dorothy Schnering, Delbert Kingston, and others stand by one of the prize-winning Curtiss cows. The little girl in this picture is Deb McFarland, one of the Schnerings' granddaughters.

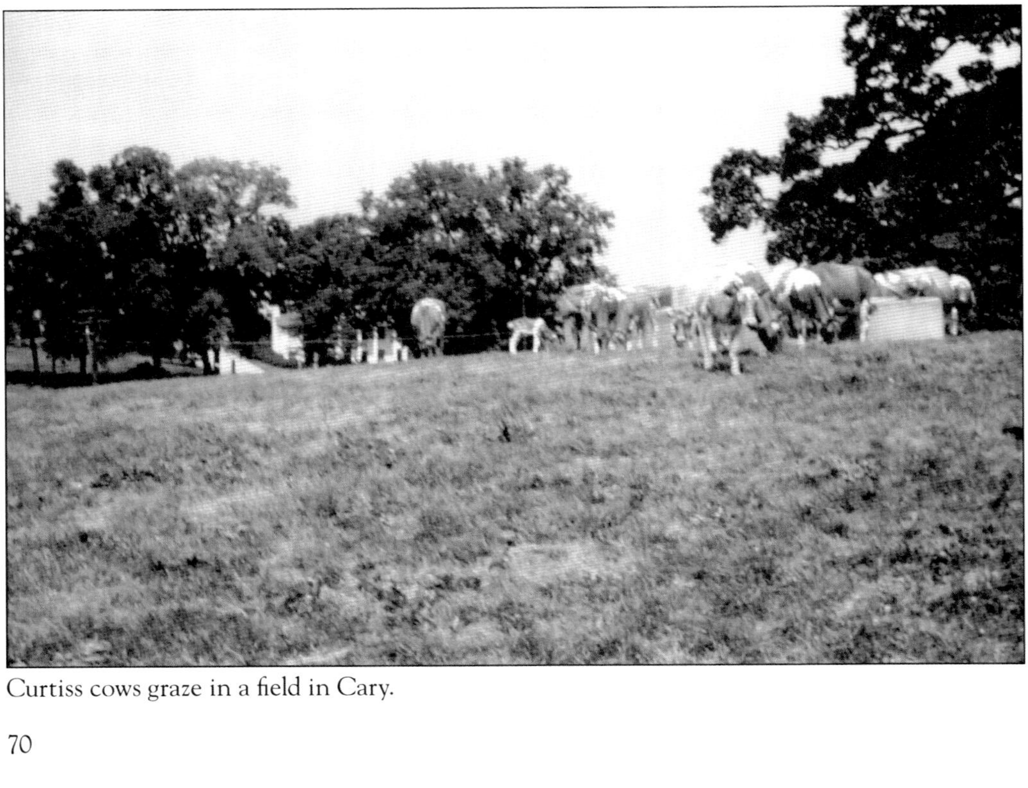

Curtiss cows graze in a field in Cary.

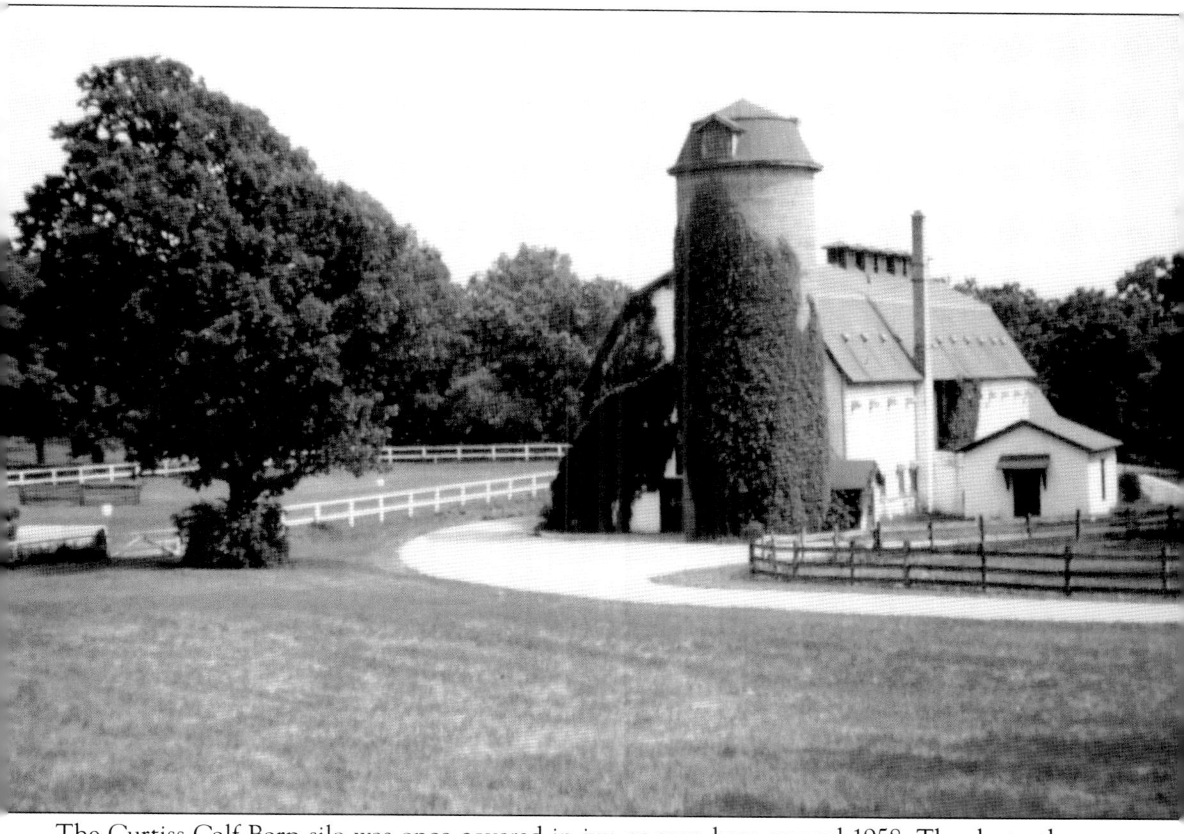

The Curtiss Calf Barn silo was once covered in ivy, as seen here around 1958. Thanks to the efforts of Shirley Beene on behalf of the McHenry County Historical Society, this barn has been recognized as an official historic landmark.

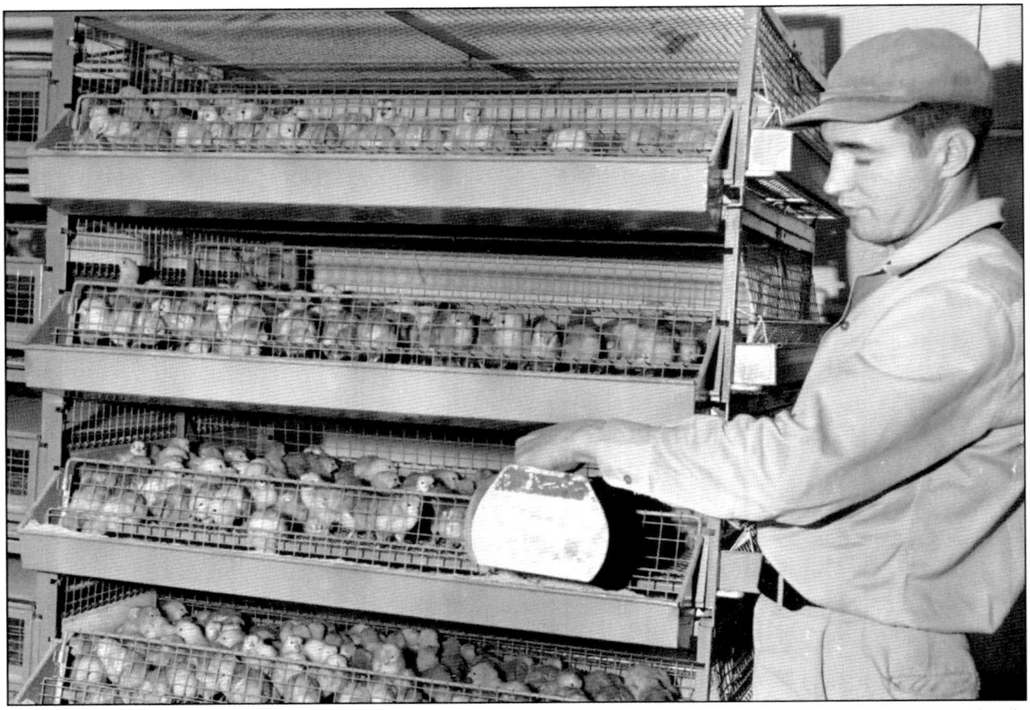

Curtiss Farm chicks were raised to maturity in large quantities. Curtiss Farm sanitation standards and diet innovations were responsible for improving the process of raising broilers.

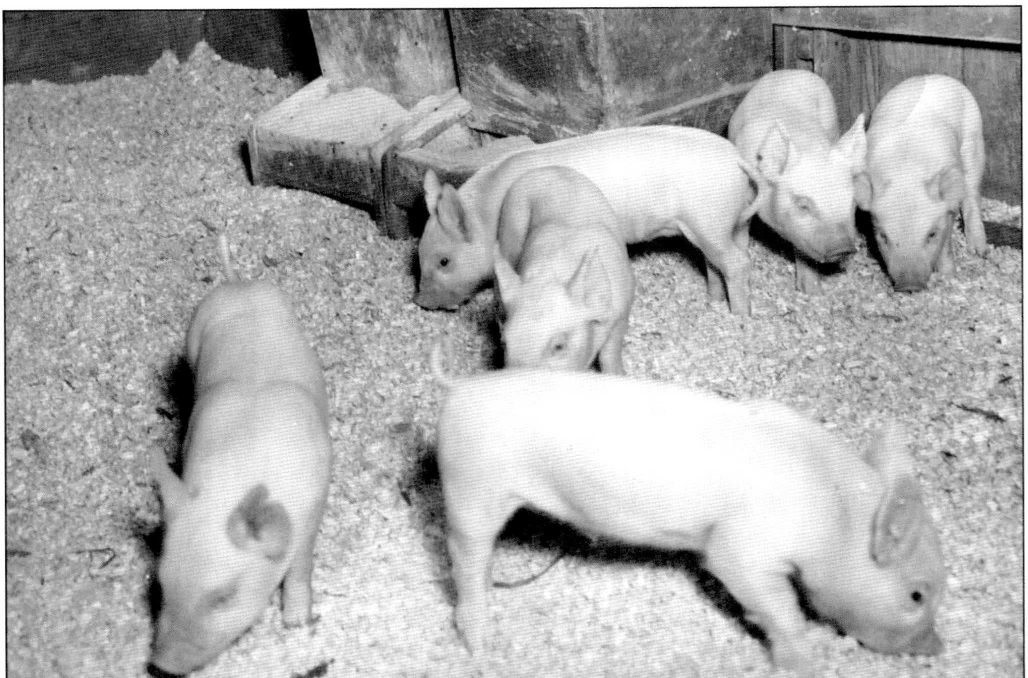

Hogs raised at Curtiss Farm were among the best in the world.

This postcard advertisement for Curtiss Breeding Service boasts the following: "The CURTiSS 4-BAR-C Beef A.I. Program is designed to produce the best-looking, best-doing and best-paying calf crops you ever raised! Top bulls of eleven beef breeds readily available."

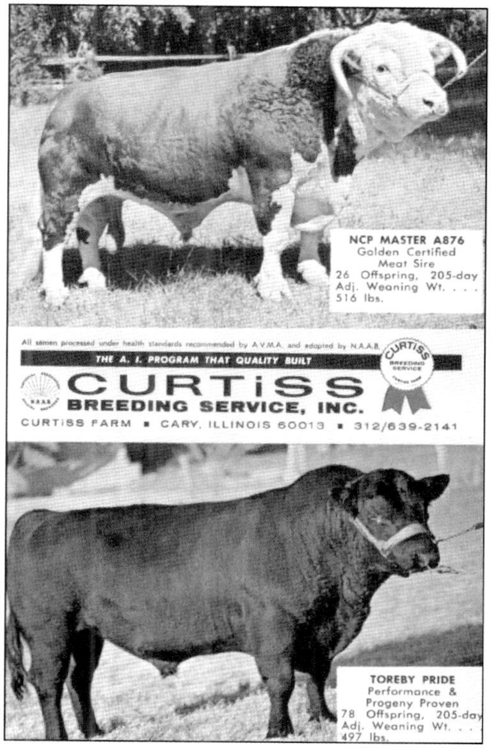

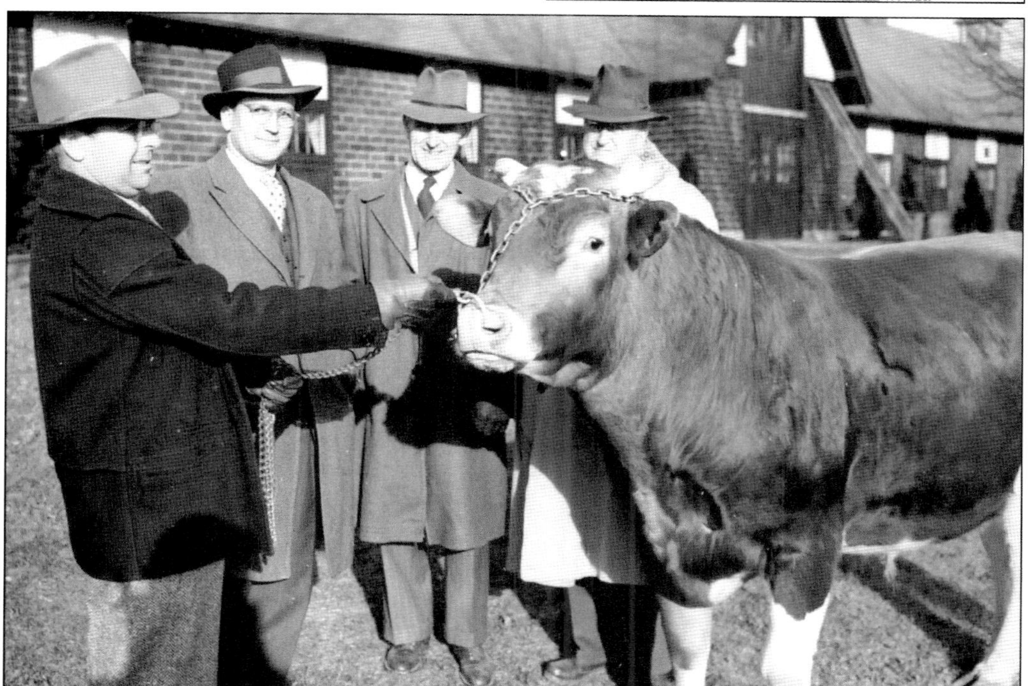

Otto Schnering, Bob Schnering, Delbert Kingston, and a Curtiss Farm staff member are next to a member of the Curtiss herd.

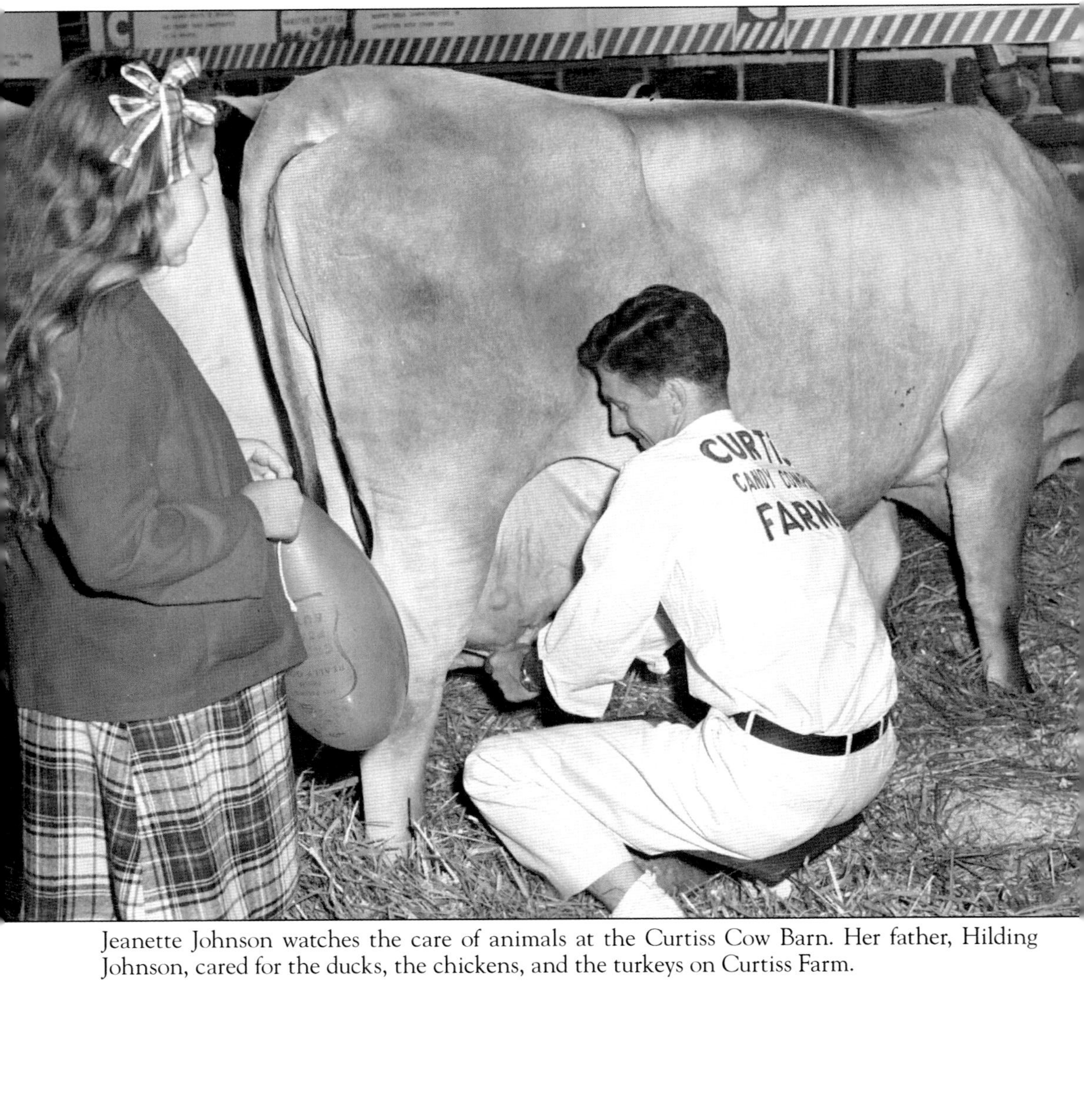

Jeanette Johnson watches the care of animals at the Curtiss Cow Barn. Her father, Hilding Johnson, cared for the ducks, the chickens, and the turkeys on Curtiss Farm.

This is a memo dated April 9, 1947, from Otto Schnering to Hilding Johnson on company letterhead. The text of this personally signed note demonstrates Schnering's ability to know and relate to his employees. Addressed by first name, the text of the memo reads: "Mrs. Schnering and I will be away for a little over two weeks. I just hope you will have very good success with the chickens while we are gone. Take good care of things, and best to Jenny and the little girls. Sincerely Yours, Otto Schnering, President."

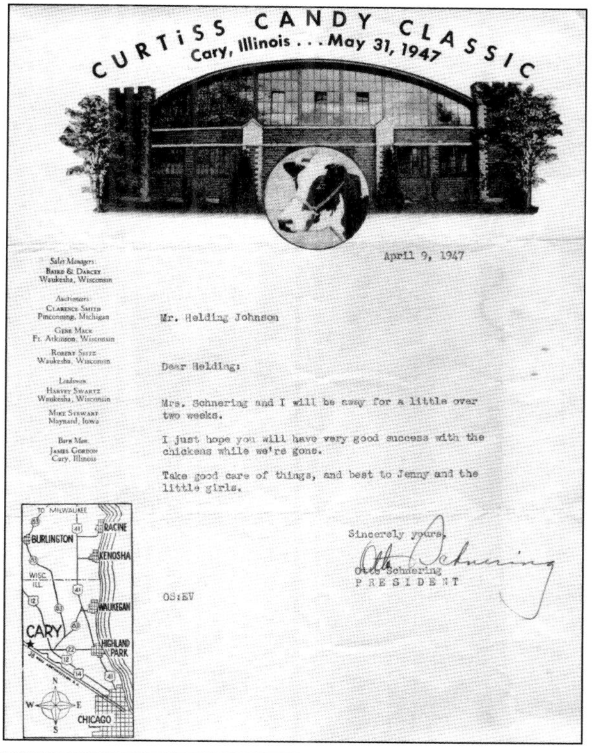
CURTISS CANDY CLASSIC
Cary, Illinois . . . May 31, 1947

Sales Managers:
Baird & Darcey
Waukesha, Wisconsin

Auctioneers:
Clarence Smith
Pinconning, Michigan

Gene Mack
Ft. Atkinson, Wisconsin

Robert Seitz
Waukesha, Wisconsin

Leadsmen:
Harvey Swartz
Waukesha, Wisconsin

Mike Stewart
Maynard, Iowa

Barn Man:
James Gordon
Cary, Illinois

April 9, 1947

Mr. Helding Johnson

Dear Helding:

Mrs. Schnering and I will be away for a little over two weeks.

I just hope you will have very good success with the chickens while we're gone.

Take good care of things, and best to Jenny and the little girls.

Sincerely yours,

Otto Schnering
PRESIDENT

OS:EV

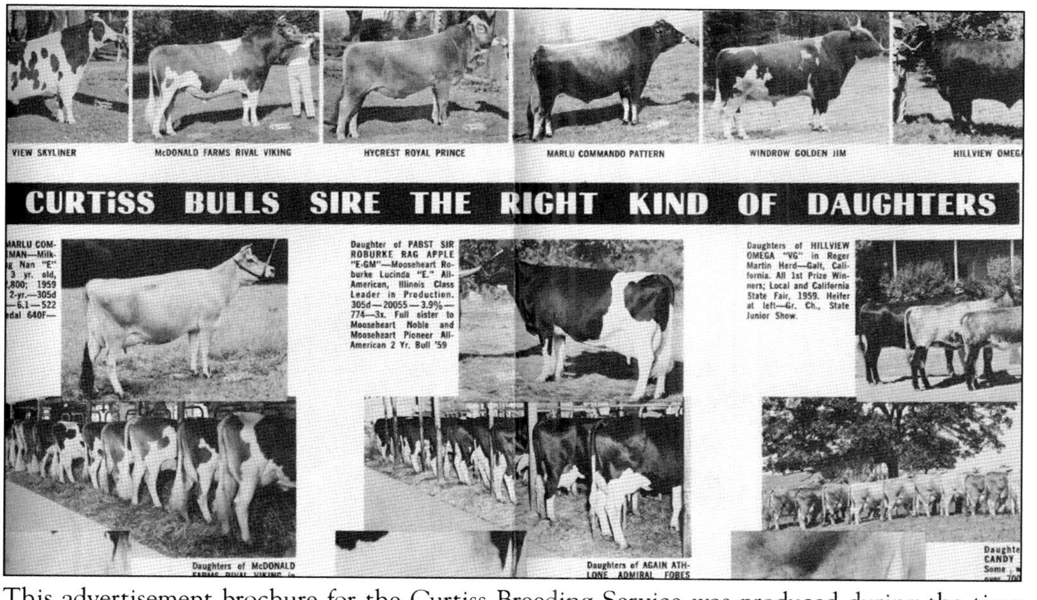

This advertisement brochure for the Curtiss Breeding Service was produced during the time period that Dorothy Schnering served as the company president. When the breeding service was considered perhaps an expendable asset after Otto Schnering's death, it was Dorothy who fought to maintain it and oversee its continued growth and success. The opening caption in the brochure reads, "The Curtiss Breeding Service is a nationwide artificial breeding program with more than 1,000 herd technicians in 44 states."

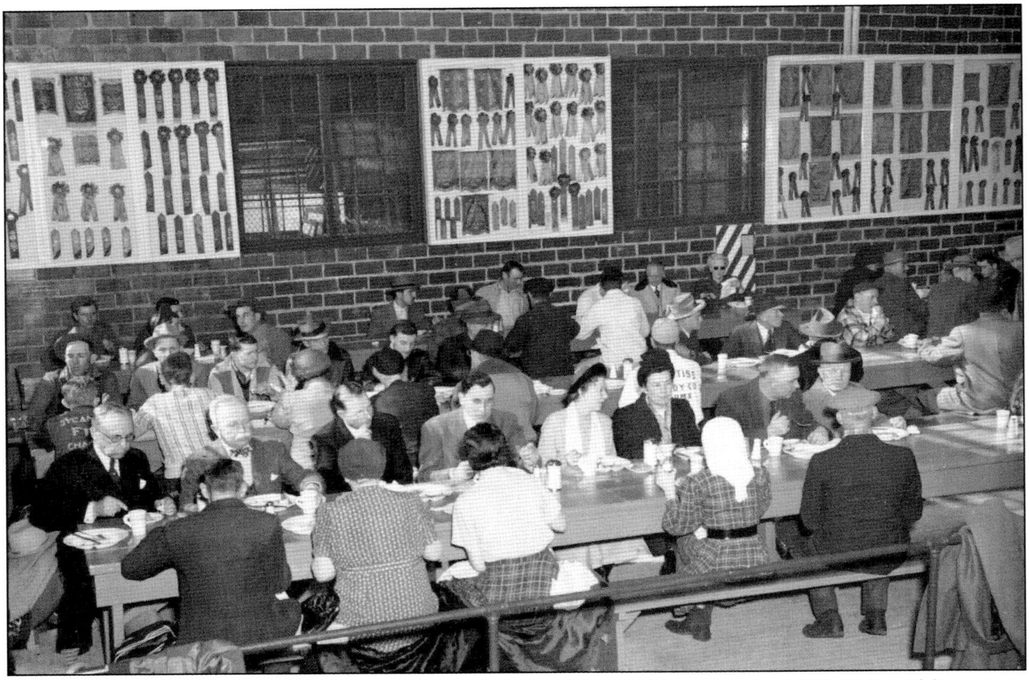

This scene took place inside the arena barn during a livestock auction in 1949. Prize ribbons can be seen displayed on the walls throughout the barn.

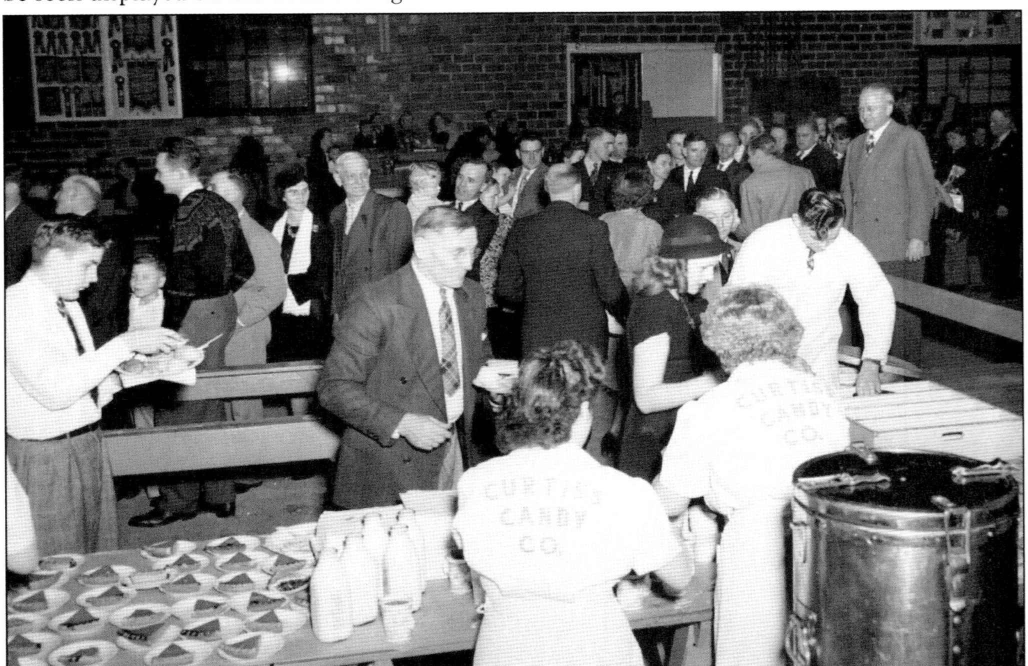

This photograph depicts one of many livestock auctions held at the arena barn. Otto Schnering can be seen greeting guests as Curtiss Candy Company employees serve pie, milk, and other tasty treats to event attendees in 1947.

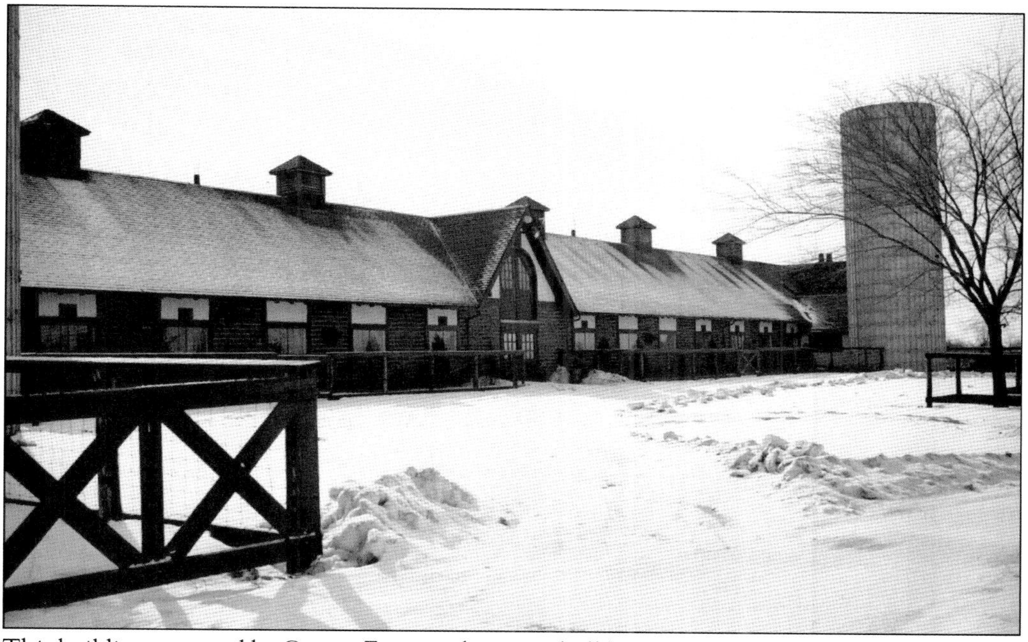

This building was used by Curtiss Farm as the arena bull barn for special events. This site is now the location of the Cary Park District Community Center. The building is seen here in 1947.

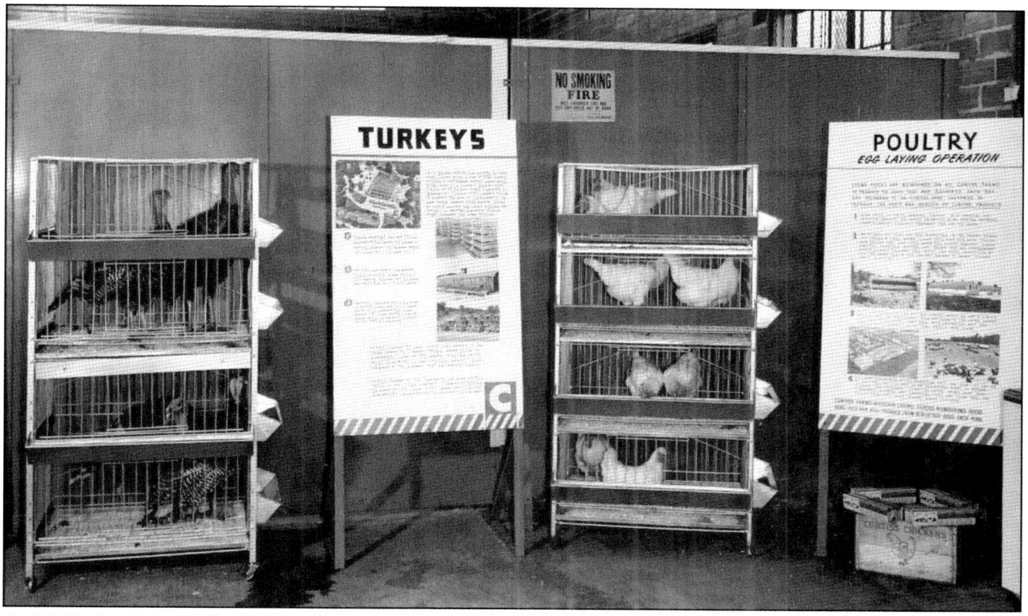

A 1948 display in the arena barn informed the viewer about the poultry operations at Curtiss Farm. One caption read, "Laying flocks are maintained on all Curtiss Farms to produce the eggs that are gathered each day and delivered to the Curtiss food factories to improve the taste and quality of Curtiss products." Turkey Hill Road got its name from the numerous turkeys that once resided there.

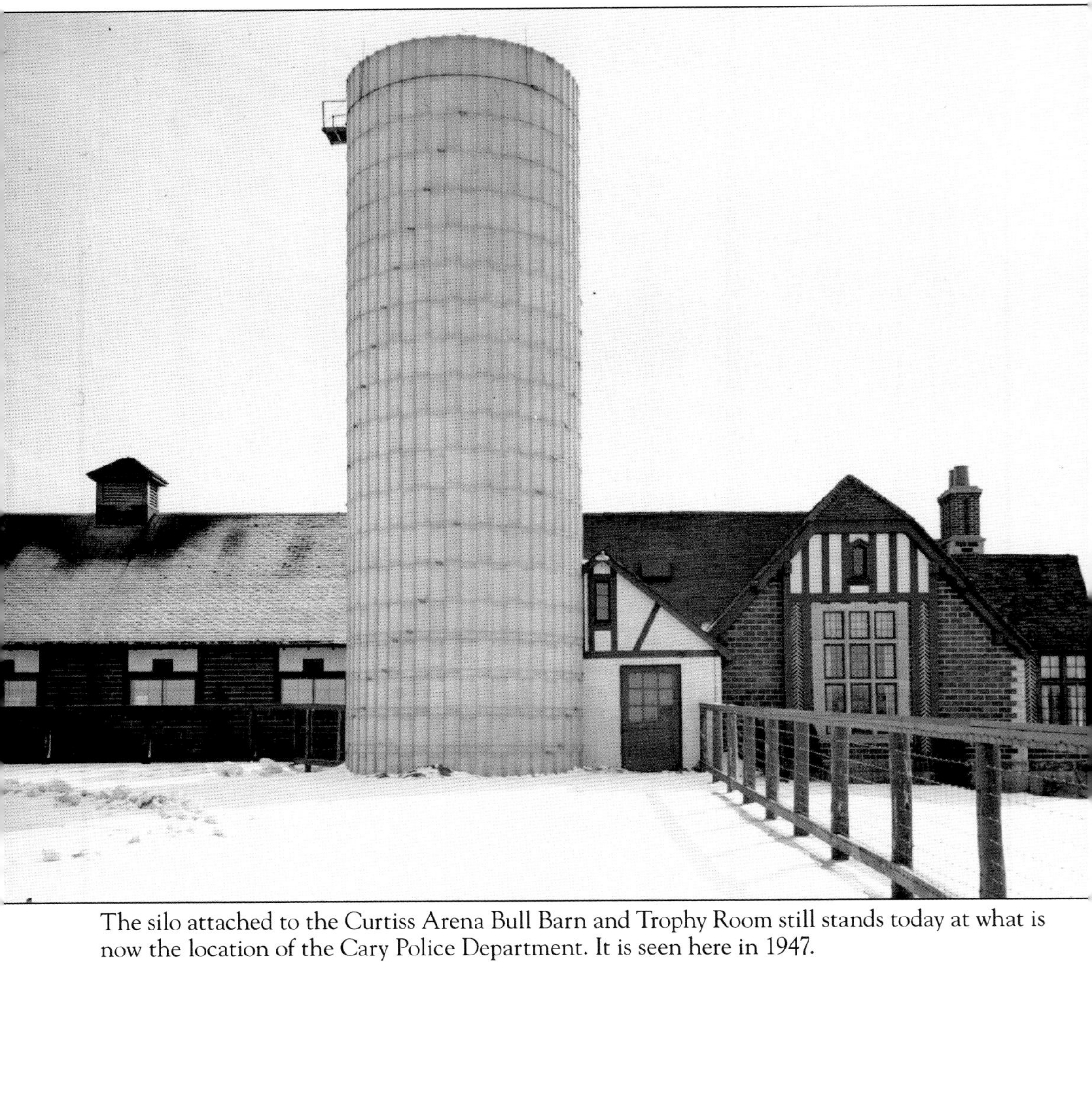

The silo attached to the Curtiss Arena Bull Barn and Trophy Room still stands today at what is now the location of the Cary Police Department. It is seen here in 1947.

Dinner was served to attendees at the legendary Curtiss Farm livestock auctions in the arena barn. People traveled from all over the world to attend these auctions and bid on Curtiss livestock. This auction took place in 1947.

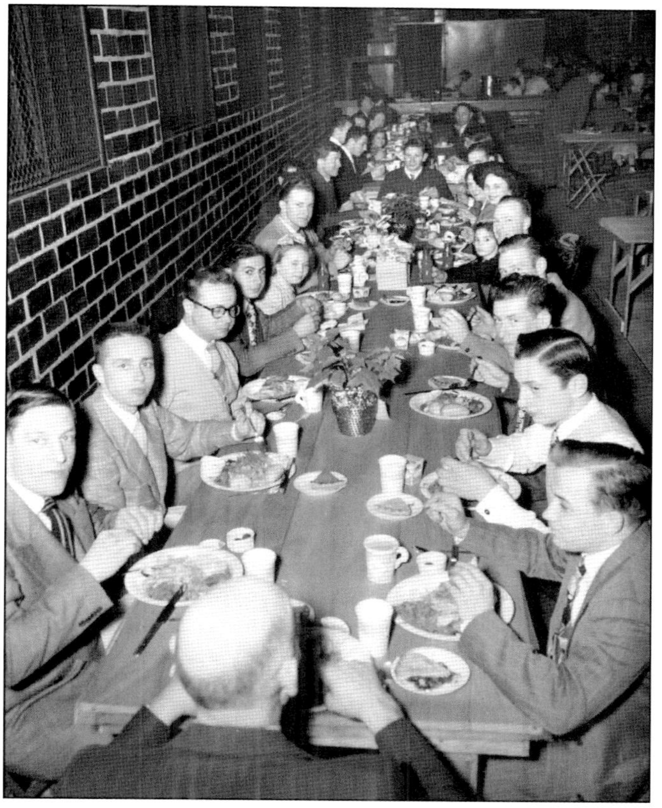

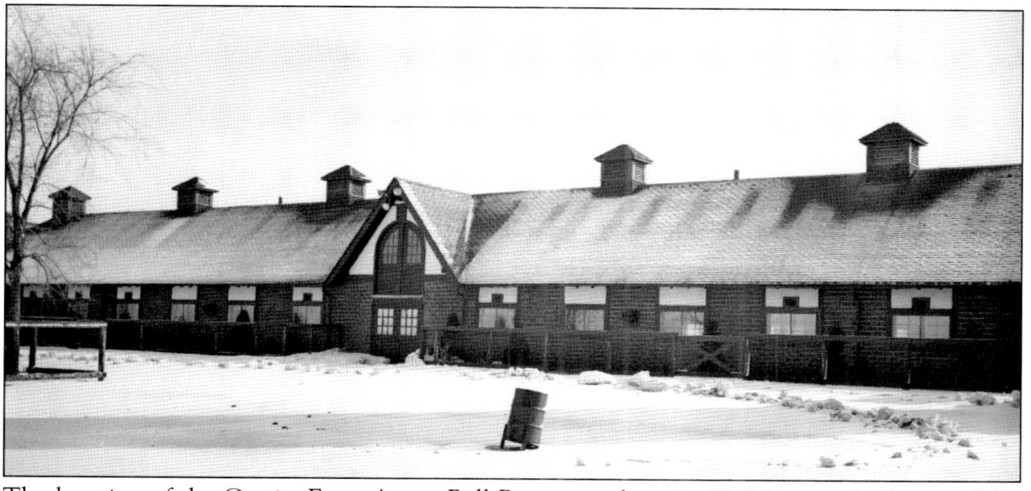

The location of the Curtiss Farm Arena Ball Barn, seen here in 1947, is now the home of the community center for the village of Cary.

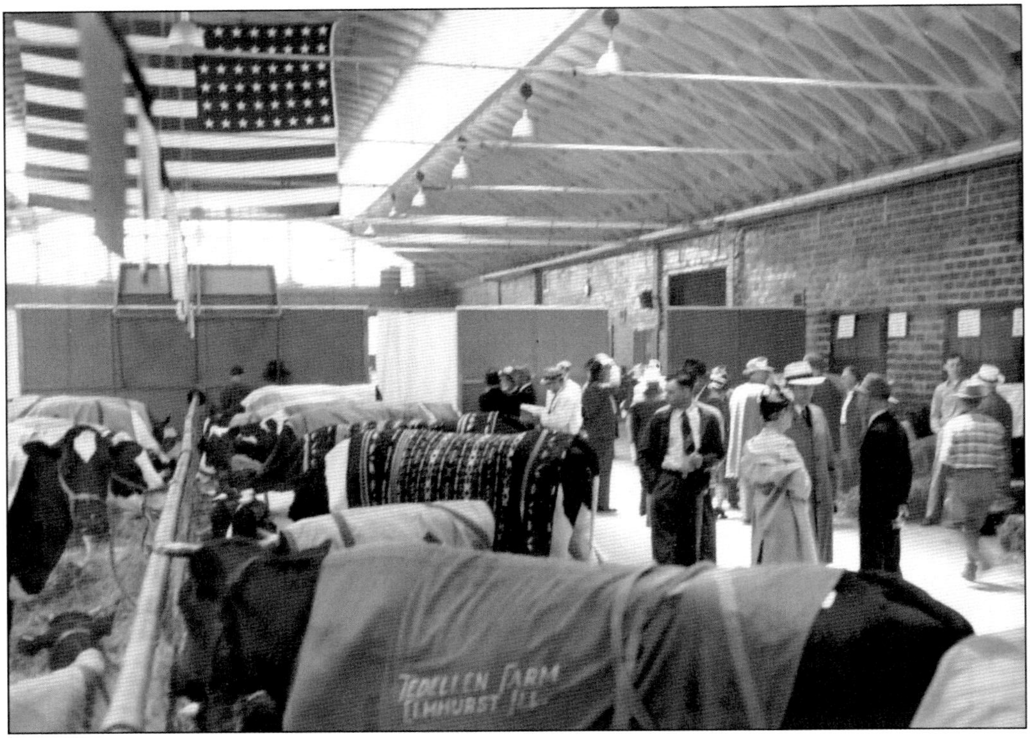

This scene is from the Curtiss Candy Classic held on June 3, 1946, where prize-winning Curtiss cows were on display.

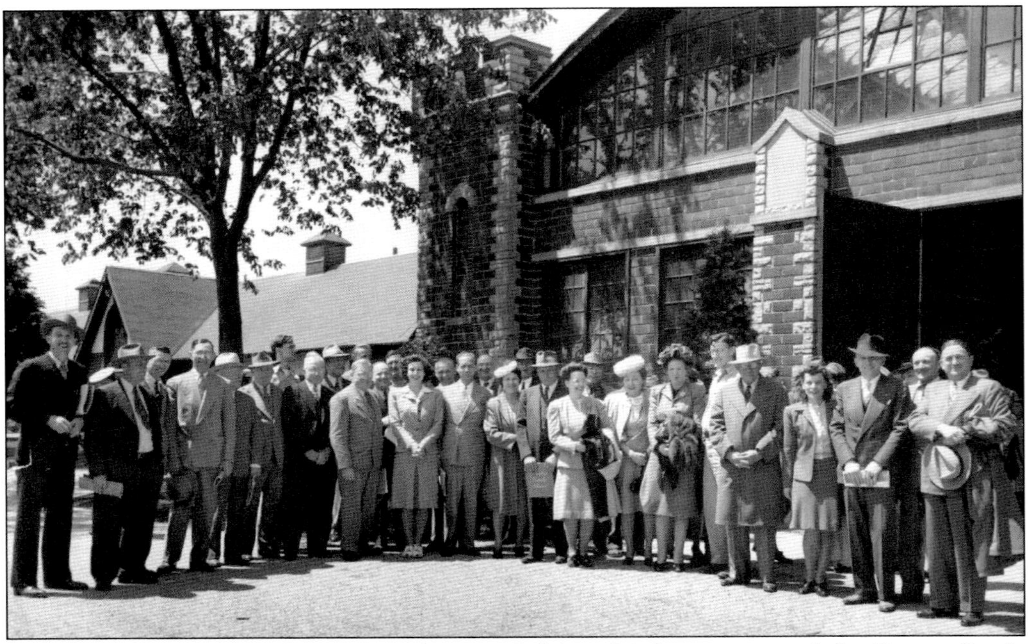

This photograph shows a large group that traveled from Michigan to attend the Curtiss Candy Classic on June 3, 1946.

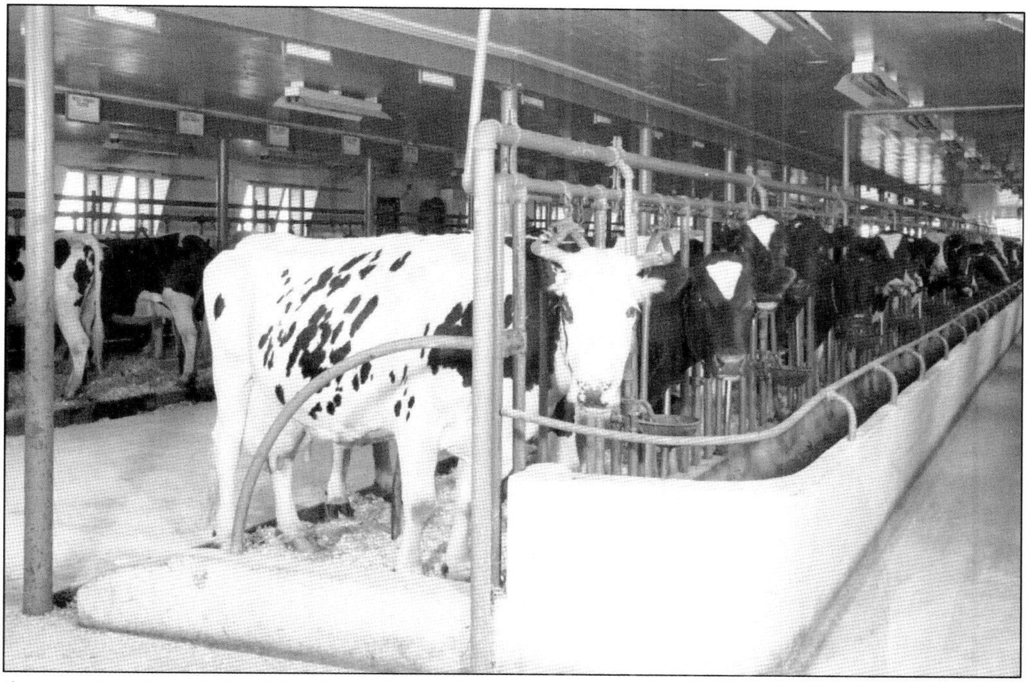

An interior view of the dairy barn shows Curtiss dairy cows lined up in large numbers in 1947.

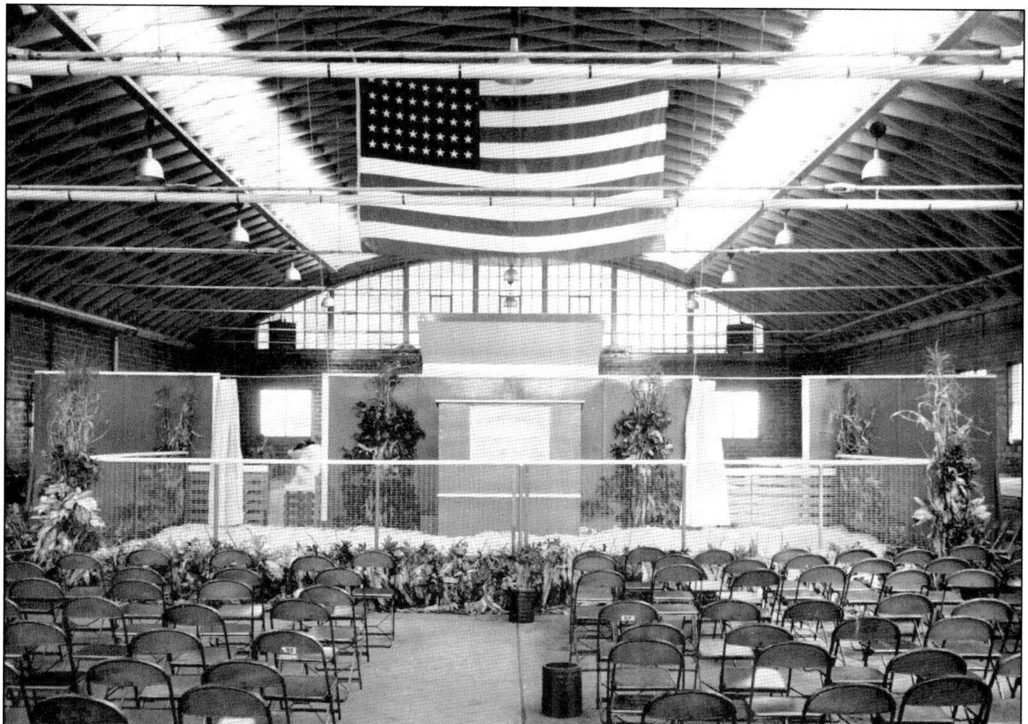

The American flag was prominently displayed above the stage at every livestock auction held at the Curtiss Farm division of the Curtiss Candy Company, seen here in 1946.

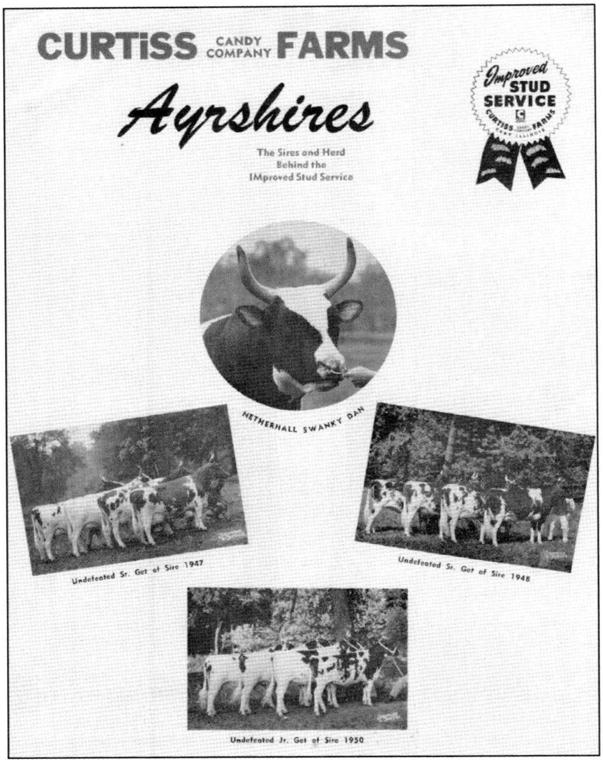

This cover of a Curtiss Candy Company farm informational brochure features pictures and information about the award-winning Ayrshire sires and herd that were a part of the Curtiss Breeding Service.

Dear Farmer-Breeder:

The way to herd development or improvement is through breeding to sires with the inherited ability to transmit profitable performance.

Such sires are not always available, except where it is possible to combine the most successful bloodlines. Great cows, generations of them, must stand behind the sire — cows great in their **production, with ability to reproduce** their greatness, desirable in their **type and conformation,** persistent in **production** and **living long productive lives.**

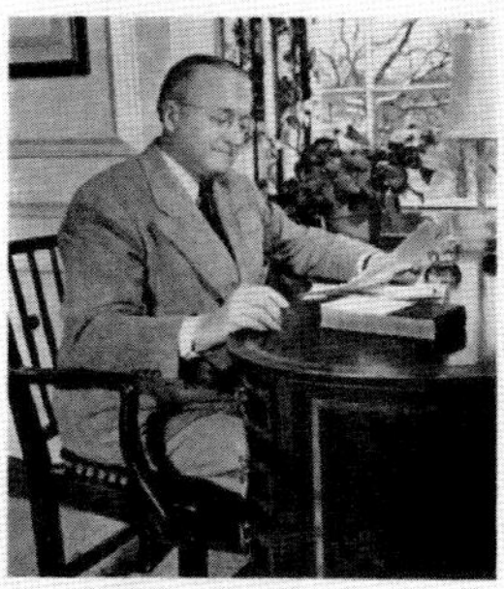

MR. OTTO SCHNERING

Curtiss Candy herd sires are precisely such sires. They are the products, the offspring, of a breeding program built on great cow families.

Through the Curtiss Candy artificial breeding program, the IMproved Stud Service, these herd sires are your herd sires. Through them, you can carry on a breeding program based on the best that comes from Curtiss Candy's own Ayrshire Herd.

You can follow up the breeding of each successive generation of Curtiss-bred animals with assurances of consistency and uniformity. For, in the Curtiss Candy herd are the great individuals — the combinations — from which will come your future sires. You can look ahead and plan ahead with them. Only Curtiss Candy presents you with this sound and distinctive program of artificial breeding.

We present this booklet as an introduction to our animals and service.

We would be pleased to have you visit our Curtiss Candy farming operation, to see our sires and herd, and to observe our program. I hope that we can expect you soon.

Sincerely,

Otto Schnering

Otto Schnering
Founder and President

A letter from Otto Schnering and a photograph of Schnering at his desk are featured on the inside cover of this Curtiss Farm brochure. The letter begins: "Dear Farmer-Breeder: The way to herd development or improvement is through breeding to sires with the inherited ability to transmit profitable performance."

This page, selected from one of the Curtiss Farm brochures, is headed by the caption "Perpetuating Breed Greatness," and highlights some of the members of the legendary Curtiss herd, such as "Netherhall Swanky Dan, with an unparalleled record of 84 Grand Championships from coast-to-coast in his 15 year life span."

PERPETUATING BREED GREATNESS

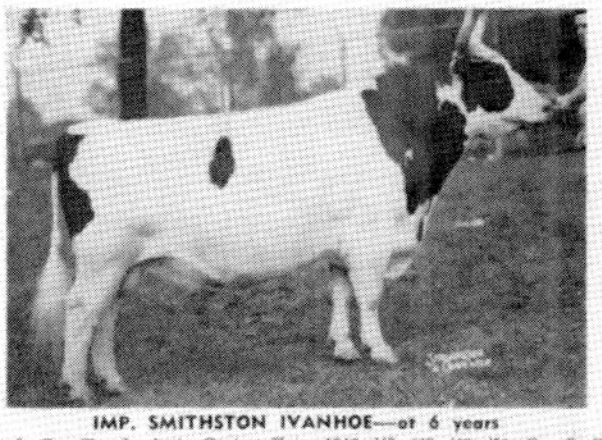

IMP. SMITHSTON IVANHOE—at 6 years

Sr. & Gr. Ch., Lachute Spring Fair, 1946, '47, '48, '49, '50; Sr. & Gr. Ch., Royal Winter Fair, 1947, '48, '49; Sr. & Gr. Ch., National Ayrshire Show, 1950; Sr. & Res. Gr. Ch., DCC, 1950; Sire of Jr. Ch. Bull, Royal Winter Fair, 1950.
Sire: Netherton Noble Art
Dam: Smithston Evergreen
Scottish Records:
9170 Milk 4.18% (H);
10300 Milk 4.38% 451 Fat 47 weeks.

The work of herd development is a continual program of putting together combinations of bloodlines that spell success in the milk pail, on the sale platform and in the show ring. The Curtiss Candy Ayrshire herd represents more than 50 years of constructive, progressive breeding. Behind the herd are individuals and families that rank with the greatest in the history of the breed. Noteworthy among them is the name Netherhall Swanky Dan, with an unparalleled record of 84 Grand Championships from coast-to-coast in his 15 year life span. His daughters at Curtiss Candy have production records up to 656 lbs. of Butterfat for a single yearly lactation. To greatness such as this, Curtiss Candy seeks out and adds to its herd individuals with the inherited ability to make the best better. The individuals on this page exemplify the caliber of animals upon which Curtiss Candy continues to build its herd.

It is from this herd - from this successful combination of desirable bloodlines - that come and will continue to come the sires and the dams of sires behind the IMproved Stud Service.

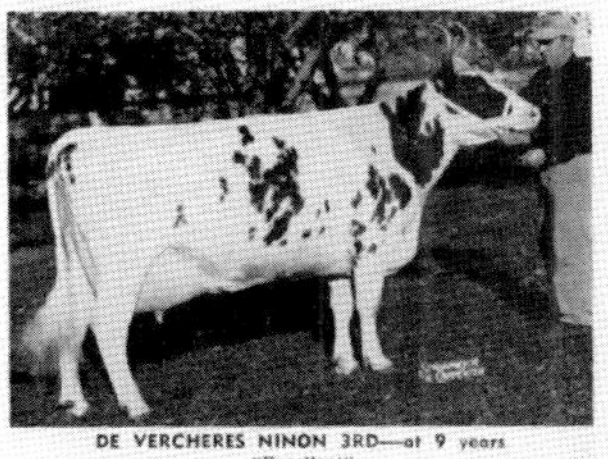

DE VERCHERES NINON 3RD—at 9 years
"Excellent"

1st Aged Cow, Sr. & Gr. Ch., DCC, 1951; 2nd Aged Cow, Res. Sr. & Res. Gr. Ch., NAS, 1951.
9314 Milk 399 Fat 268d 2X at 3 yrs.;
12147 Milk 569 Fat 337d 2X at 4 yrs.;
11177 Milk 458 Fat 365d 2X at 5 yrs.;
14924 Milk 596 Fat 365d 2X at 6 yrs.;
10965 Milk 444 Fat 305d 2X at 7 yrs.;
(On test) 3821 Milk 162 Fat 80d 2X at 8 yrs.
Sire: Cherry Bank Cupbearer
Dam: De Vercheres Ninon 2nd
8526 Milk 361 Fat 305d at 2 yrs.

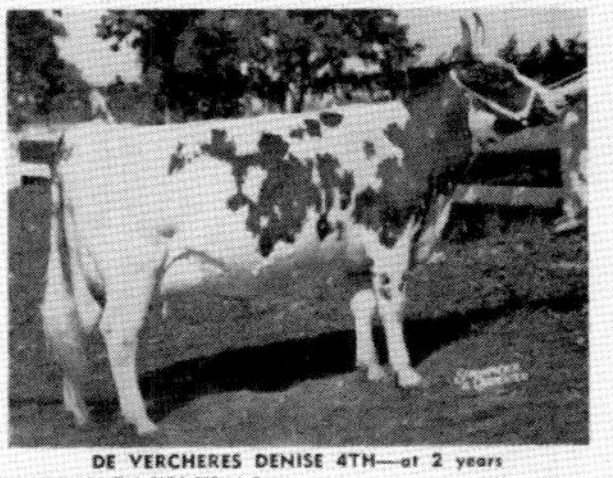

DE VERCHERES DENISE 4TH—at 2 years

10770 Milk 426 Fat 305d 2X at 2 yrs.
Sire: De Vercheres Bombardier
Dam: Denise E 127th "VG"
12949 Milk 519 Fat at 2 yrs.

CURTiSS CANDY COMPANY FARMS
IMPROVED STUD SERVICE

Curtiss is the only artificial breeding organization owning its own farms, its own foundation herds . . . producing its own herd sires from its own great cow families.

Featuring

1. **SELECTED MATINGS (planned mating of a particular bull to a certain cow at a specified time or date, with conception guaranteed)**
2. **STUD POOL MATINGS (mating from a bull available at the time of call for service, without previous selection)**

ONLY the CURTiSS CANDY IMproved Stud Service offers this 10-Point Artificial Breeding Service to make possible the economic breeding of cattle that will develop into profitable producers:

1. An opportunity to follow a well-defined, successful breeding program as carried on at the CURTiSS CANDY COMPANY FARMS — mating to present herd sires and looking ahead to future sires combining the most desirable bloodlines.
2. Association with a business organization founded and developed on the principles of quality service and continued progress to give the consumer the greatest amount of value at a minimum cost.
3. All bulls in the stud represent the concentrated goodness of great cow families with inherited ability to transmit. All are line-bred for uniformity and conform to the 5-Points of the CURTiSS CANDY breeding program.
4. All bulls are used in the CURTiSS CANDY FARMS' own high-producing and show winning herds, where their progeny is carefully observed to determine early their "proof of goodness" thereby utilizing their greatness over a longer span of years.
5. The semen is collected from vigorous bulls, adequately housed and properly managed.
6. The semen receives expert handling from our staff of veterinarians and laboratory technicians.
7. All Herd Technicians are carefully trained in the latest techniques of artificially breeding cattle; they are equipped with the best available scientific instruments, and are properly supervised to render the highest quality performance.
8. Fresh semen is delivered with the necessary frequency to insure peak breeding efficiency for conception.
9. A plastic tube, used only once and then destroyed after the breeding, is utilized along with all other necessary sanitary measures to insure safety and herd health.
10. Prompt, efficient service by CURTiSS CANDY Herd Technicians who feel a genuine responsibility toward each herd in which they work.

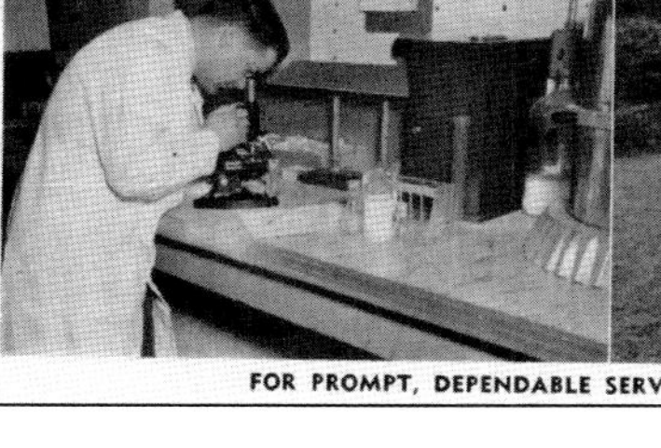

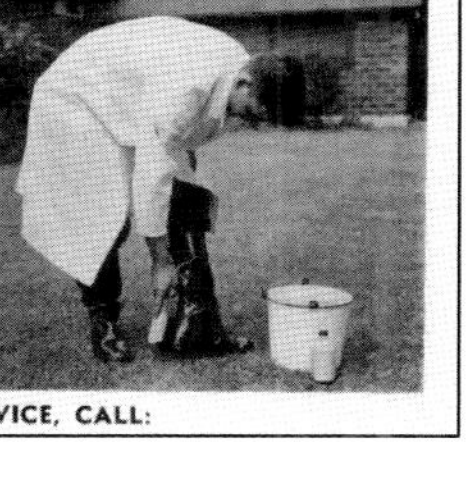

FOR PROMPT, DEPENDABLE SERVICE, CALL:

The back cover of this Curtiss Farm breeding service informational brochure says it all: "Curtiss is the only artificial breeding organization owning its own farms, its own foundation herds . . . producing its own herd sires from its own great cow families."

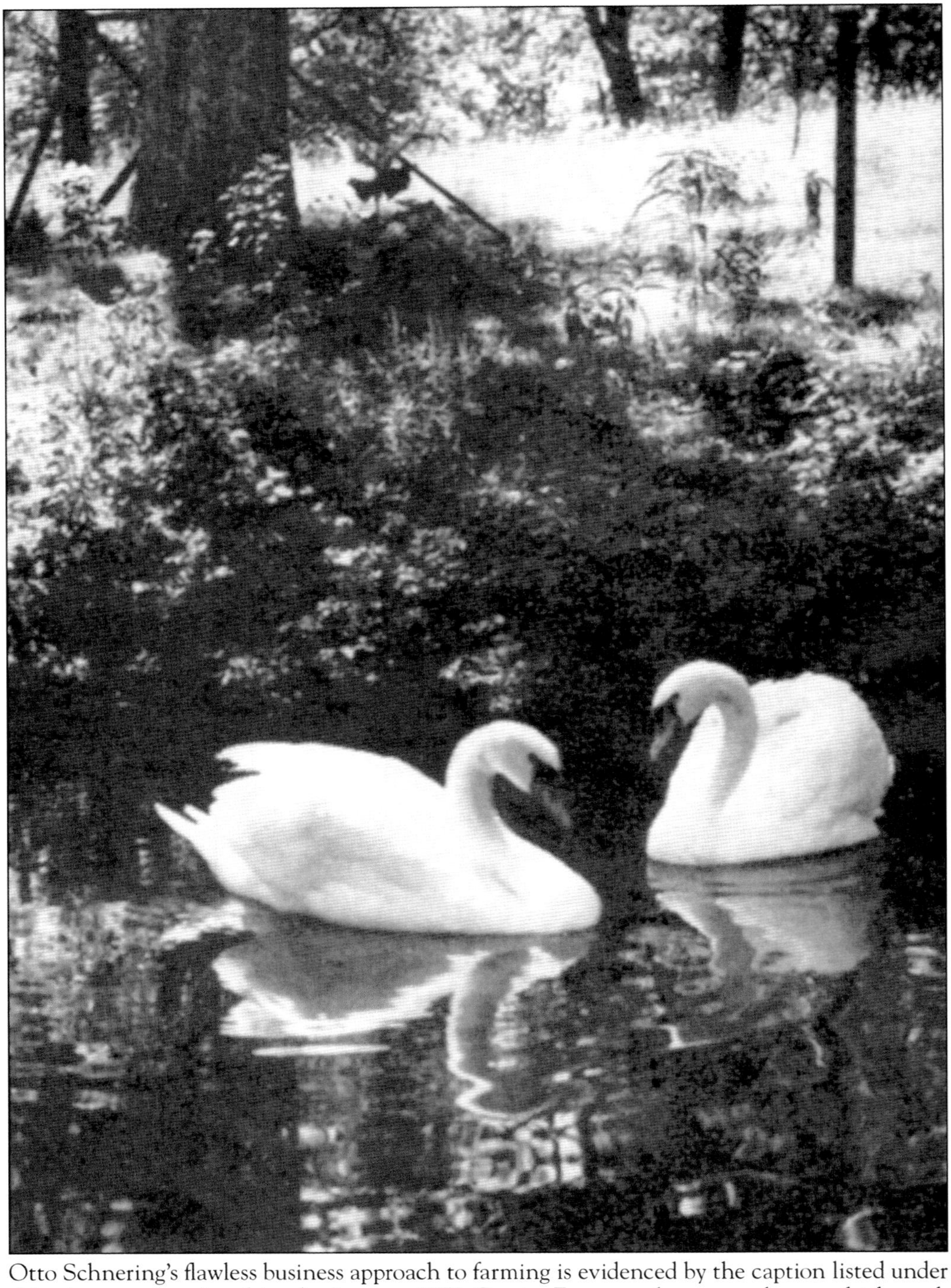

Otto Schnering's flawless business approach to farming is evidenced by the caption listed under this photograph printed in the January 1950 Curtiss Farm employee newsletter, which read: "Only luxury items Otto Schnering will admit on the Curtiss farms are the pair of swans shown here in the pool near his residence. Schnering raised sheep for awhile, but sold them when they failed to show a profit."

Four

Scenic Trout Valley and Continuing Tradition

Honoring the contributions made by both the Hertz and the Schnering families, the Trout Valley homeowners strive to maintain the scenic beauty of this unique section of land. With its rolling hills, dramatic variety of wildflowers and old-growth trees, deeded horse trails and grazing fields, historic architecture, riverfront vantage point, and natural spring-fed ponds, there is no other place in the Midwest quite like it.

Residents owe a debt of thanks to the famous landscape architect Jens Jensen, hired by John D. Hertz in 1919 to conduct a topographical survey and design a landscape for this area. Jensen is associated with Frank Lloyd Wright, having not only collaborated with him on several projects, but also displaying a similar aesthetic vision and conservation principles. Jensen had the talent to tap into the natural beauty of an area, further enhancing its splendor while preserving and strengthening its long-term viability. He often worked with water and limestone as underlying themes. Trout Valley resident Holly Schaller Guge perhaps said it best: "Jensen's landscapes were created to increase in beauty with the passage of time as they mature. They were not created for instant gratification." For this reason, current residents are able to enjoy the treasure of Trout Valley's scenic landscape to this day and witness its beauty grow with each passing year.

When this area was developed into a community of privately owned homes by Don and Norm Maxon, beginning in 1955, the architect brothers committed themselves to conserving the environment while developing the area. Trout Valley village residents are dedicated to preserving the community's rich legacy and continue to fund projects and donate their time toward enhancing this picturesque landscape.

Thanks to the efforts of Trout Valley village trustee David Hall and others, Trout Valley has been designated as an official tree city by the National Arbor Day Foundation, in cooperation with the U.S. Department of Agriculture Forest Service and the National Association of State Foresters. There are countless present and former residents—Louise Wolters, Sue Murphy, the Liautaud family, Kerry Johnson, Judy Olsen, Steve Hildebrand, Howard Willman, and so many others too numerous to list—who have been instrumental in preserving the trout ponds and surrounding fen, conserving the health of the majestic woods, caring for the wildflowers that flourish along the garden-walk trails, and maintaining the horse trails, grazing pastures, hiking trails, riverfront park, and other dedicated green spaces so that they might be enjoyed for generations to come.

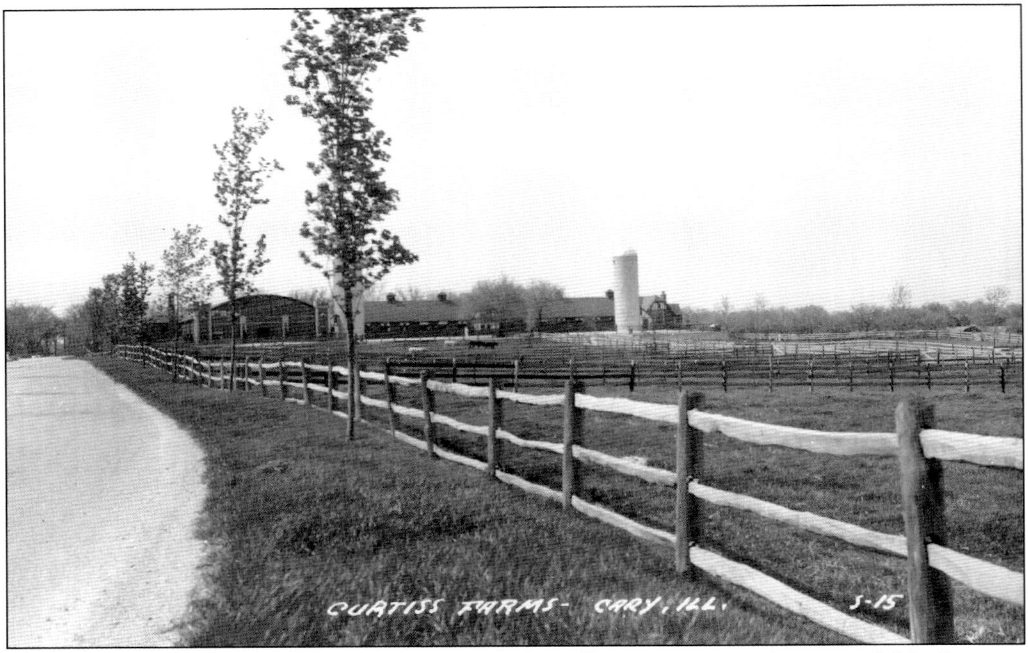

The early postcards for Curtiss Farm featured the rolling pastures and grazing fields during a time when there were only a handful of buildings. The original fences shown depicted in this 1940s postcard are the style that is maintained to this day throughout Trout Valley.

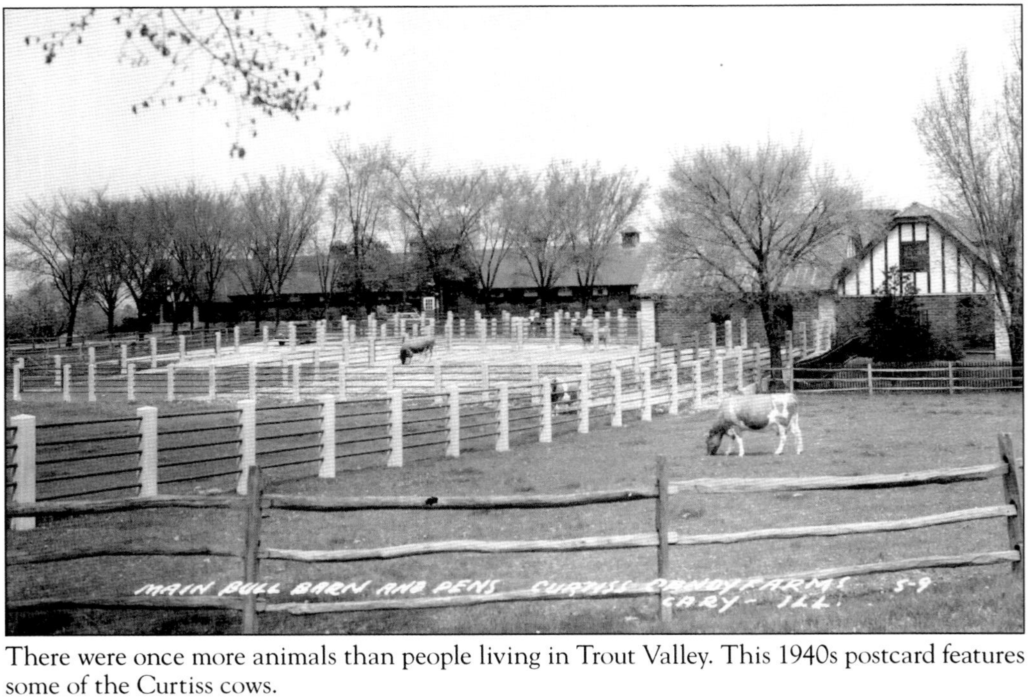
There were once more animals than people living in Trout Valley. This 1940s postcard features some of the Curtiss cows.

The Trout Valley barn is one of the original structures that is still in use today. It is seen here in 1970.

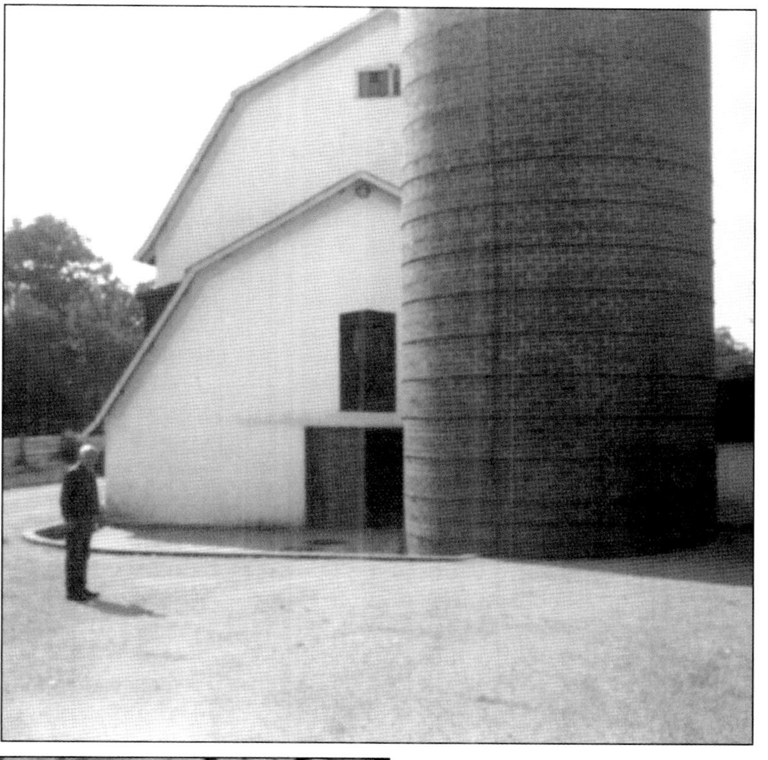

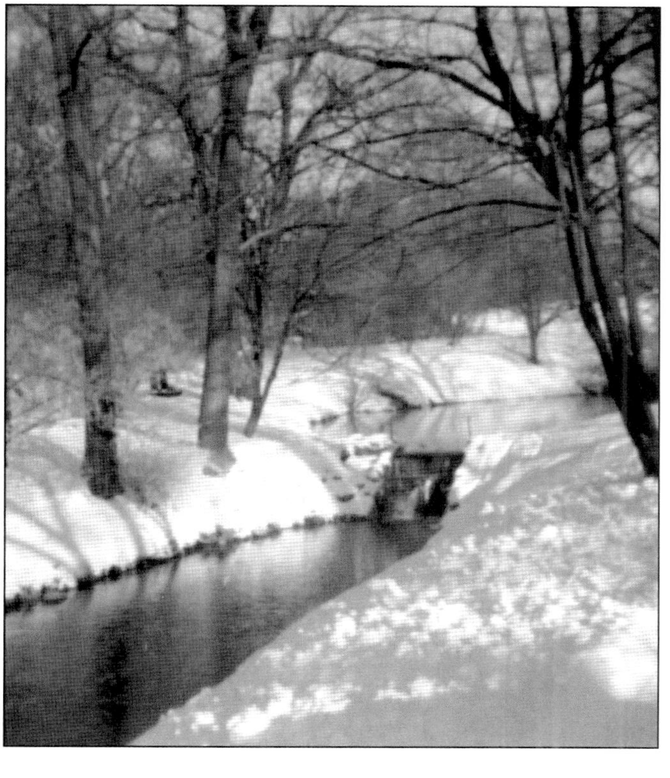

Even in the winter of 1970 the small waterfalls flowing through the spring-fed trout ponds added to Trout Valley's pristine beauty.

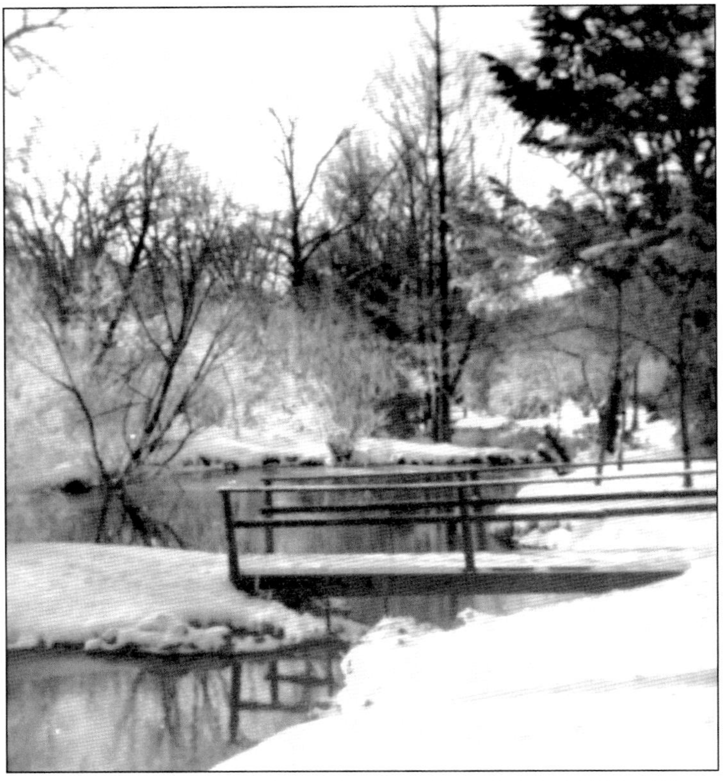

This picture shows Rainbow Bridge, spanning the trout ponds, in 1970.

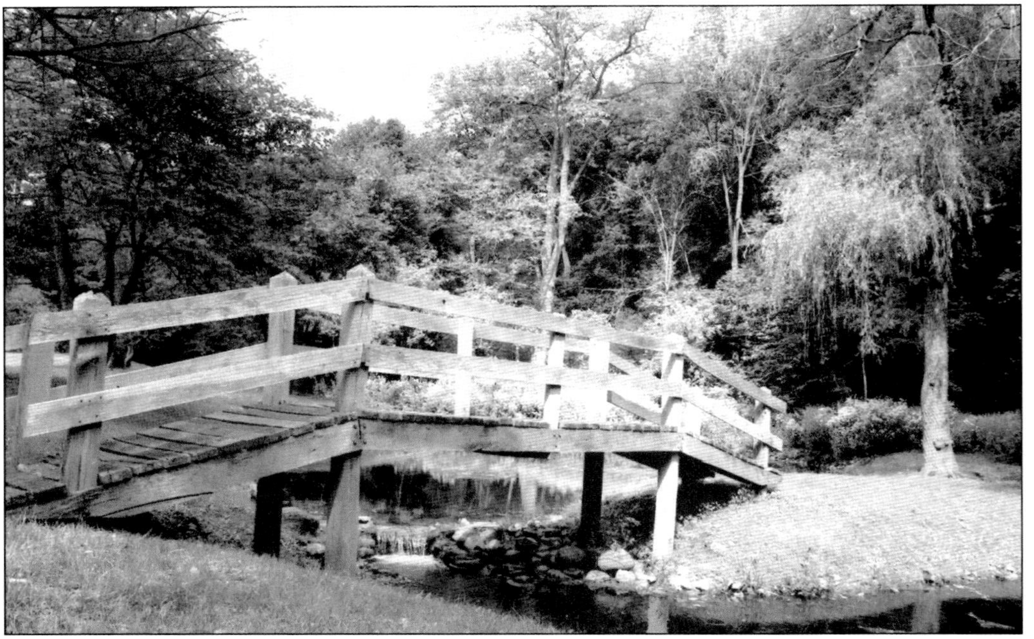

Rainbow Bridge was eventually rebuilt in a more elevated design. This photograph depicts Rainbow Bridge in the spring. Donations have been periodically gathered over the years from private residents to help maintain the stock of the trout ponds.

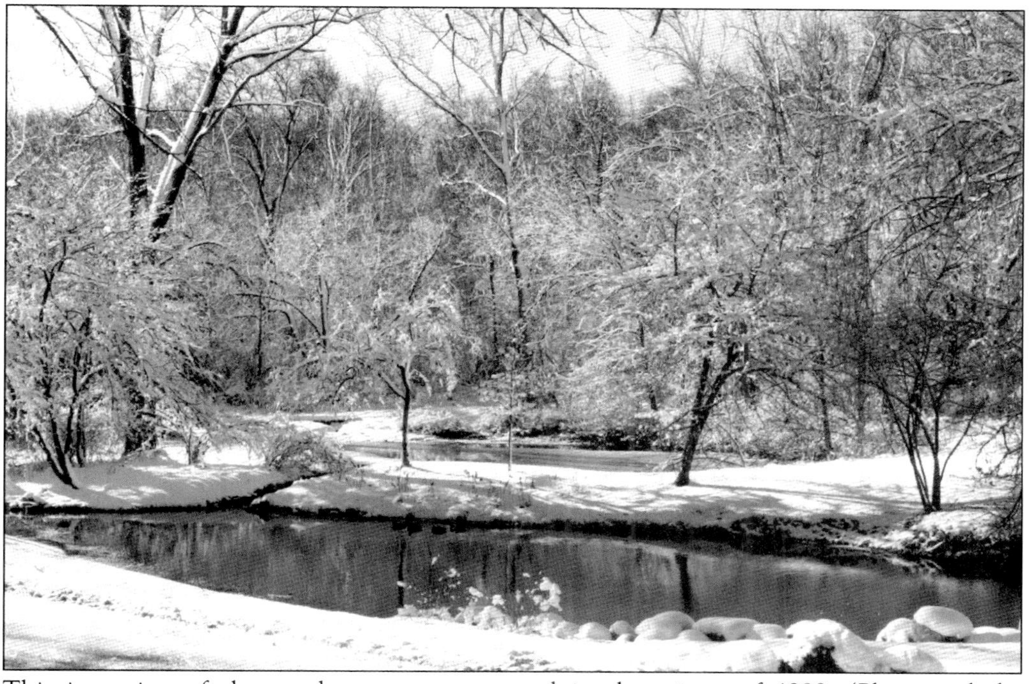

This is a view of the northernmost trout pond in the winter of 1998. (Photograph by Lorette Dodt.)

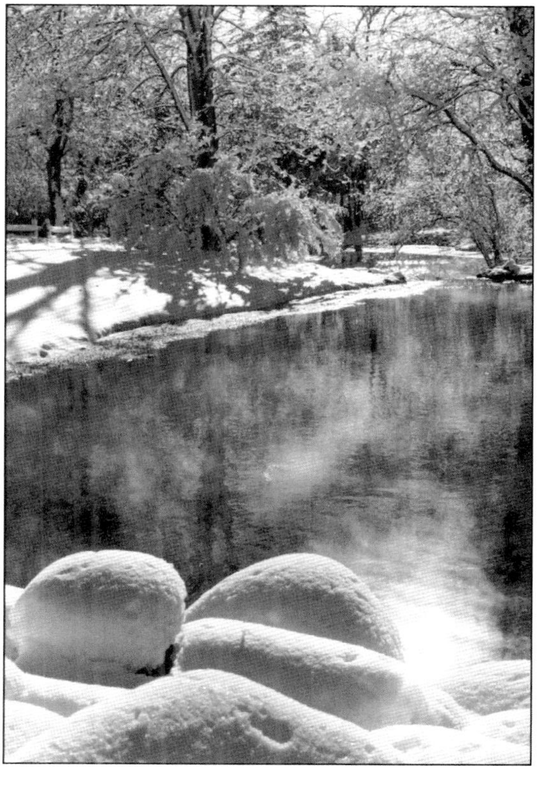

As the first in a system of naturally spring-fed ponds, the northernmost trout pond rarely freezes, as seen here in the winter of 1998. (Photograph by Lorette Dodt.)

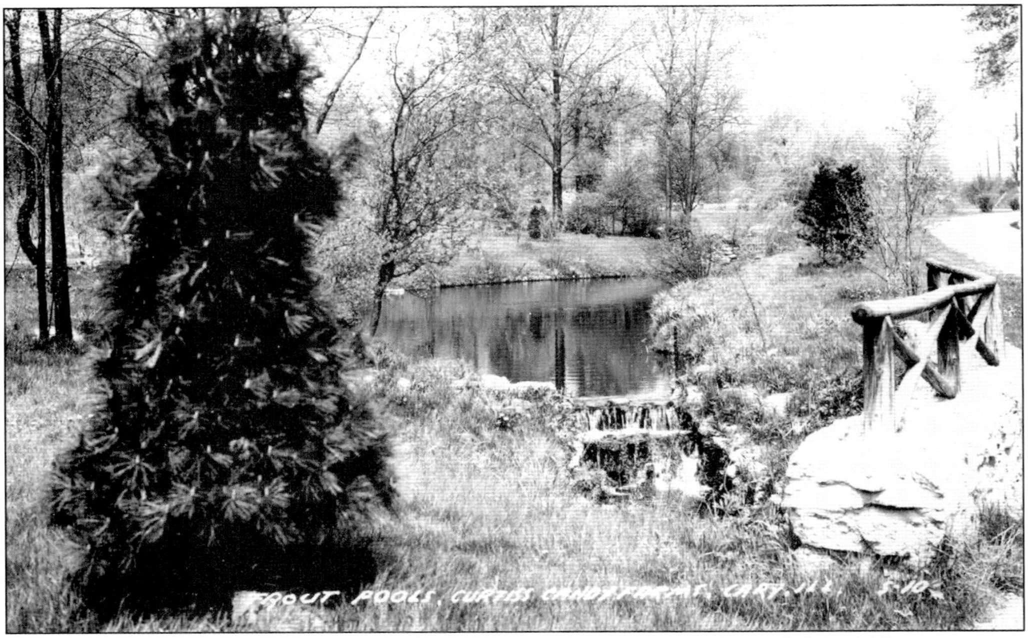

This postcard displays the trout pool during the Curtiss Farm era, around the 1940s.

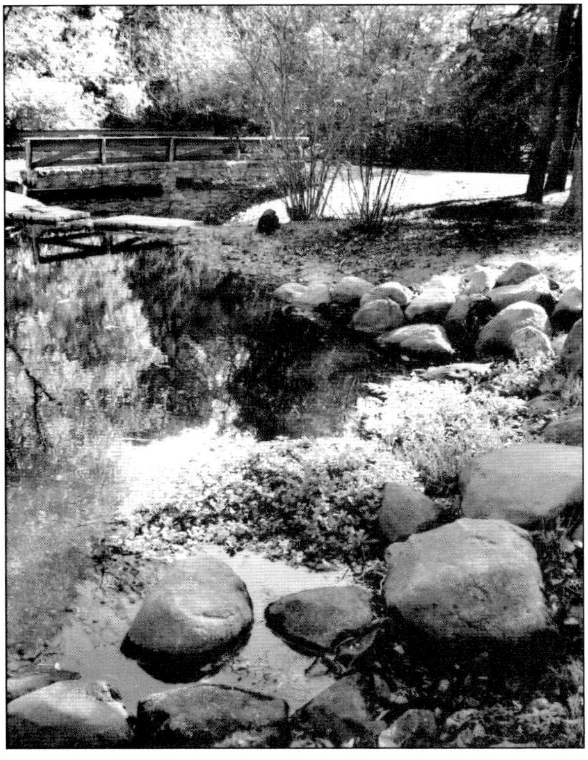

This picture shows some of the variety of fauna that flourishes around the trout ponds.

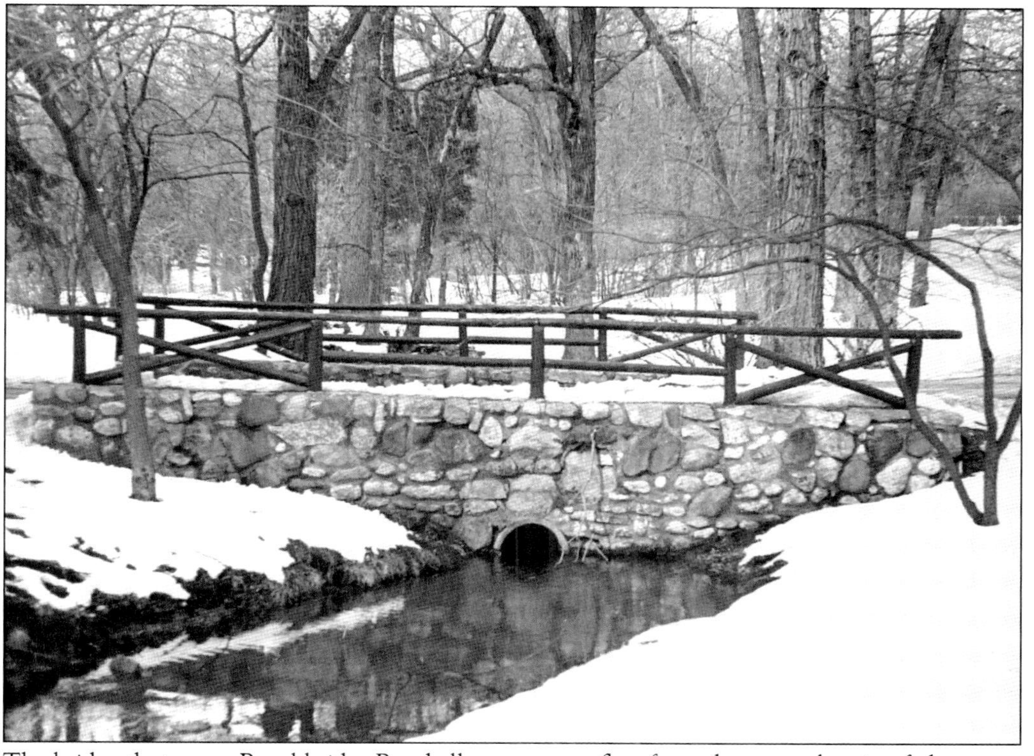

The bridge that spans Brookbridge Road allows water to flow from the natural spring-fed streams and ponds into Tom Sawyer Pond, as seen here around 1940.

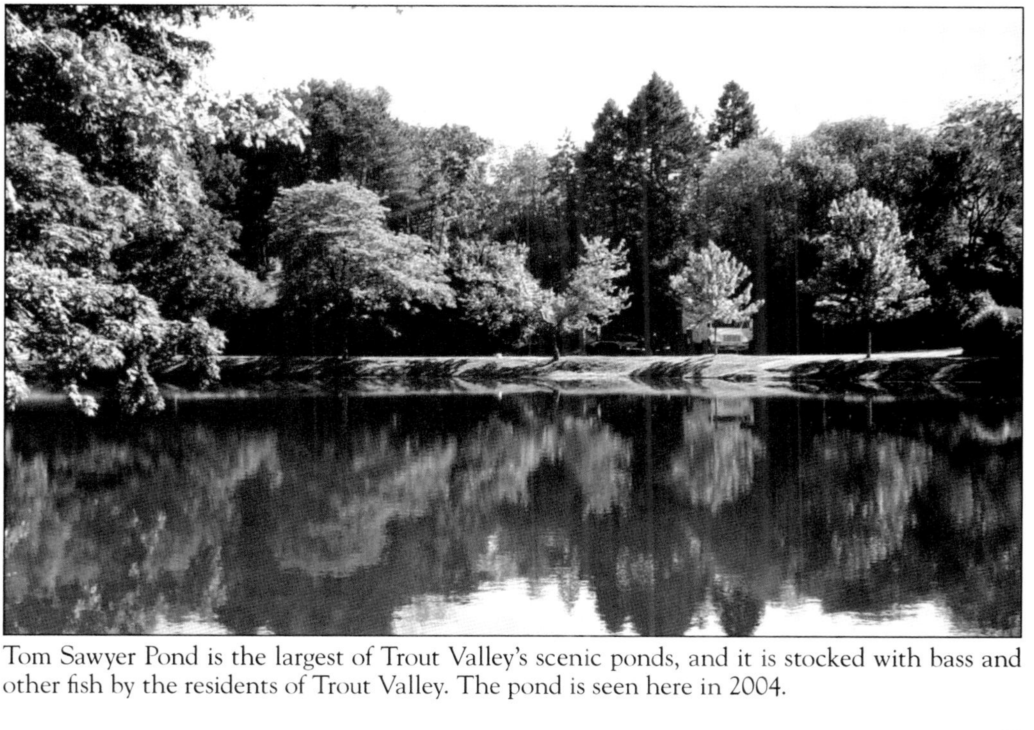

Tom Sawyer Pond is the largest of Trout Valley's scenic ponds, and it is stocked with bass and other fish by the residents of Trout Valley. The pond is seen here in 2004.

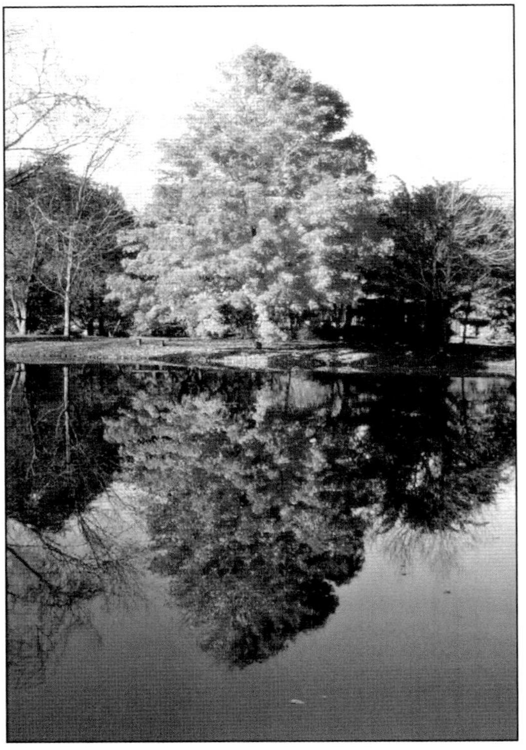

The variety of maple trees throughout the valley produces magnificent colors in the fall. The reflection of the trees can be seen on the mirrorlike water of Tom Sawyer Pond on calm days, as seen here in 2003.

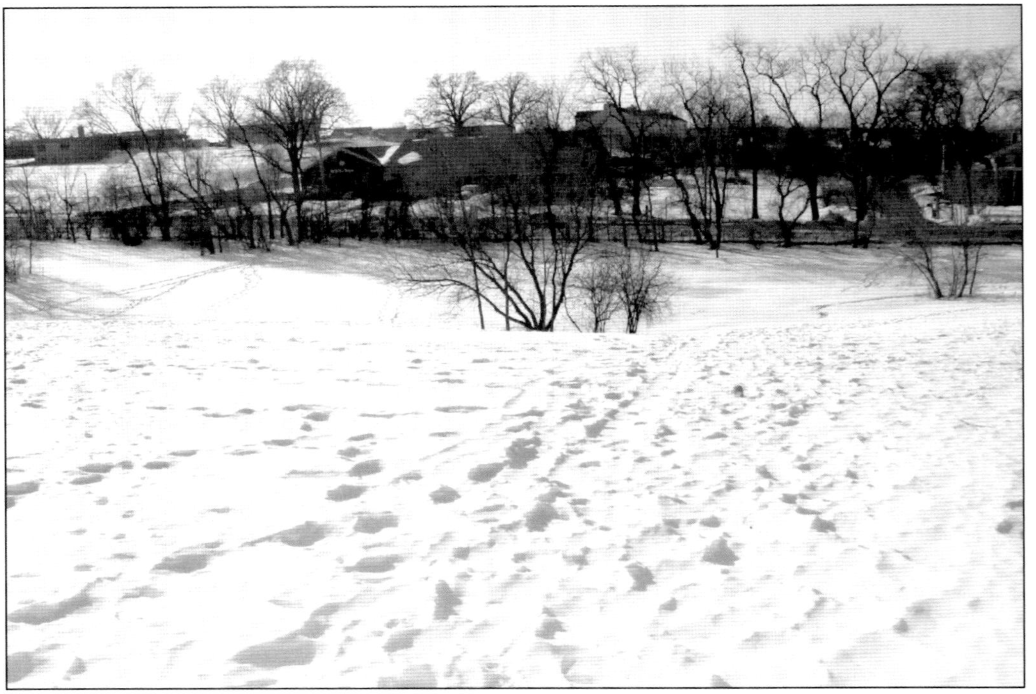

The horse pasture at the entrance of Country Commons Road, seen here in 2008, makes a delightful sledding hill where children can play during the winter.

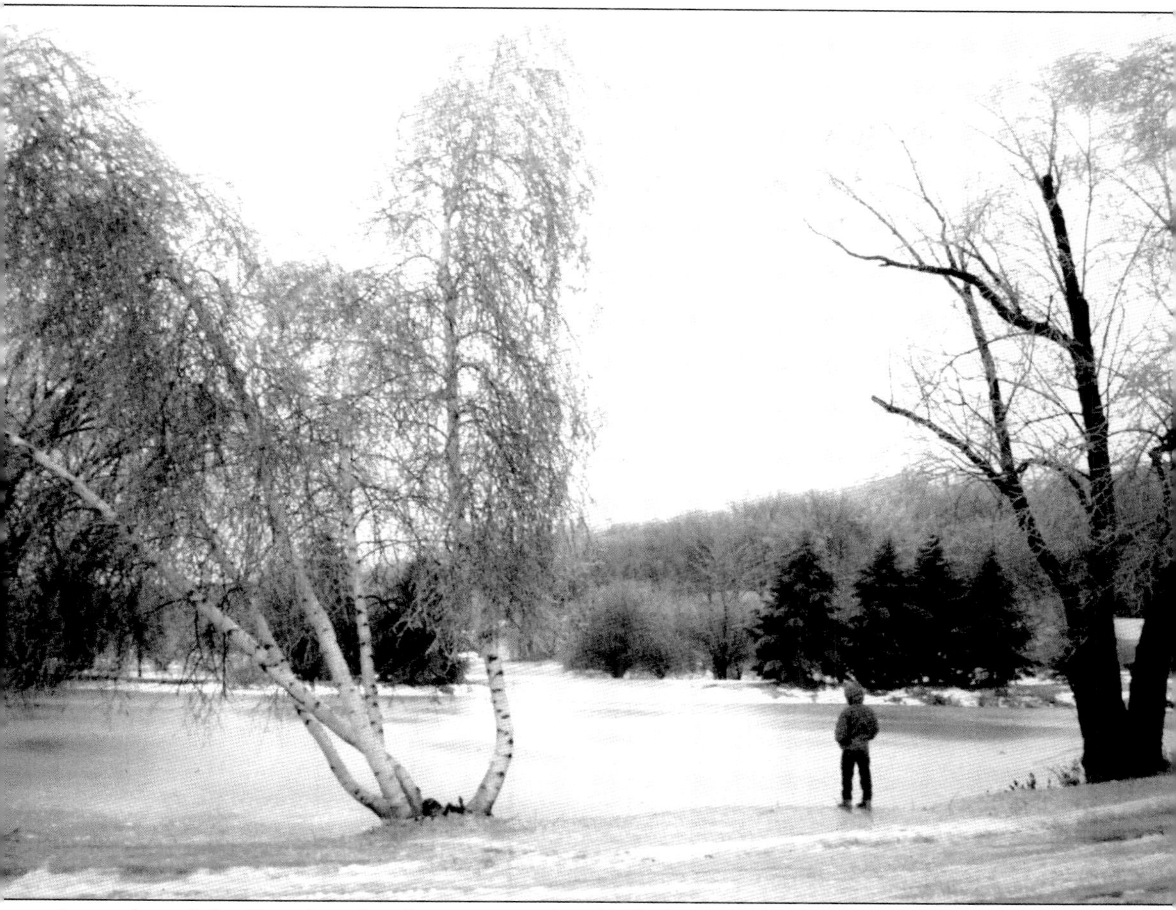

A member of the Trentlage family is seen in this 1965 photograph admiring the view of Tom Sawyer Pond on a quiet winter morning.

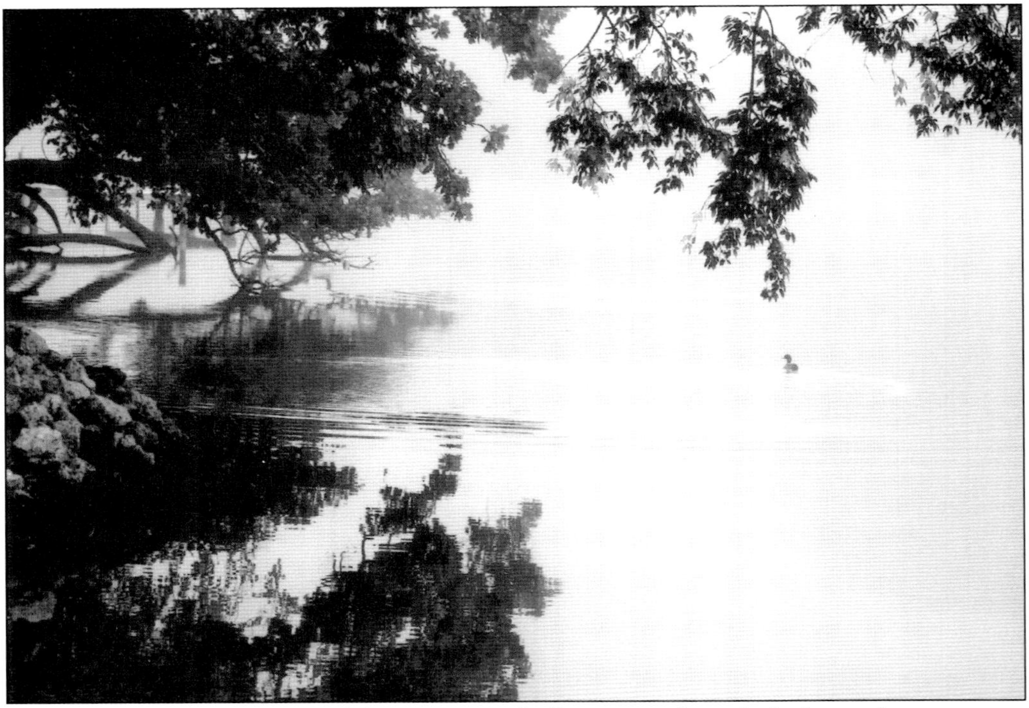

Trout Valley borders the beautiful Fox River and offers private boat docks for residents.

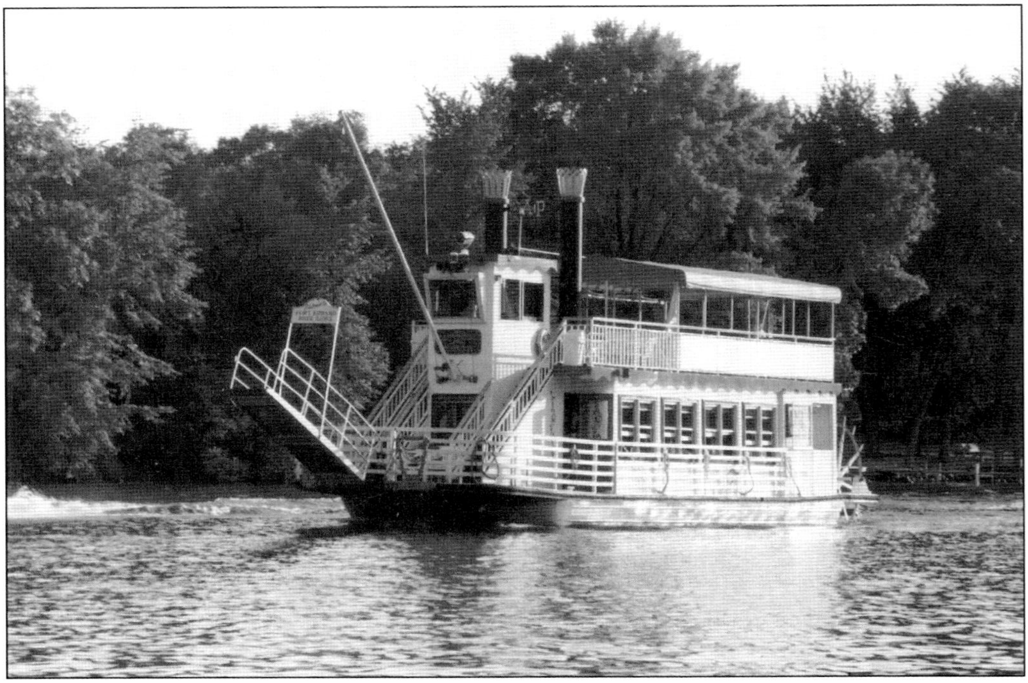

The *Algonquin Princess* riverboat offered dinner cruises and passenger cruises along the Fox River, where it could be seen from the shores of Trout Valley on its way from Port Edwards. (Photograph by Lorette Dodt.)

A cherry tree in full bloom can be seen from this home once known as the hay barn, seen in 1977. (Courtesy of Richard Trentlage.)

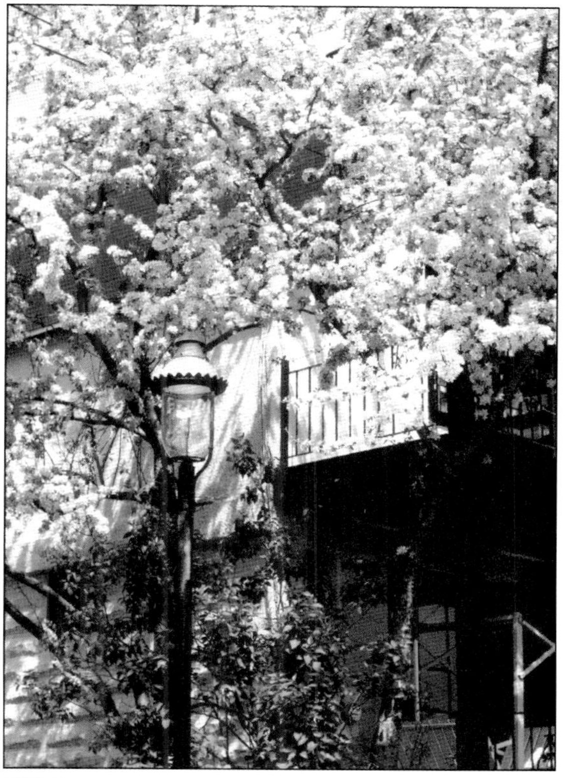

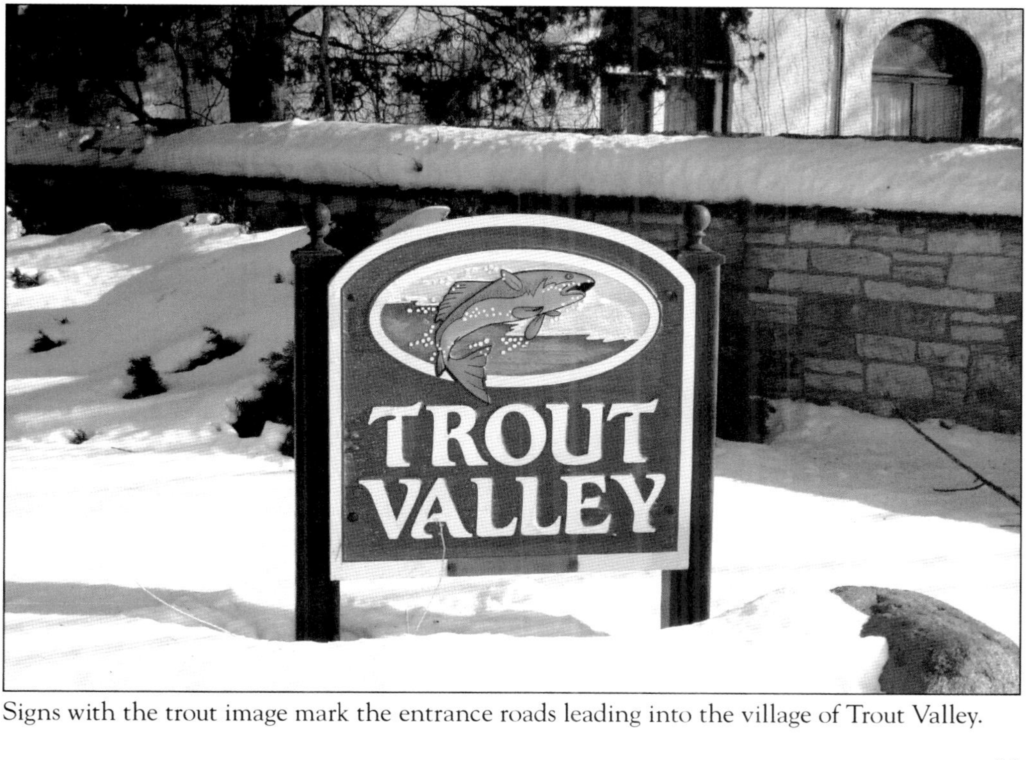

Signs with the trout image mark the entrance roads leading into the village of Trout Valley.

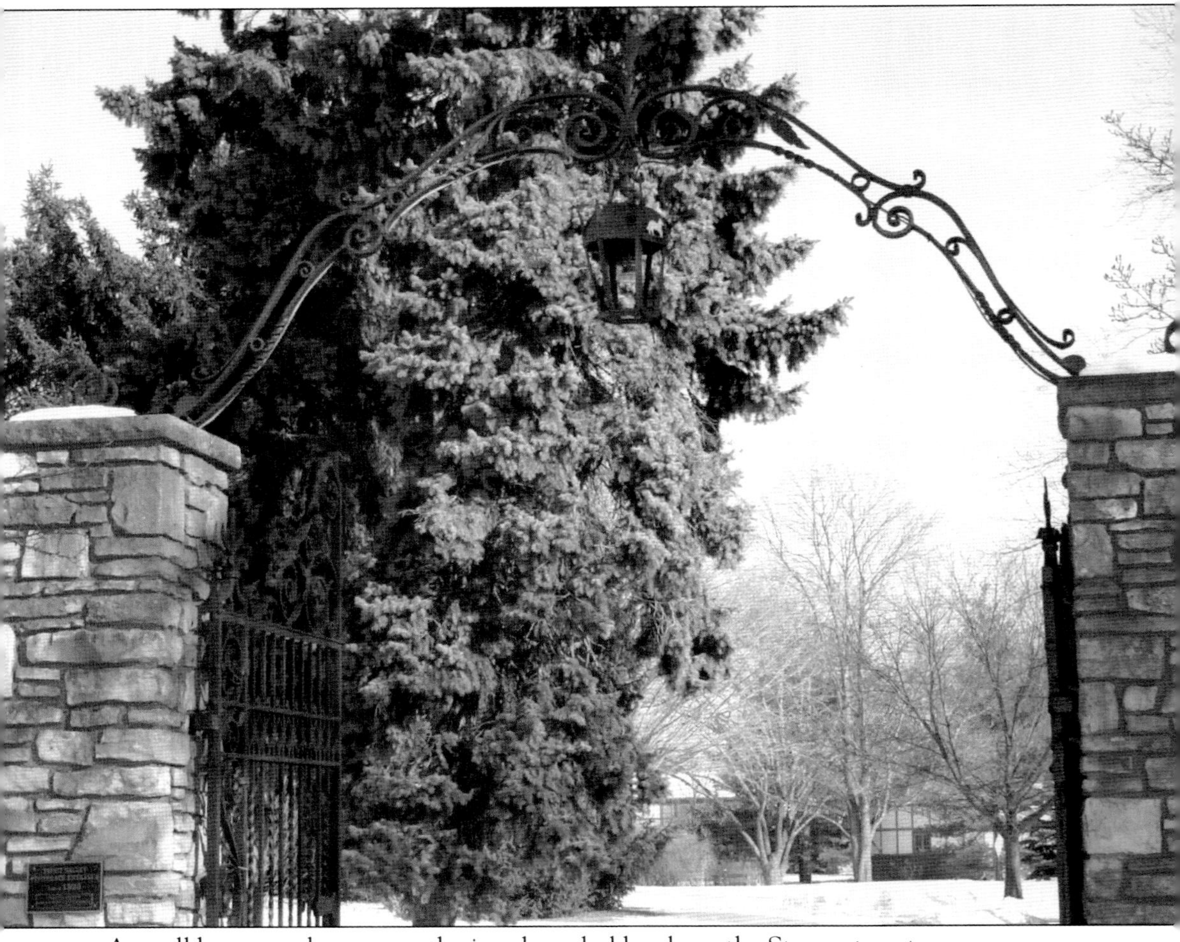

A small horse can be seen on the iron lamp holder above the Stonegate entrance.

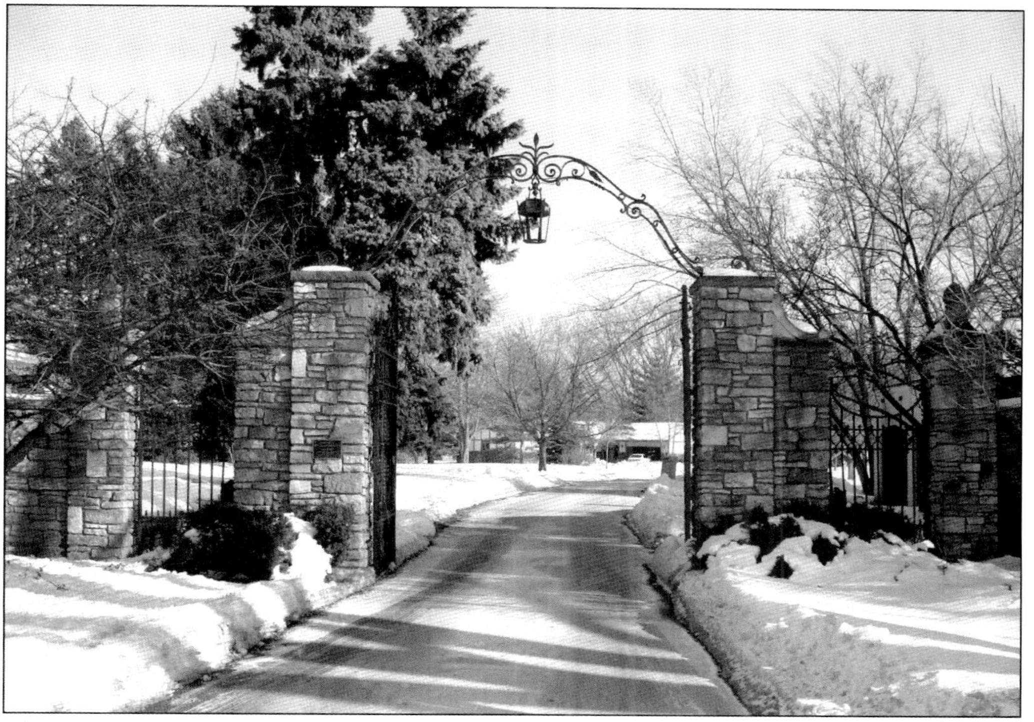

The original stone-pillared gate with ironwork marks the entrance at Stonegate Road.

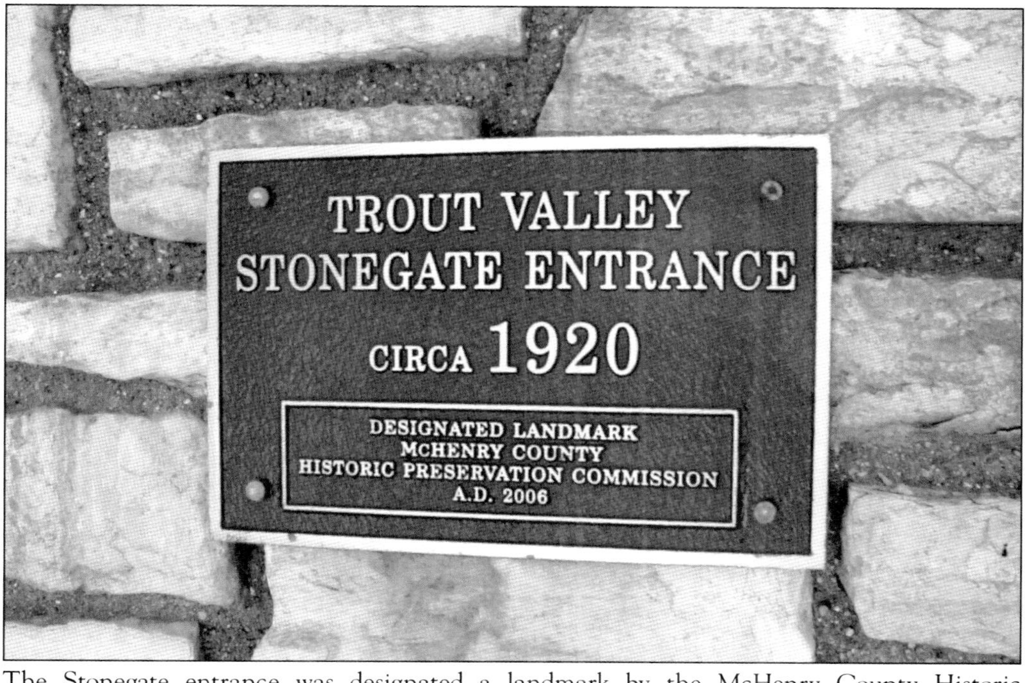

The Stonegate entrance was designated a landmark by the McHenry County Historic Preservation Commission in 2006, thanks to the dedicated efforts of Trout Valley resident Shirley Beene.

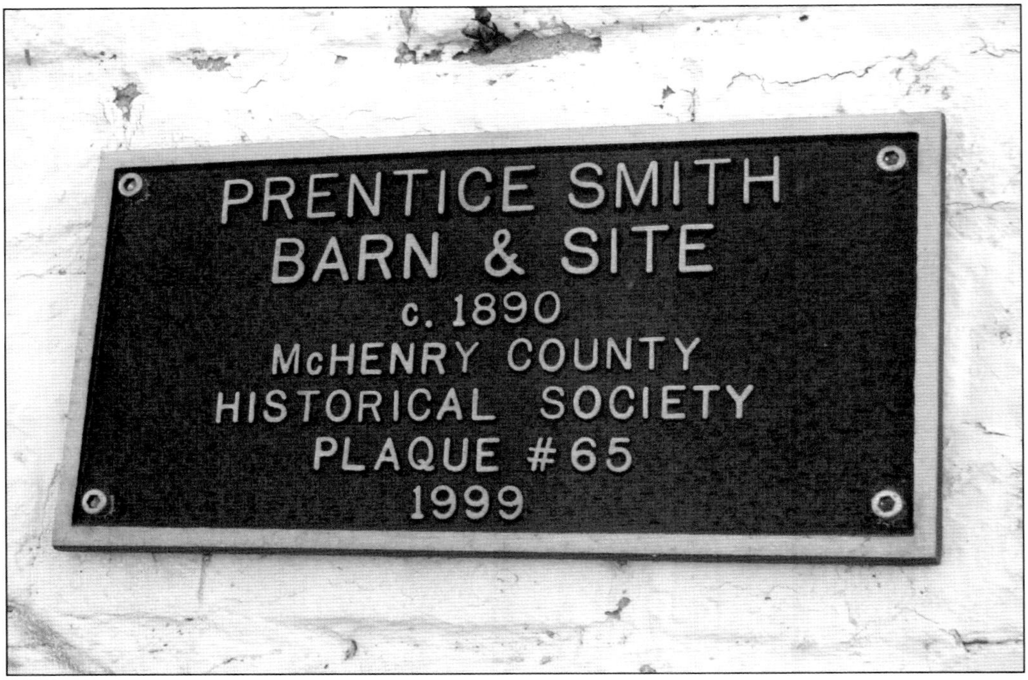

Shirley Beene spearheaded the effort to have the barn named an official historic site by the McHenry County Historical Society in 1999.

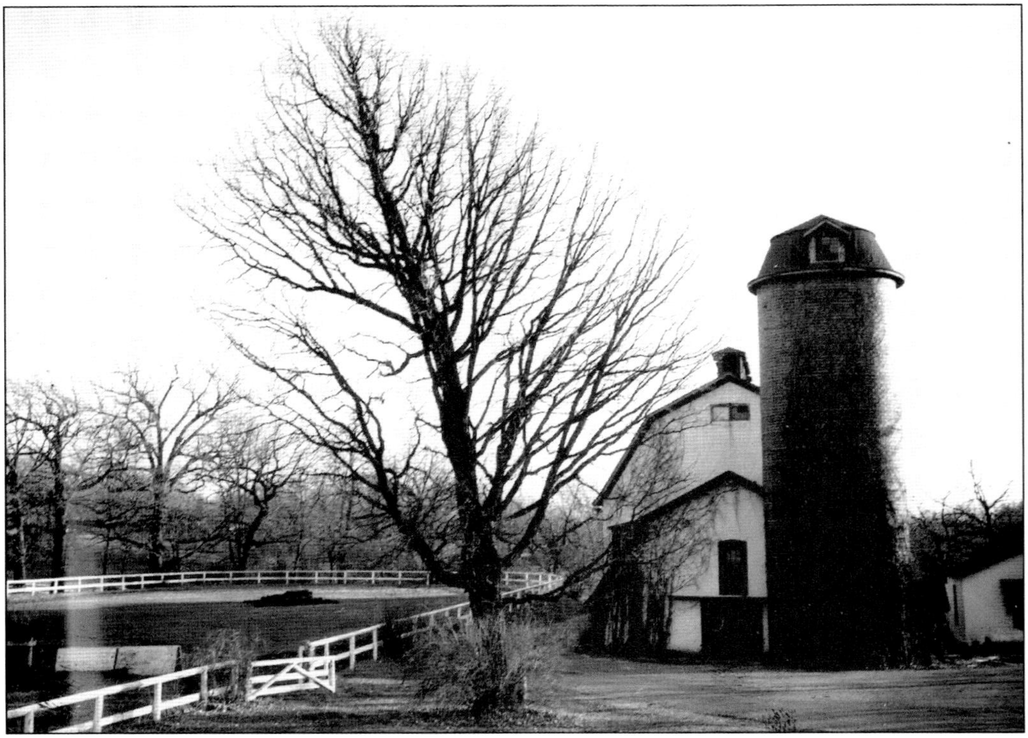

It is estimated that the Trout Valley barn was built in 1890.

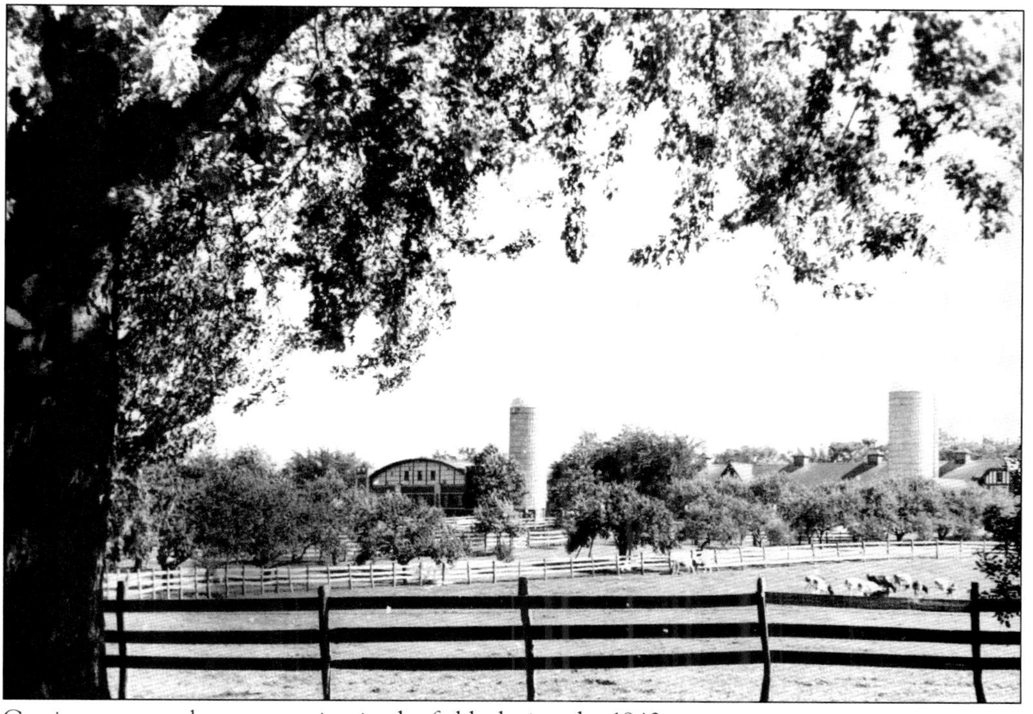

Curtiss cows can be seen grazing in the fields during the 1940s.

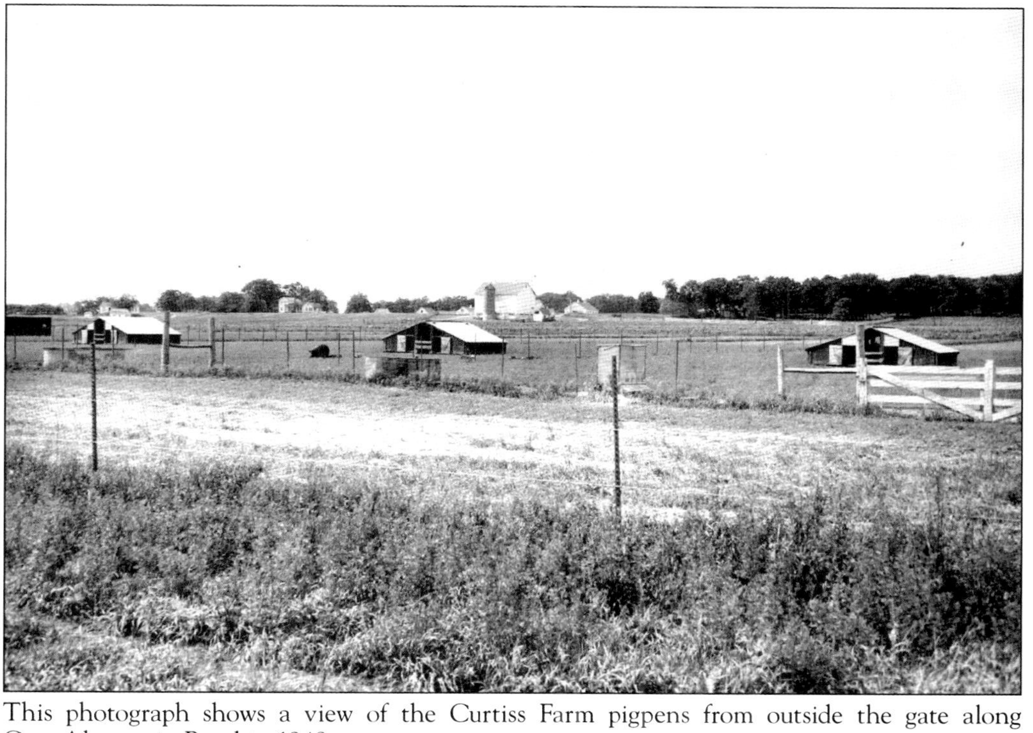

This photograph shows a view of the Curtiss Farm pigpens from outside the gate along Cary-Algonquin Road in 1948.

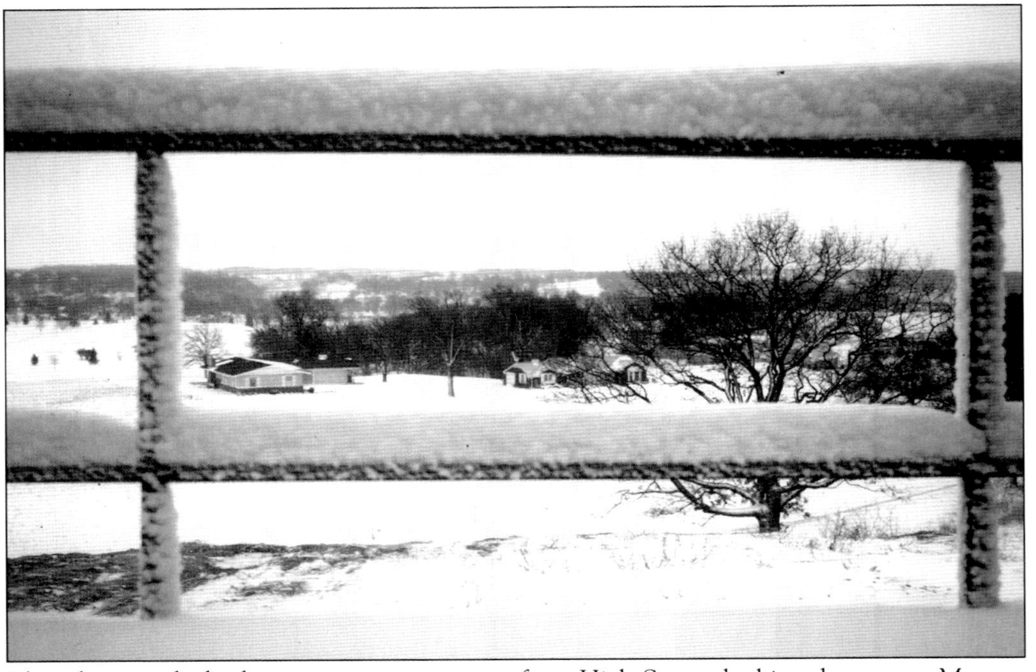

This photograph displays a scenic winter view from High Street, looking down onto Marryat Road, with the Cary Country Club golf course off to the left, around 1960. (Courtesy of Richard Trentlage.)

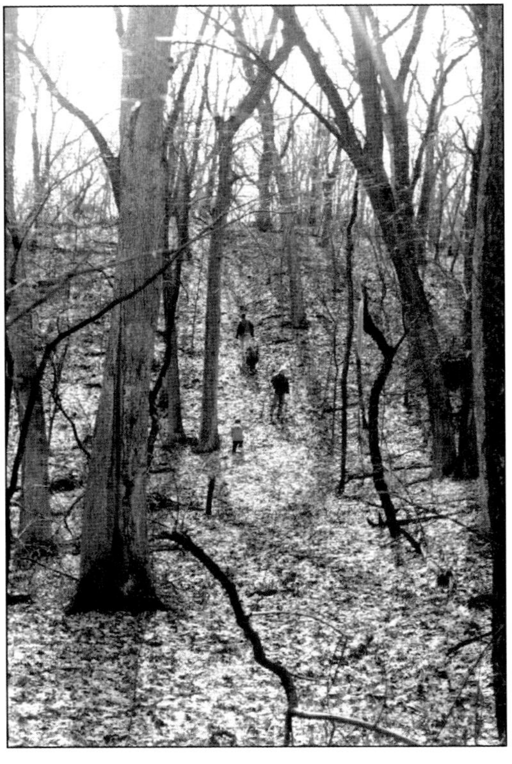

Residents are shown here enjoying a hike up Turkey Hill in the autumn of 1998. One of the Hertz homes at the top of the hill had an escape route through the floor into the basement, which led into a tunnel with an exit at the foot of the hill. (Photograph by Lorette Dodt.)

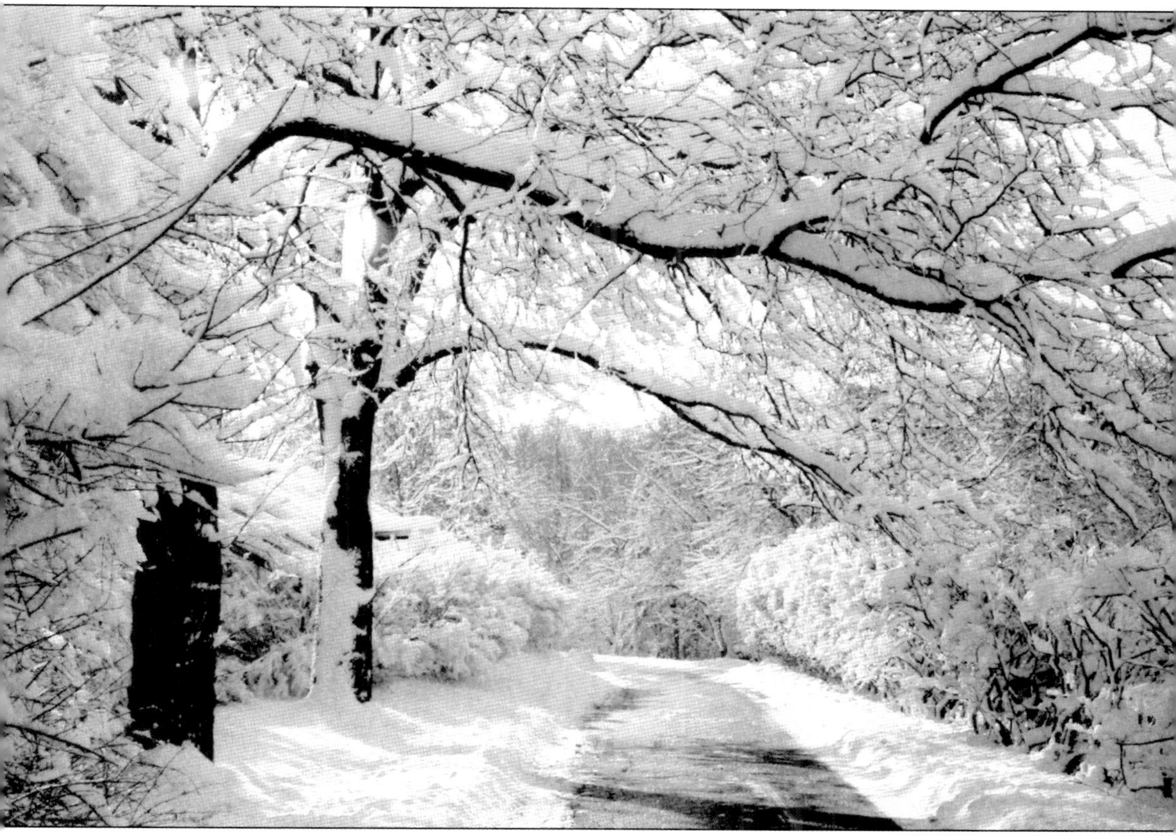

Here is a winter scene along Stonegate Road. (Photograph by Lorette Dodt.)

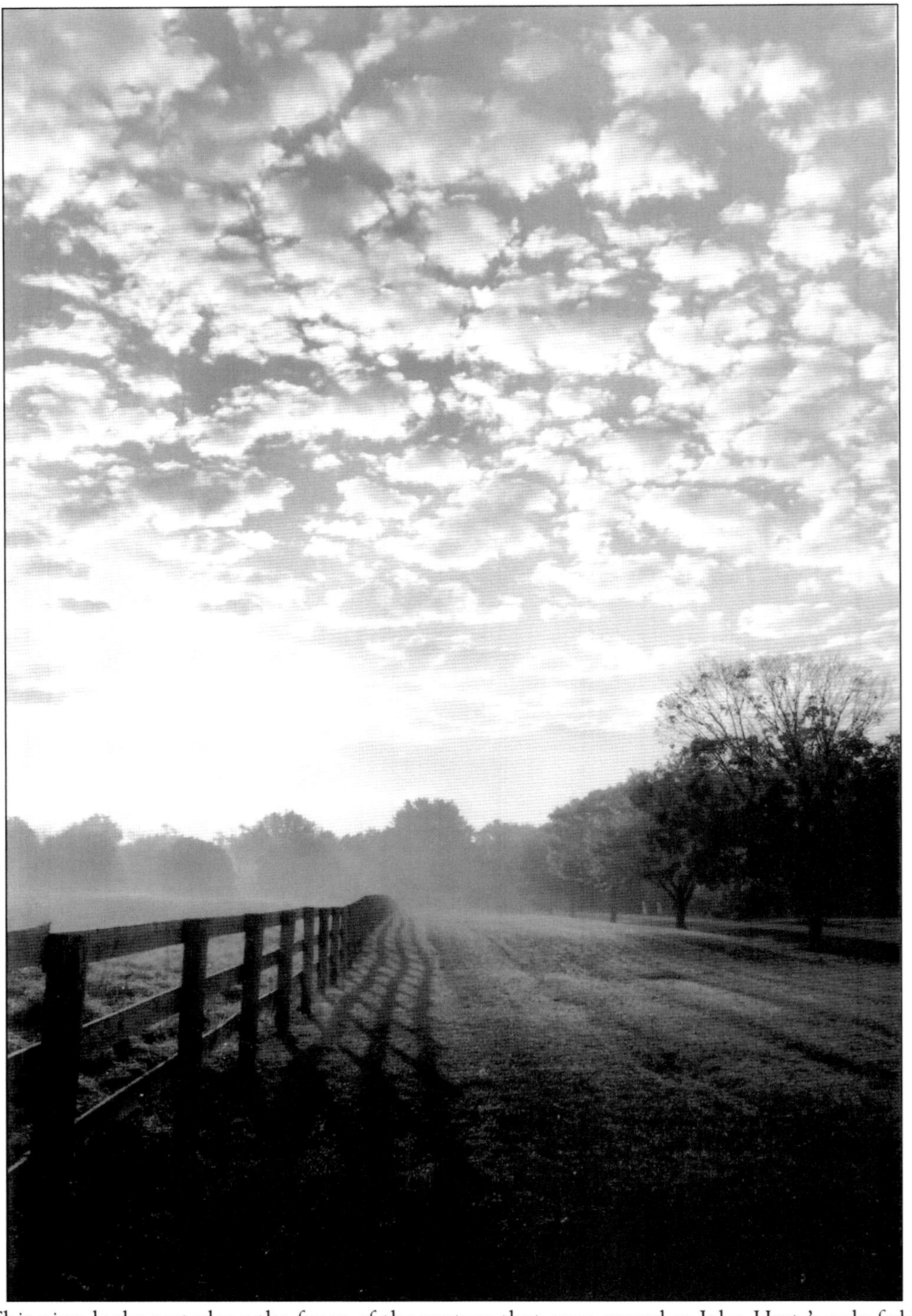

This view looks east along the fence of the pasture that once served as John Hertz's polo field. The Trout Valley Homeowner's Association obtained title to this 22-acre parcel during the 1960s by hosting a horse show on this spot for 10 consecutive years. (Photograph by Lorette Dodt.)

Displayed here is a cover from the souvenir program of the 1963 Trout Valley Horse Show, one of the equestrian traditions that continued in Trout Valley for many years.

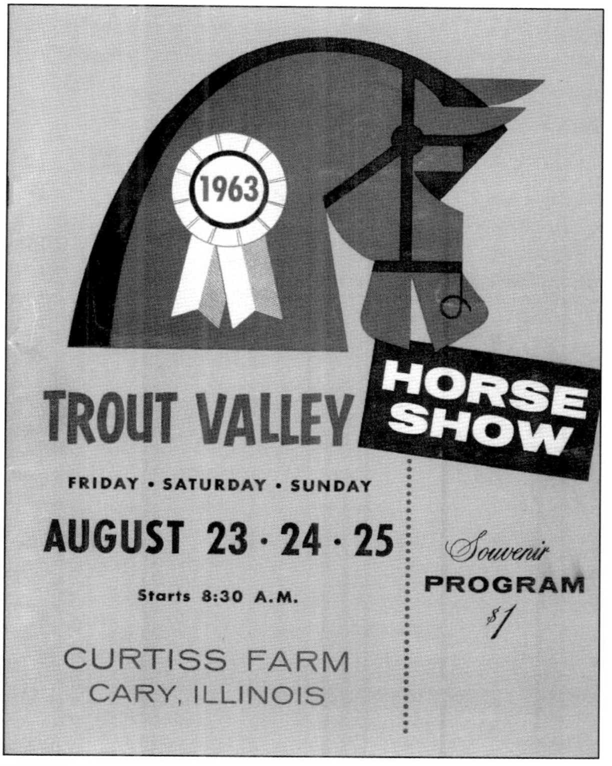

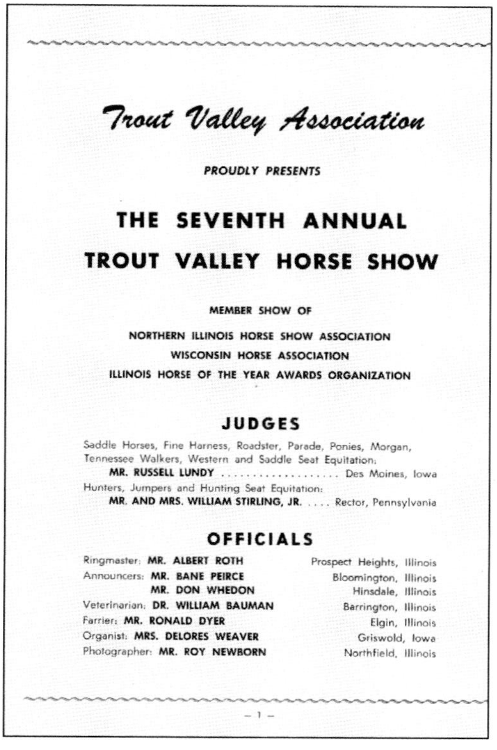

Trout Valley Association

PROUDLY PRESENTS

THE SEVENTH ANNUAL

TROUT VALLEY HORSE SHOW

MEMBER SHOW OF

NORTHERN ILLINOIS HORSE SHOW ASSOCIATION
WISCONSIN HORSE ASSOCIATION
ILLINOIS HORSE OF THE YEAR AWARDS ORGANIZATION

JUDGES

Saddle Horses, Fine Harness, Roadster, Parade, Ponies, Morgan, Tennessee Walkers, Western and Saddle Seat Equitation:
MR. RUSSELL LUNDY .... Des Moines, Iowa
Hunters, Jumpers and Hunting Seat Equitation:
MR. AND MRS. WILLIAM STIRLING, JR. .... Rector, Pennsylvania

OFFICIALS

Ringmaster: **MR. ALBERT ROTH** Prospect Heights, Illinois
Announcers: **MR. BANE PEIRCE** Bloomington, Illinois
MR. DON WHEDON Hinsdale, Illinois
Veterinarian: **DR. WILLIAM BAUMAN** Barrington, Illinois
Farrier: **MR. RONALD DYER** Elgin, Illinois
Organist: **MRS. DELORES WEAVER** Griswold, Iowa
Photographer: **MR. ROY NEWBORN** Northfield, Illinois

– 1 –

The Trout Valley horse shows typically ran over a three-day period and featured a tightly packed schedule of riding and show contest events, as briefly summarized in the opening page of the souvenir program shown here. The weekend also entailed a dinner and dance social event held at the Trout Valley barn. This image is from the 1963 event.

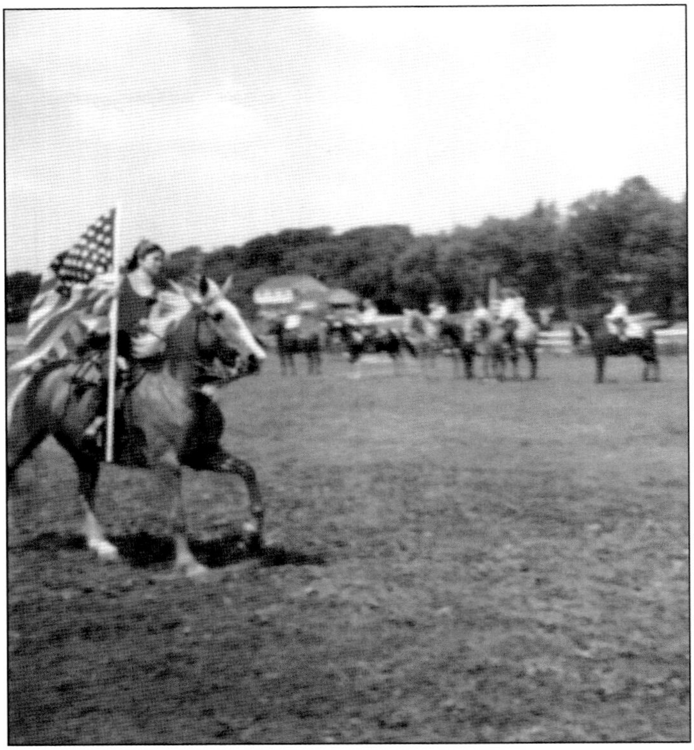

Sue Himes rides her horse Bee Bee in the Trout Valley Fourth of July horse parade around 1972.

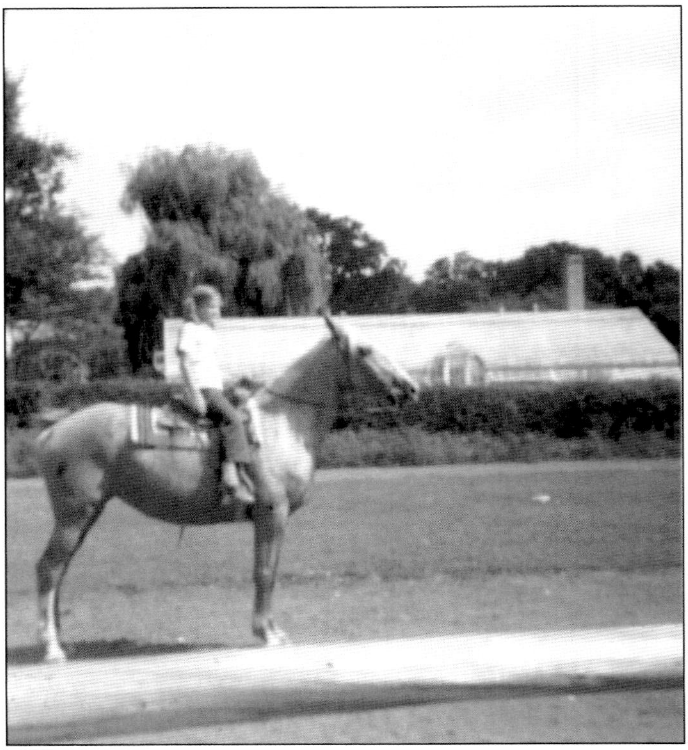

Practicing in the neighborhood horse training ring, Sue Himes sits astride her horse Bee Bee. The historic greenhouse can be seen in the background of this 1972 photograph.

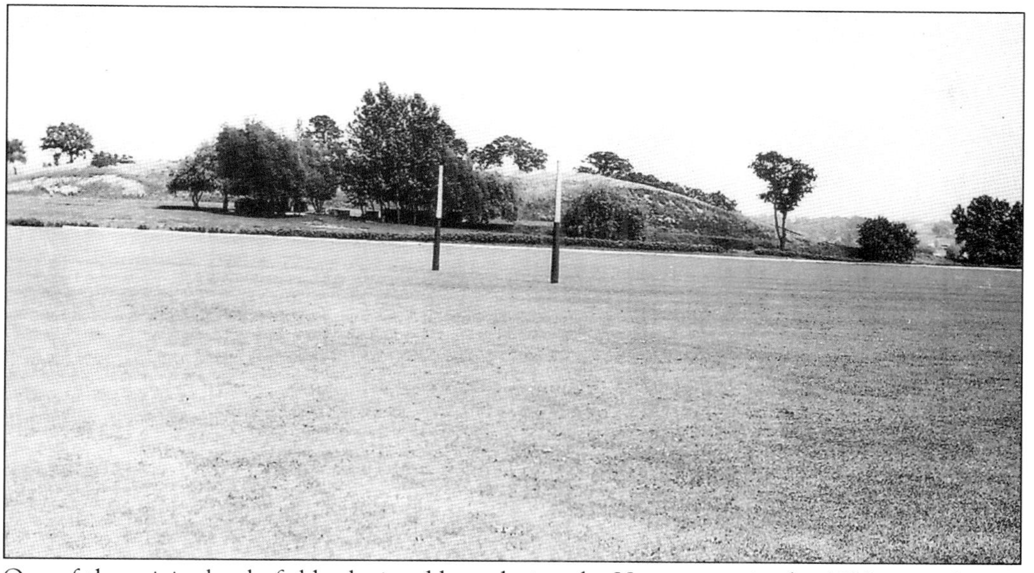

One of the original polo fields, depicted here during the Hertz estate in the 1920s, was the site of many practice sessions and formal polo events.

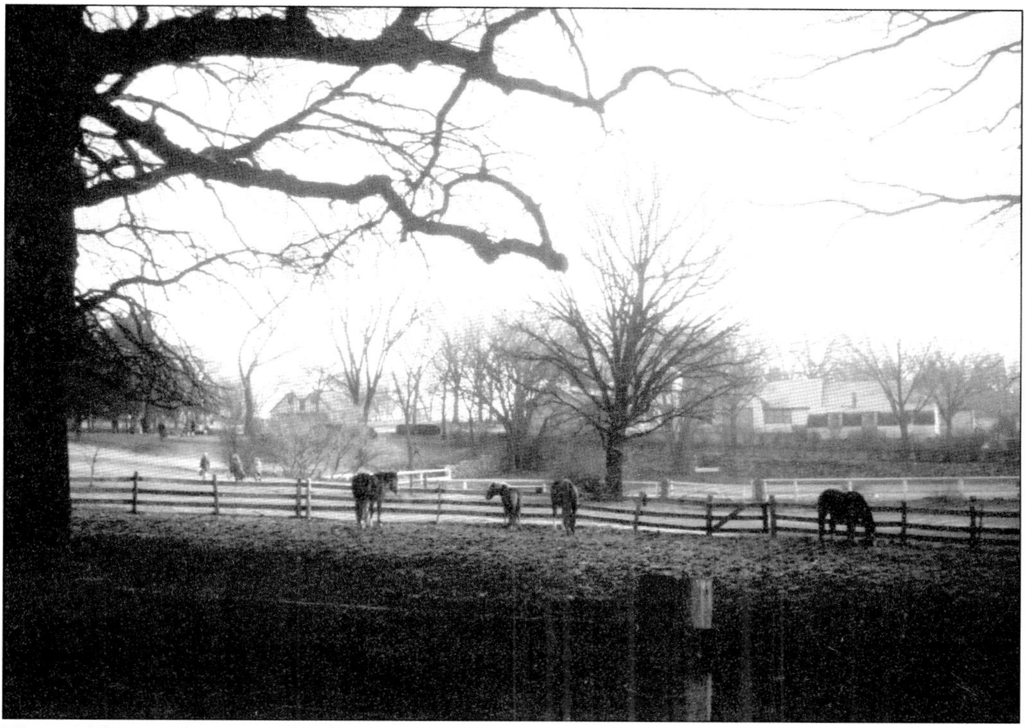

This 1965 view of Trout Valley horses was taken from the building that serves as the maintenance shed. Residents have the opportunity to participate in the Trout Valley riding club, which helps to provide the neighborhood's stables, training rings, riding trails, and horse pastures.

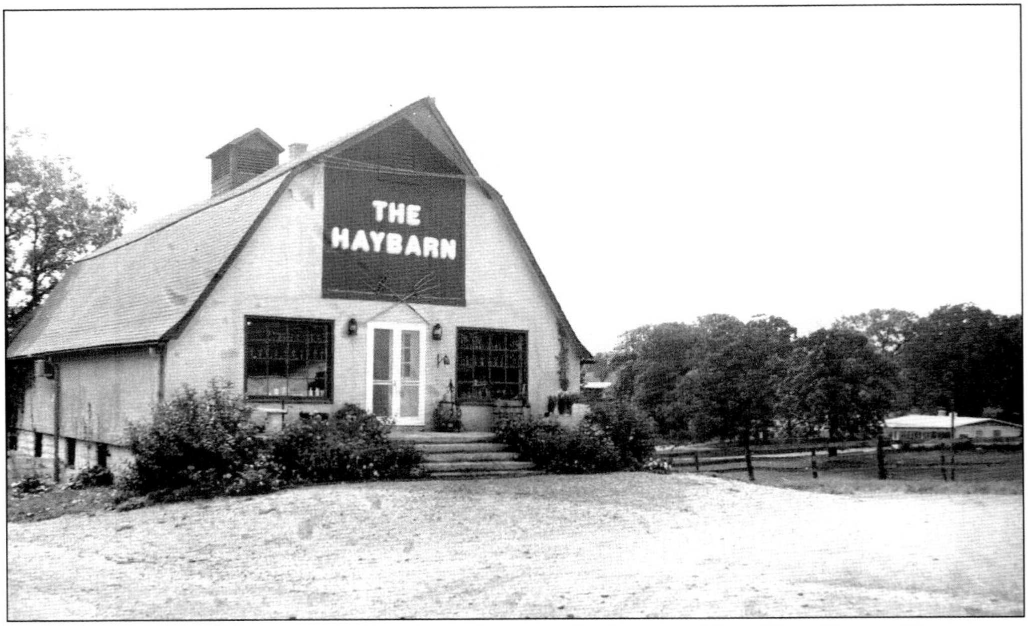

The building once known as the hay barn became the home of The Clap Trap, selling penny candy, ice cream, and antiques to locals on the lower walk-out level. Occupied jointly at the opposite end of the building was the Cary Fine Arts Center, providing dance lessons in the rooms once occupied by ponies during the Hertz era. Both businesses were owned and managed by Richard and Vivian Trentlage. This image is from the 1960s.

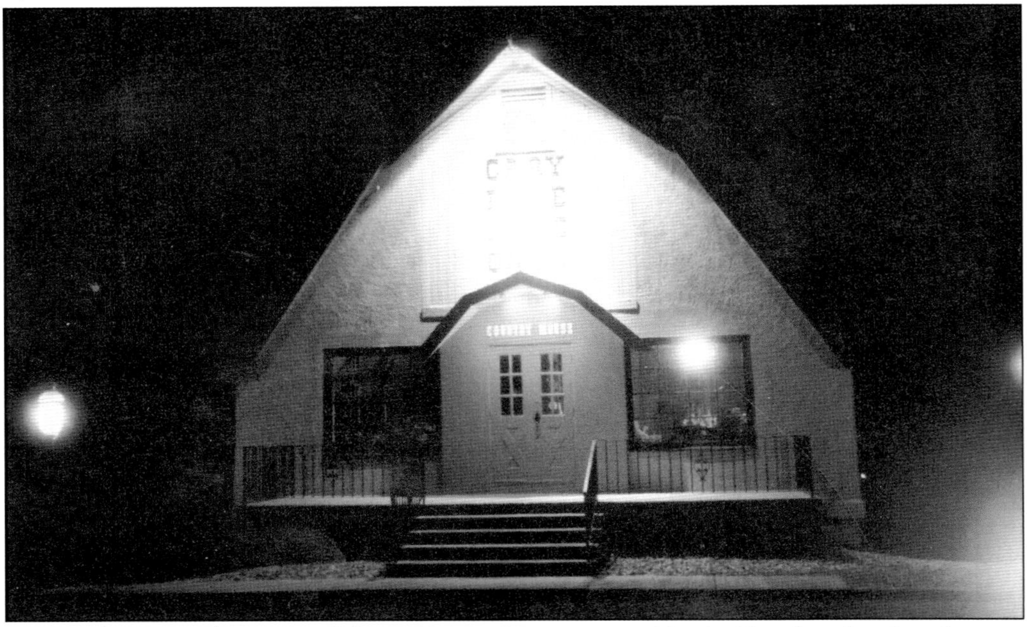

The hay barn, seen here around the 1960s, was later renovated by the Trentlage family to become the site of the Cary Fine Arts Center. Music lessons were one of the services available. In more recent years, it has housed a beauty salon, Delphi Card Business, and P&S Midwest, which provided industrial refrigeration equipment.

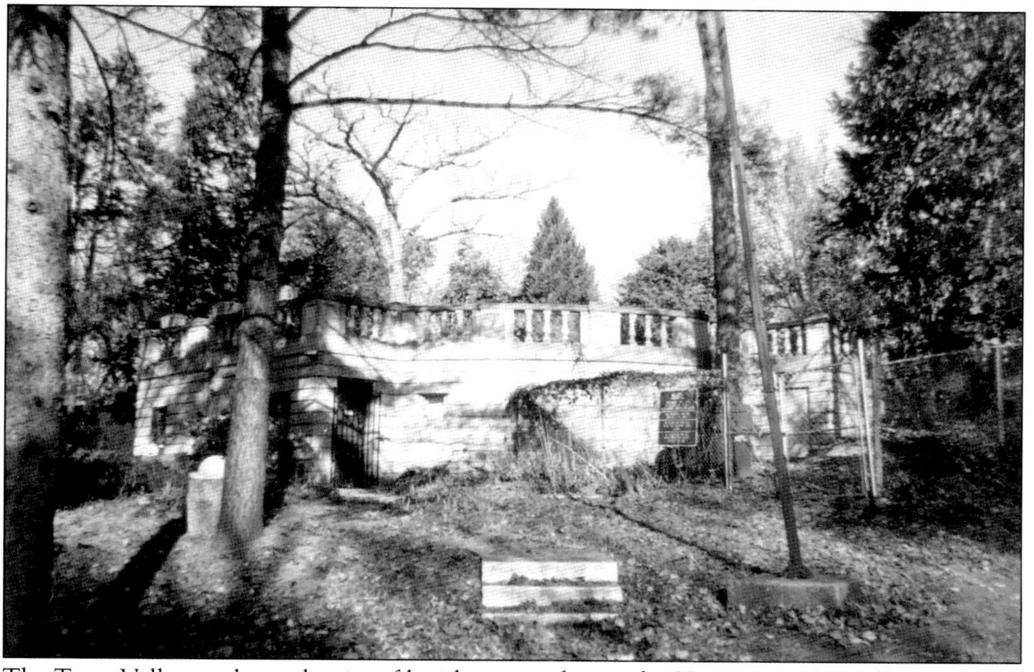

The Trout Valley pool was the site of lavish parties during the Hertz era and is still used during the summers by Trout Valley residents. (Courtesy of Todd Somers.)

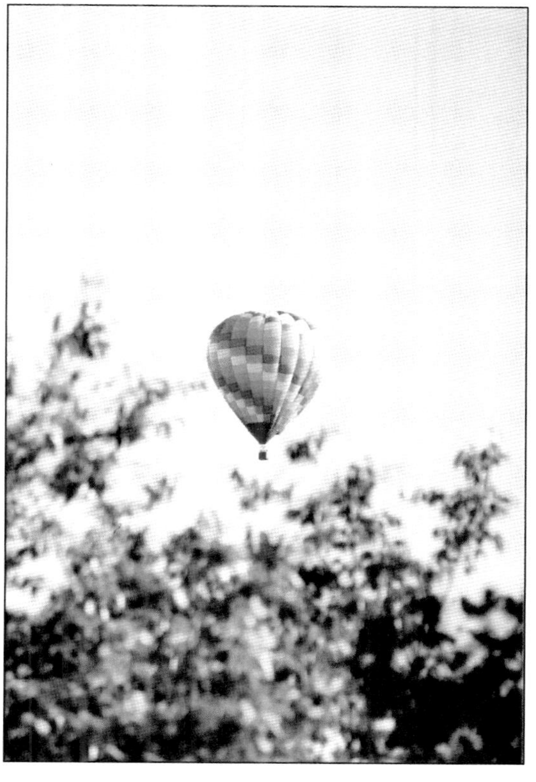

Hot air balloons have been known to drift over Trout Valley to add to the beauty of a calm sunny day. (Photograph by Lorette Dodt.)

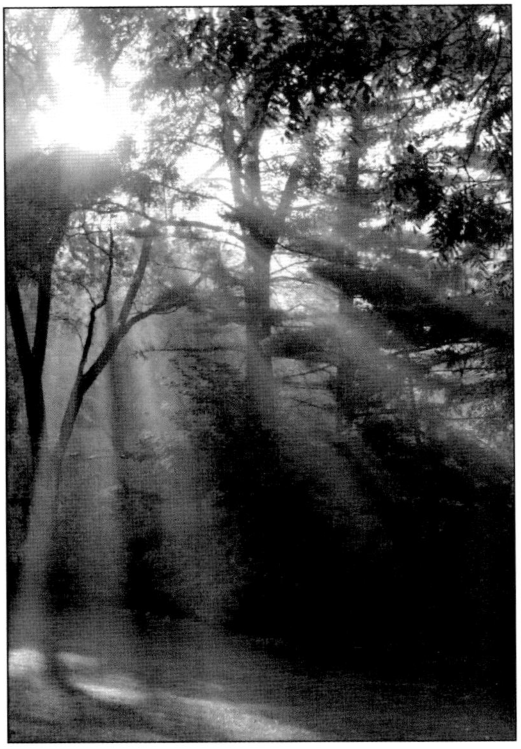

Sunbeams stream through the tree canopy in this heavily wooded neighborhood.

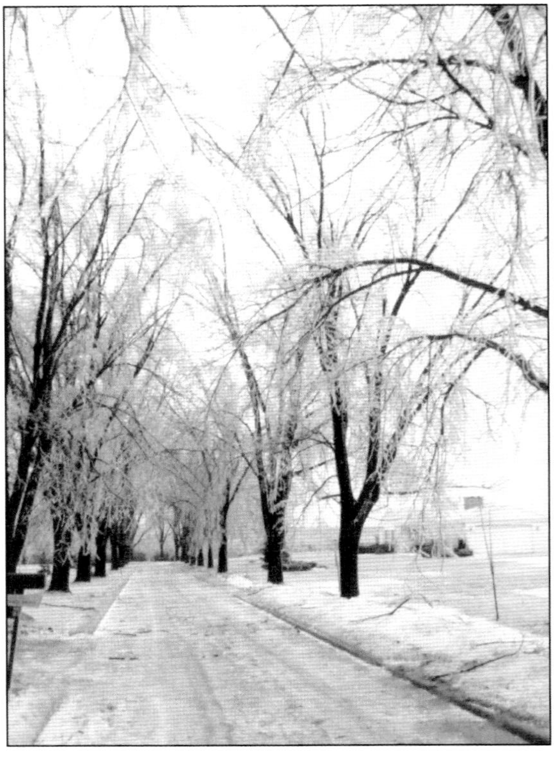

The midwestern seasons display dramatically different views of Trout Valley throughout the year, as can be seen in this photograph taken after an ice storm in 1965.

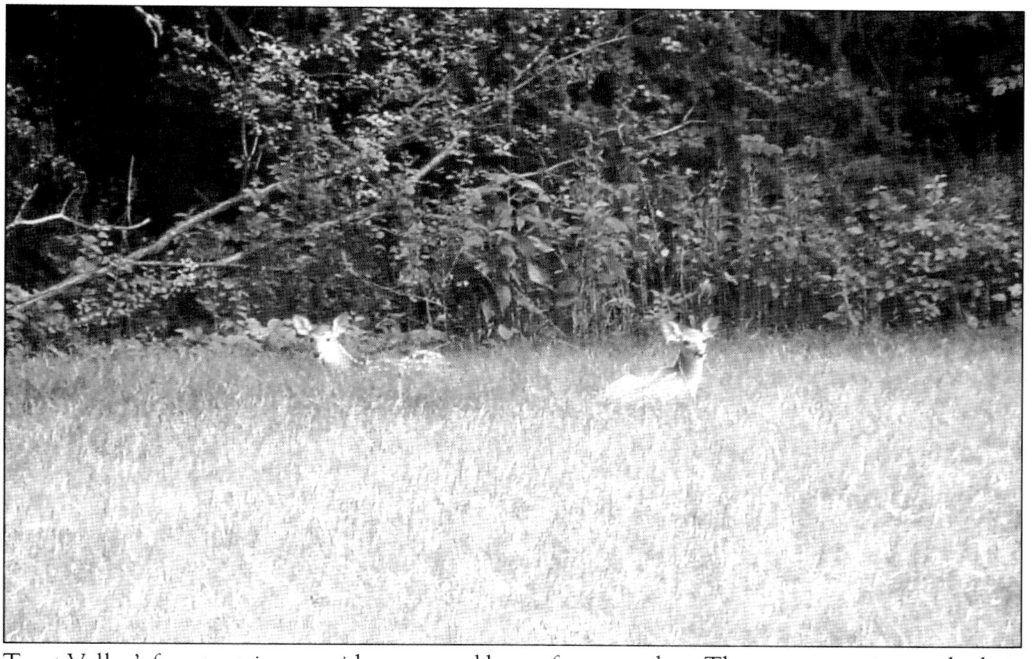

Trout Valley's forest setting provides a natural home for many deer. These young twins made their home in the Kidder backyard off River Drive in 2006, occasionally watching two-year-old Talia Kidder play just a few feet away. They were originally spotted within an estimated hour or two of birth and encouraged by their mother to try walking on their shaky legs for the first time.

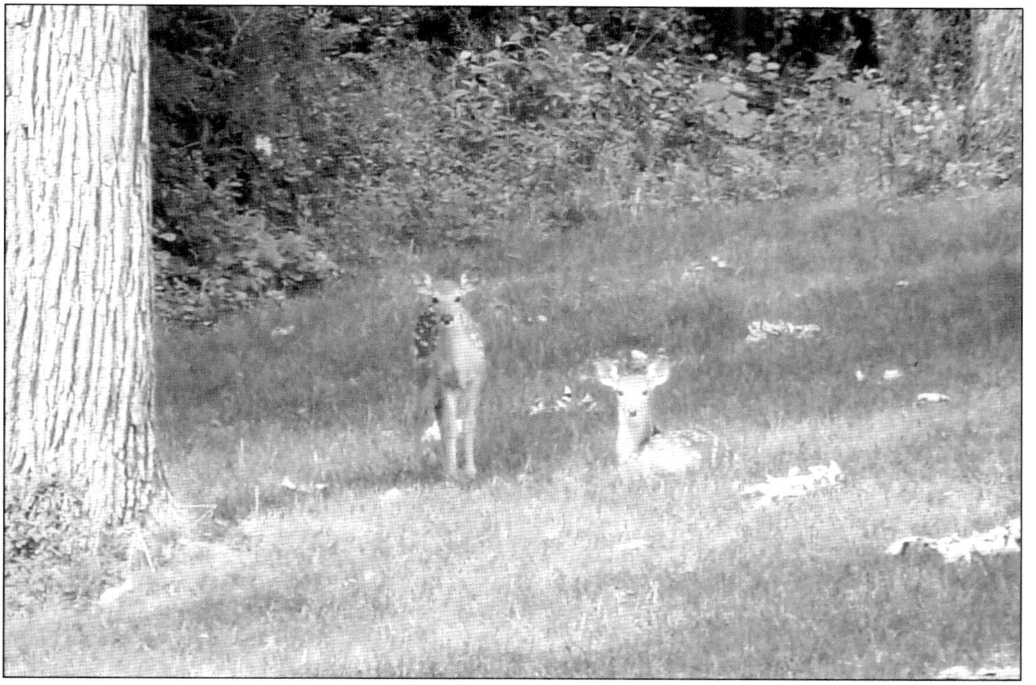

Deer, fox, raccoons, groundhogs, numerous species of birds, and other wildlife flourish in the lush Trout Valley landscape as evidenced here in 2006.

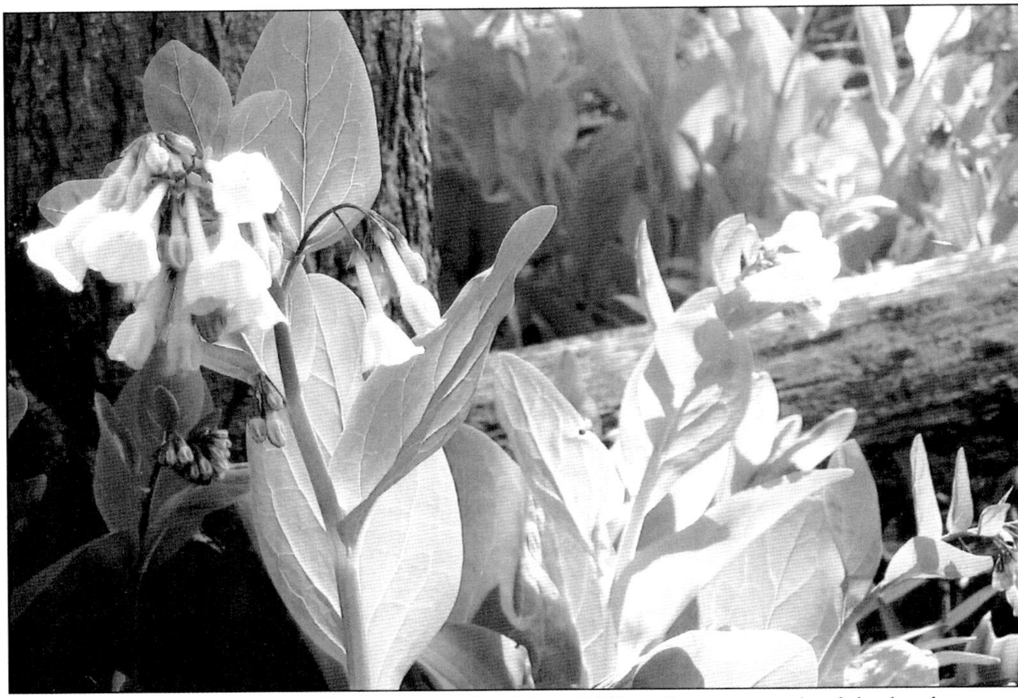

Wildflowers are well-protected treasures within Trout Valley. Because much of the land remains untouched, they can be seen throughout the various trails, streams, and fields during the spring and summer months.

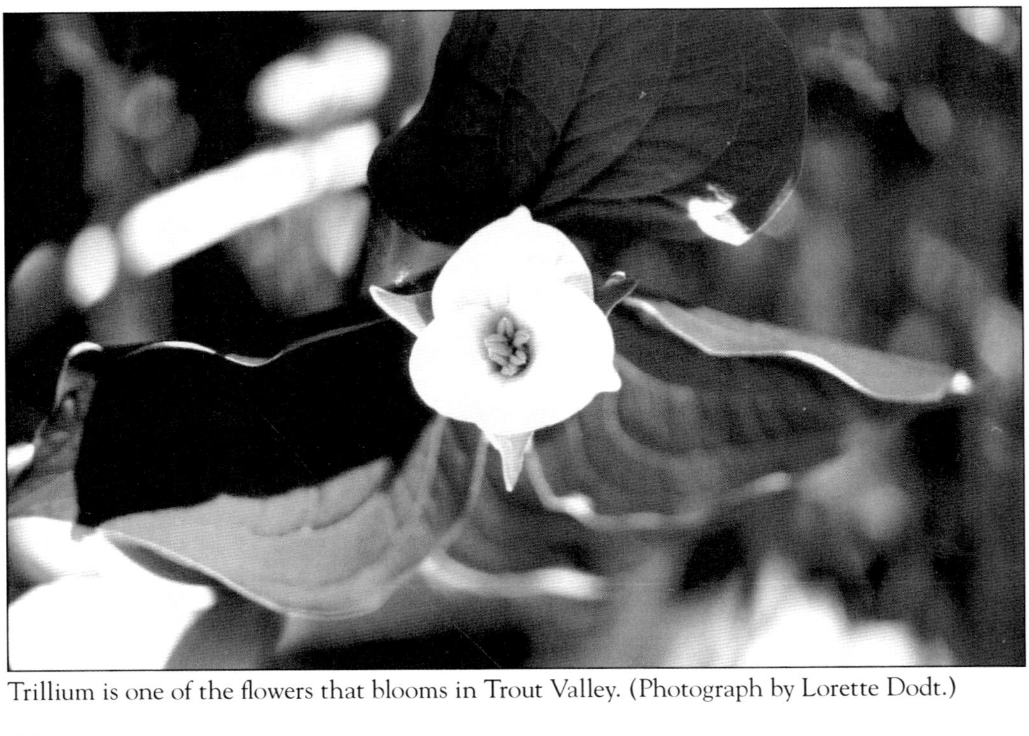

Trillium is one of the flowers that blooms in Trout Valley. (Photograph by Lorette Dodt.)

Dutchman's britches can be seen blooming along certain trails and walking paths. (Photograph by Lorette Dodt.)

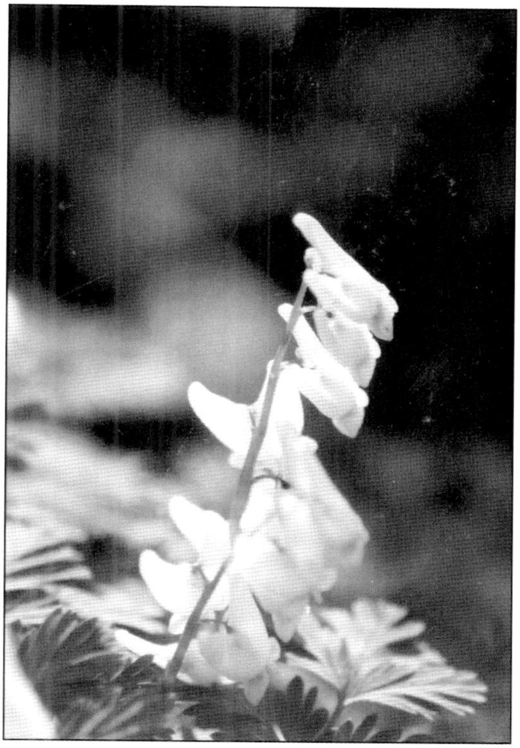

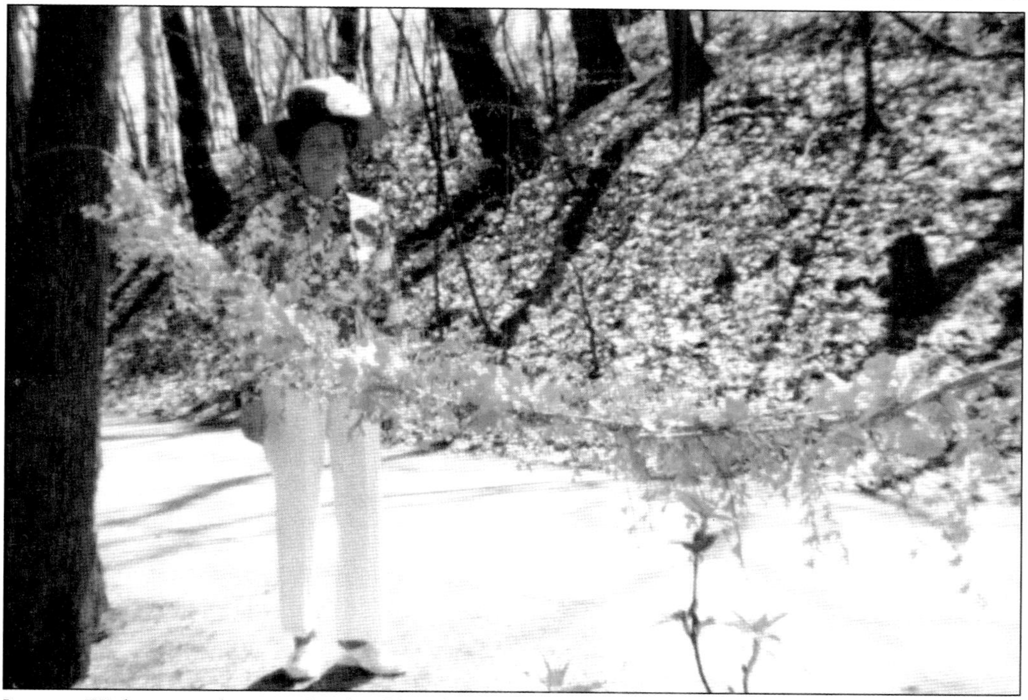

Louise Wolters made a garland of bright yellow daffodil blossoms for the 1975 dedication ceremony of the Trout Valley Wildflower Trail.

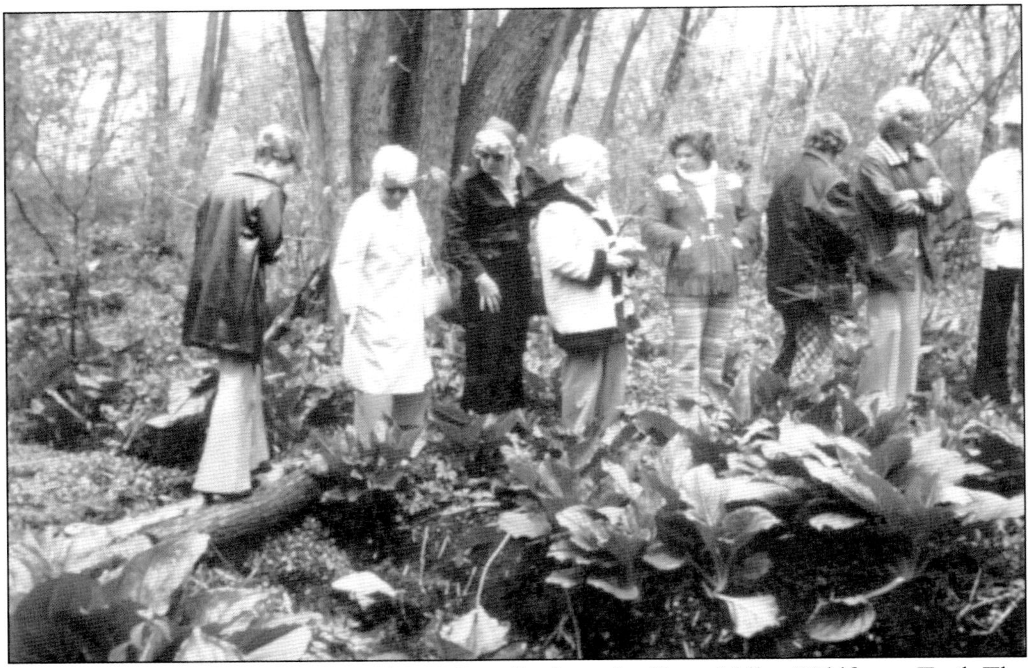

Residents are seen here enjoying a leisurely walk along the Trout Valley Wildflower Trail. The Hill 'n' Dale Garden Club was comprised of Trout Valley residents who volunteered their time to plant and care for the flora that flourishes throughout Trout Valley.

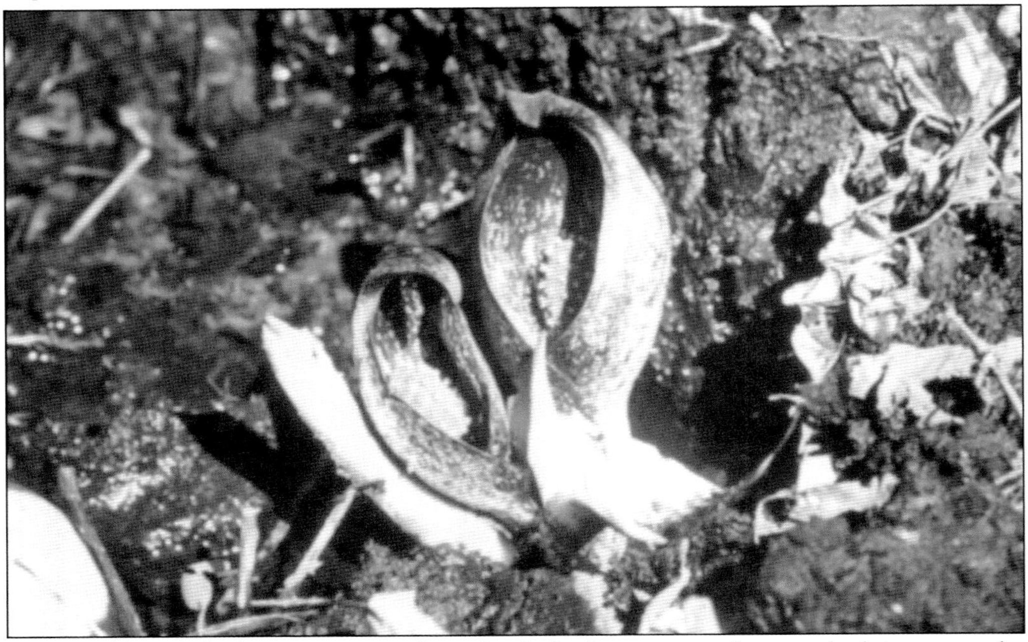

Skunk cabbage, which gets its name from the foul odor it emits when crushed, is among the first plants to emerge in late winter. With its 72 degree internal temperature, it is able to melt the snow around it, the spathe pushing through first and the leaves growing next. It is said that Native Americans ate the leaves and roots of young plants.

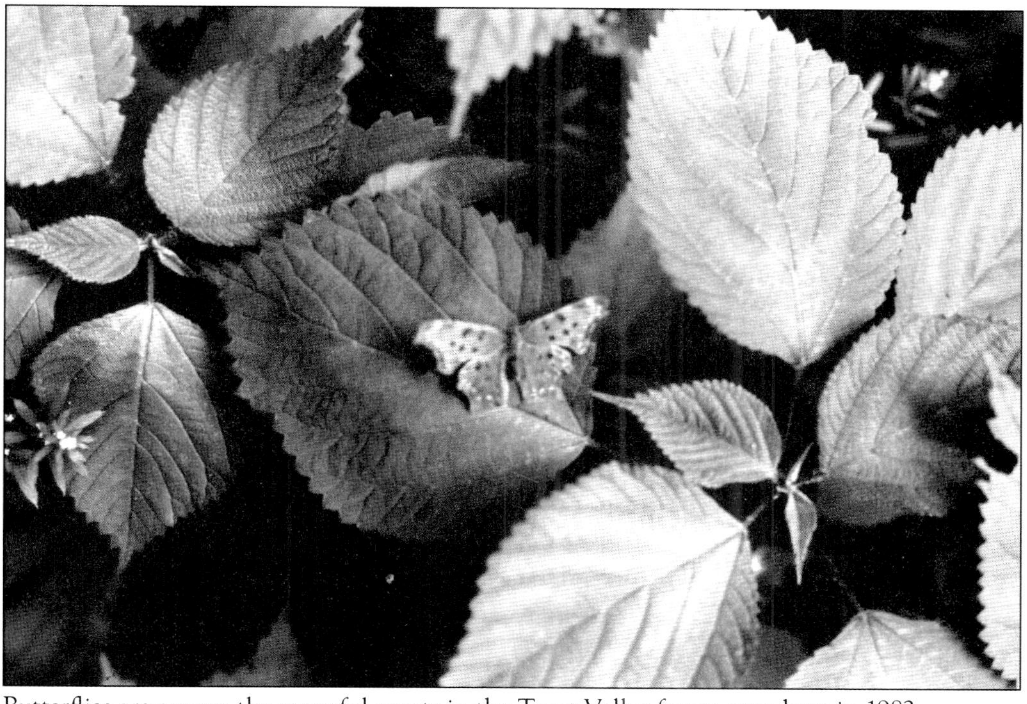

Butterflies are among the peaceful guests in the Trout Valley forest, seen here in 1982.

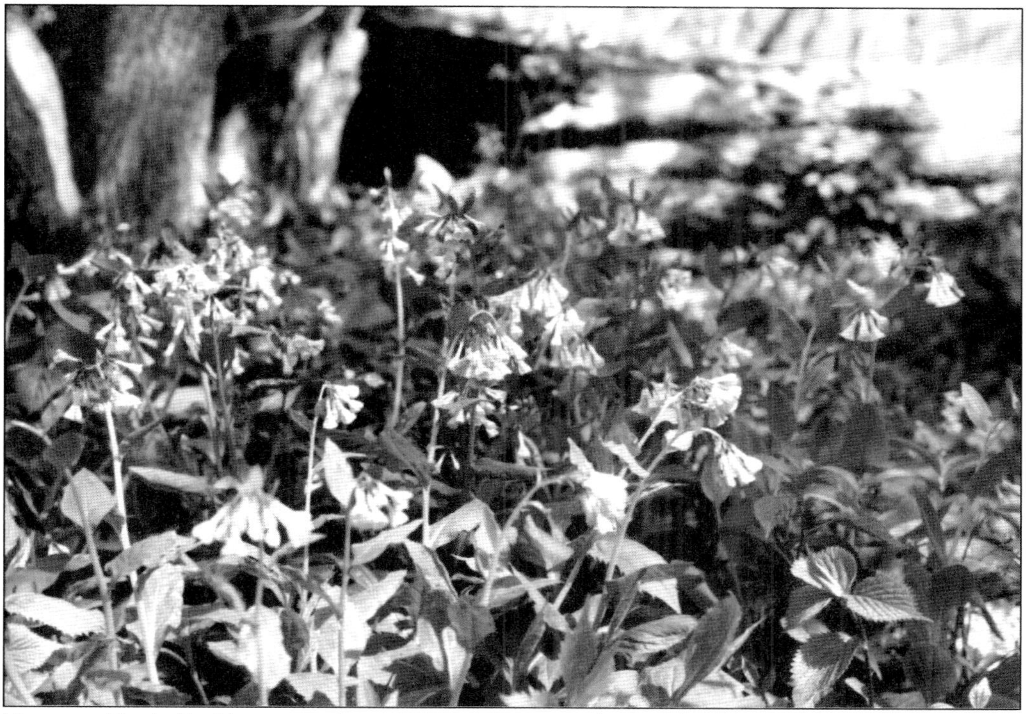

Virginia bluebells bloom in large quantities near the pool and other areas throughout Trout Valley.

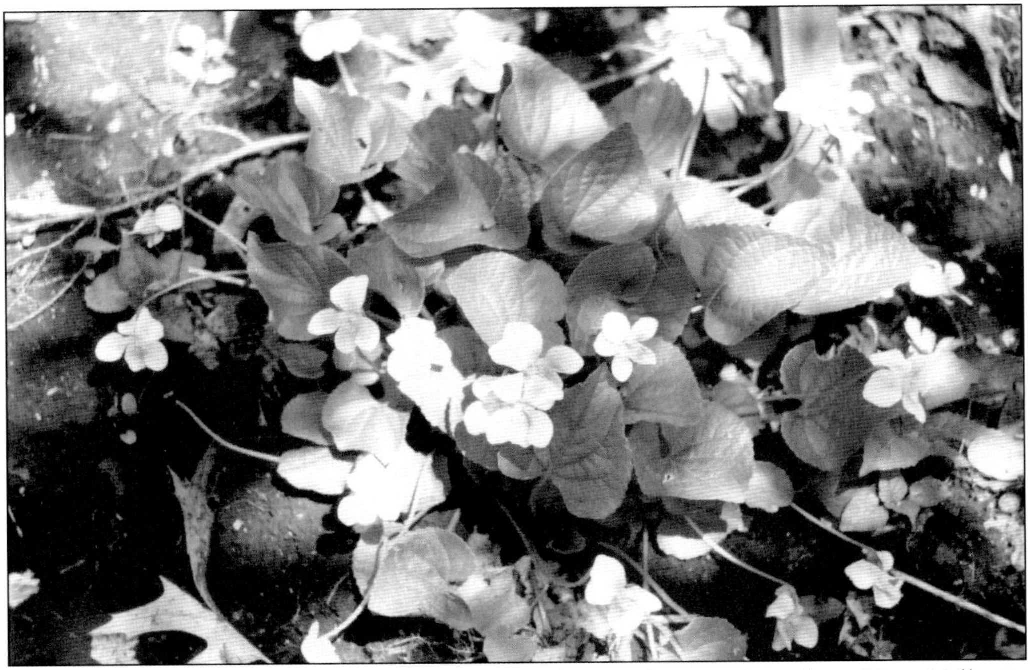

These white violets are one of the many varieties that can be seen throughout Trout Valley in the spring. Other colors include blue, yellow, and a mixture of white and blue.

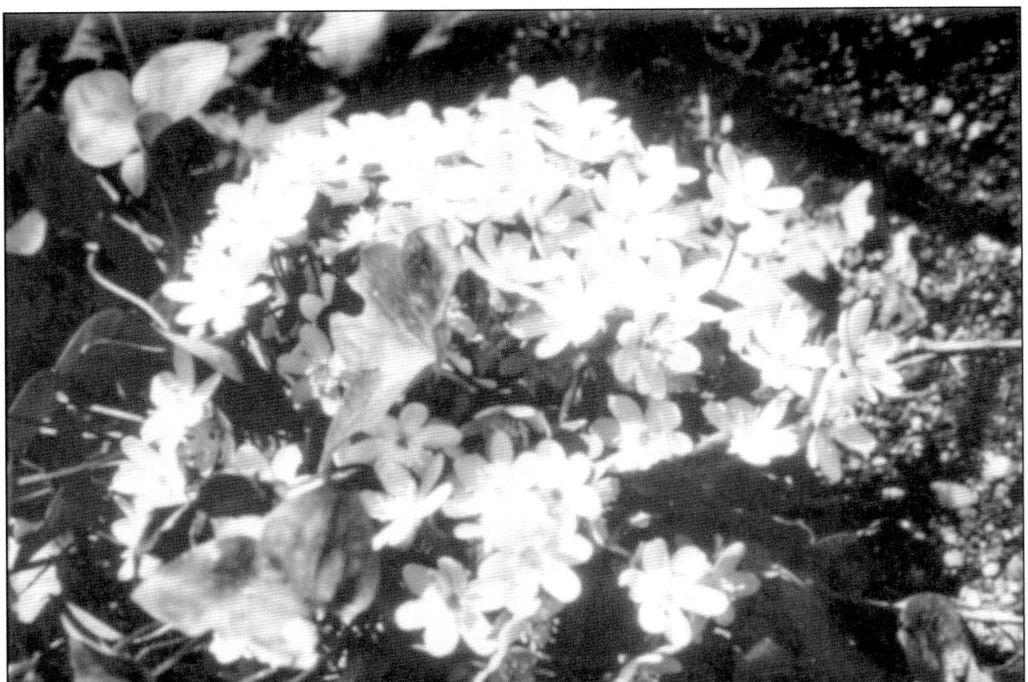

Hepatica with its bluish-purple petals can be seen growing in dry leaf-covered soil in the woods of Trout Valley.

Bright yellow marsh marigolds can be seen some years blooming along the streams of Trout Valley.

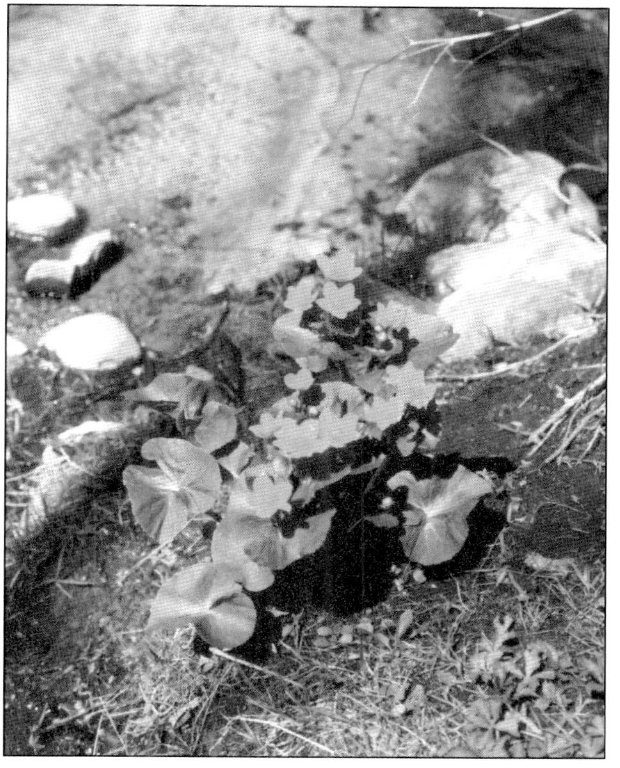

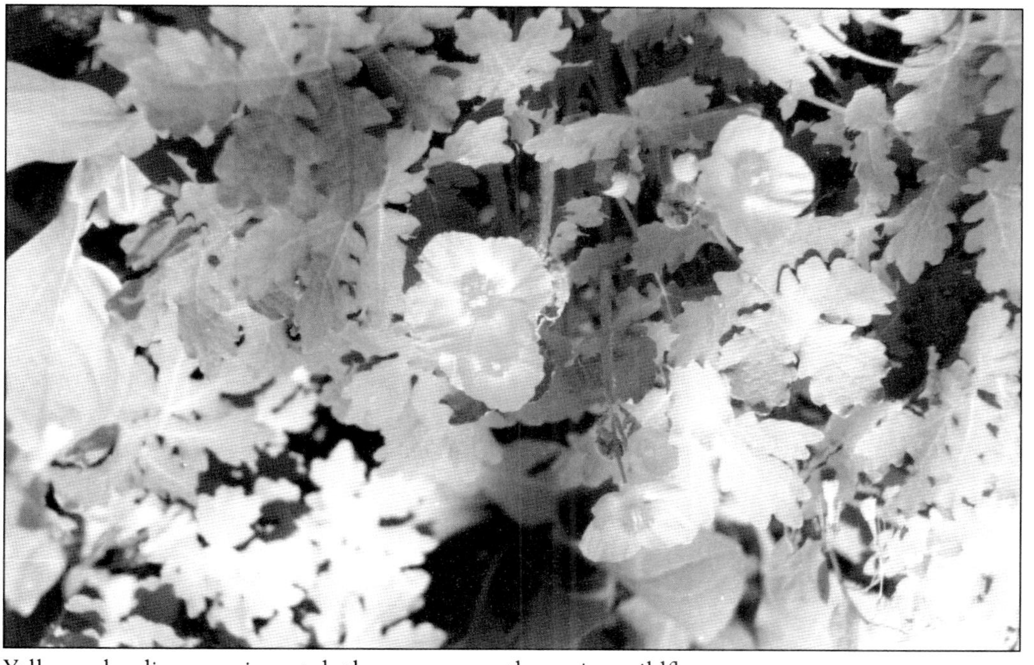

Yellow celandine poppies catch the eye among the spring wildflowers.

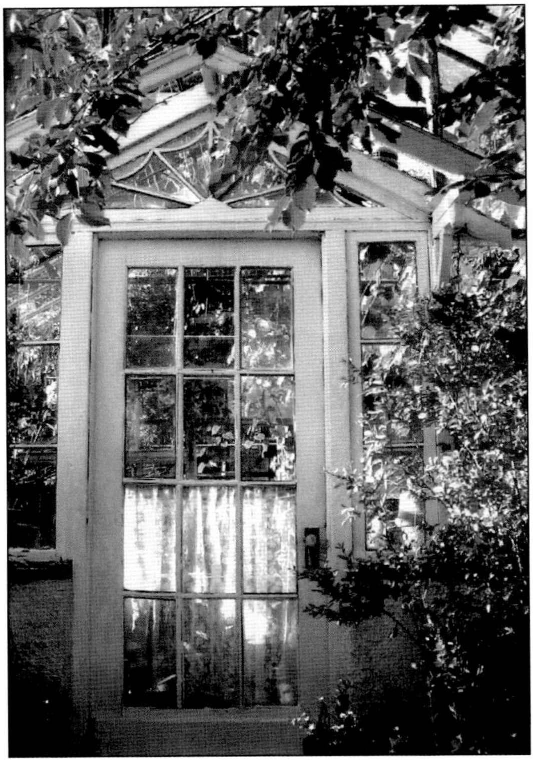

The greenhouse was built for John D. Hertz by the Lord and Burnham Company in the early 1920s. Originally built of iron and cypress wood, it has served the function of both greenhouse and aviary in decades past.

The greenhouse has been a memorable landmark in Trout Valley for almost a century.

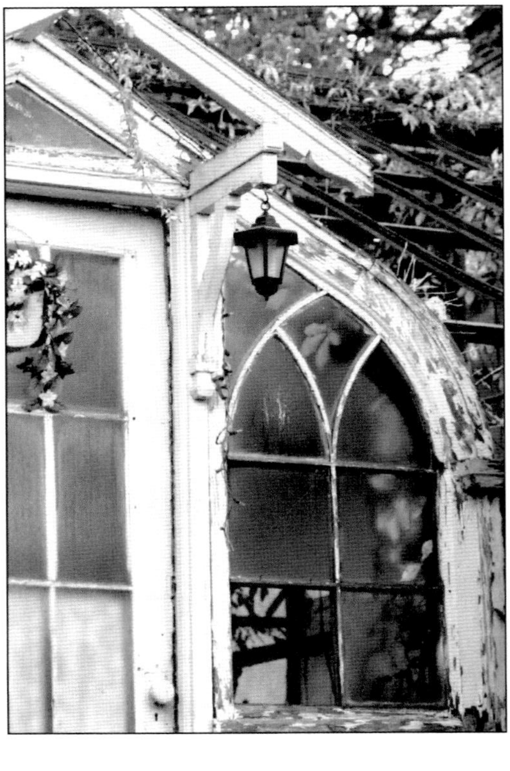

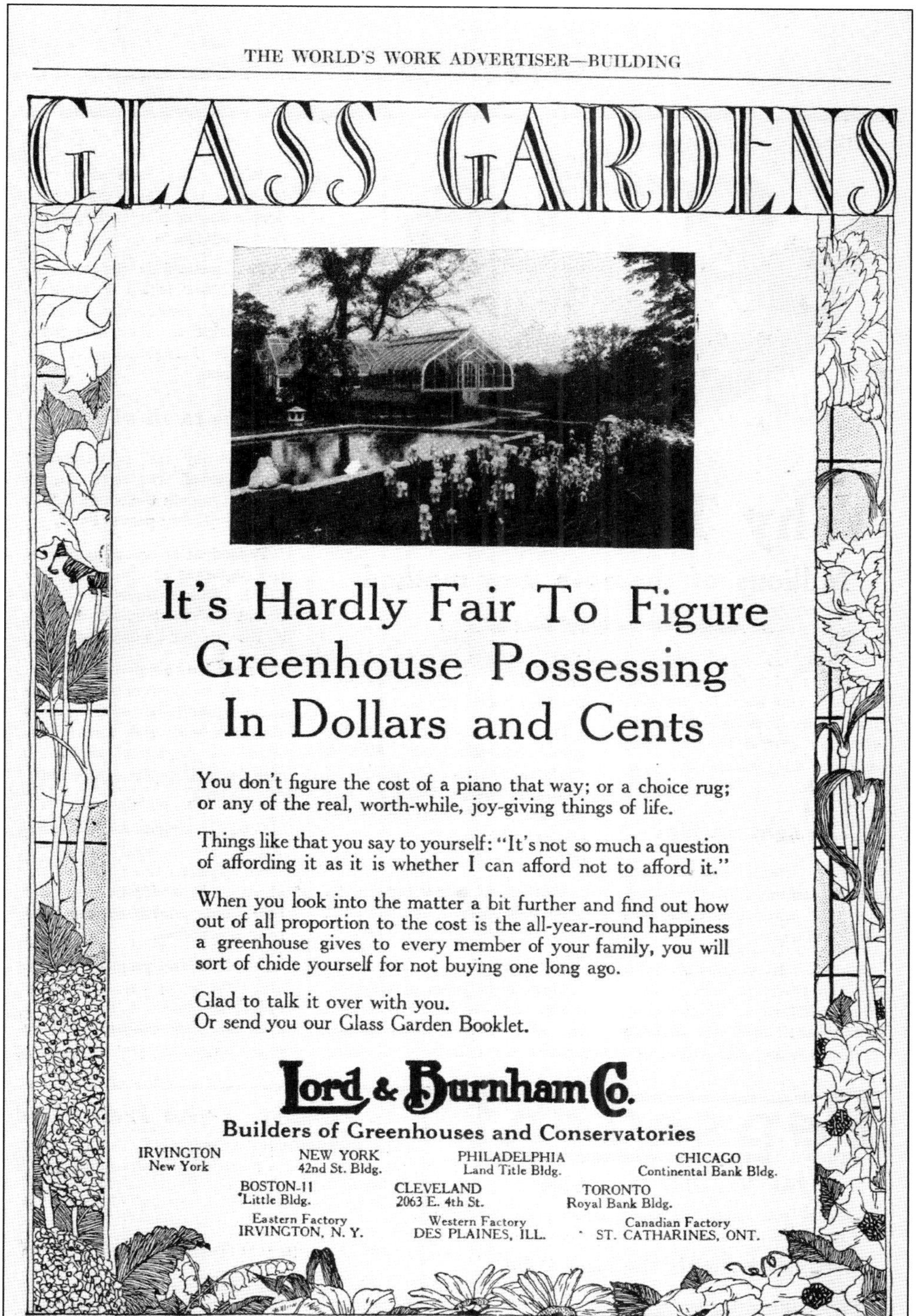

Here is an advertisement for the Lord and Burnham Company, the premier builders of greenhouses, which designed and built the greenhouse during the Hertz era.

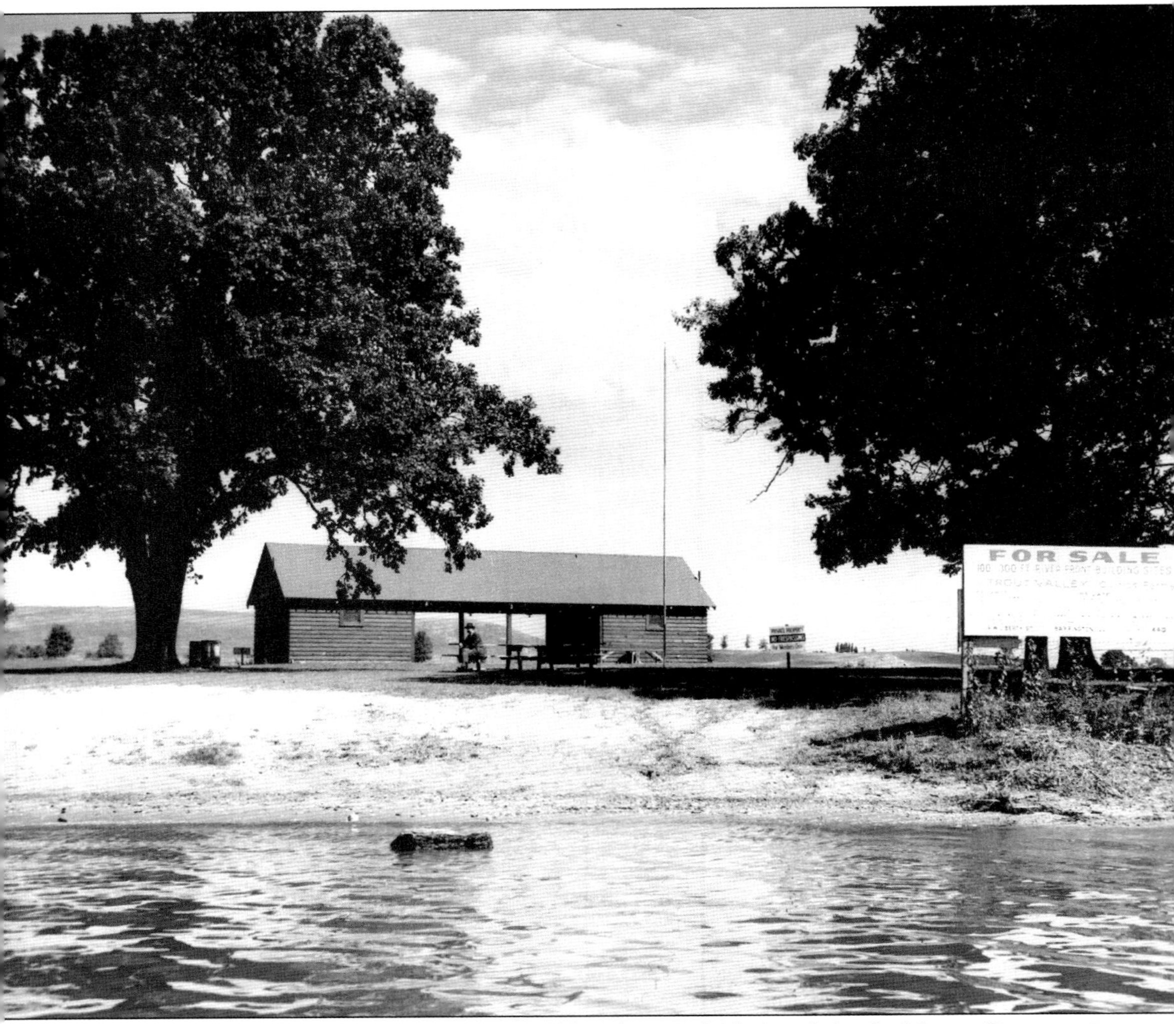

This sign along the Fox River advertises building lots available for sale by the Maxon Construction Company around 1955.

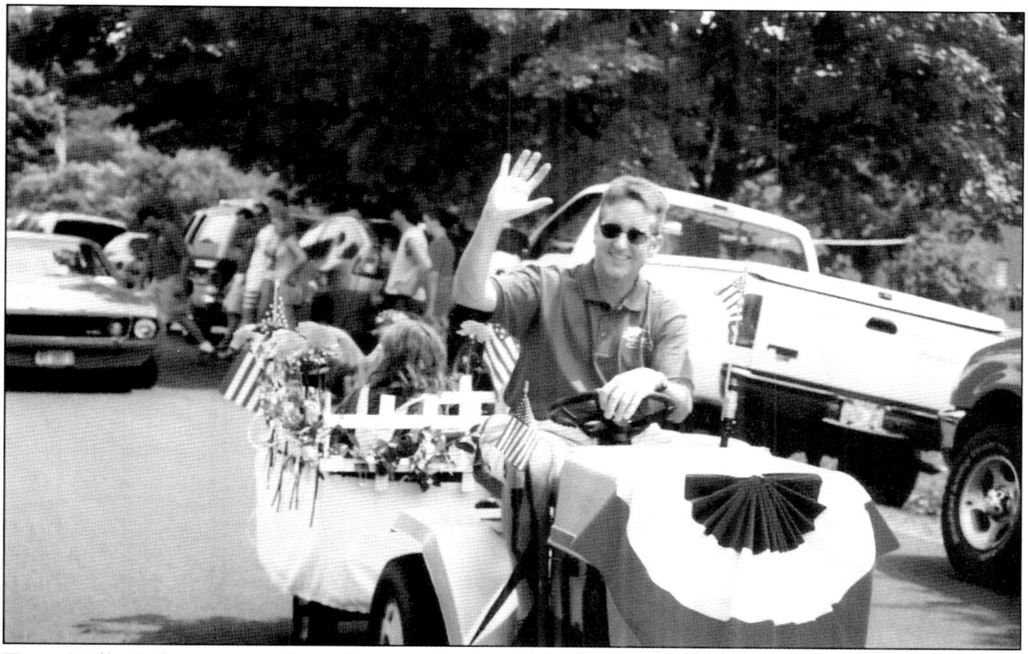

Trout Valley's first mayor, Steve Barrett, kicks off the festivities with his decorated lawn tractor in the Fourth of July parade in 2001, which typically begins on Bluff Road and ends at Trout Park. (Photograph by Lorette Dodt.)

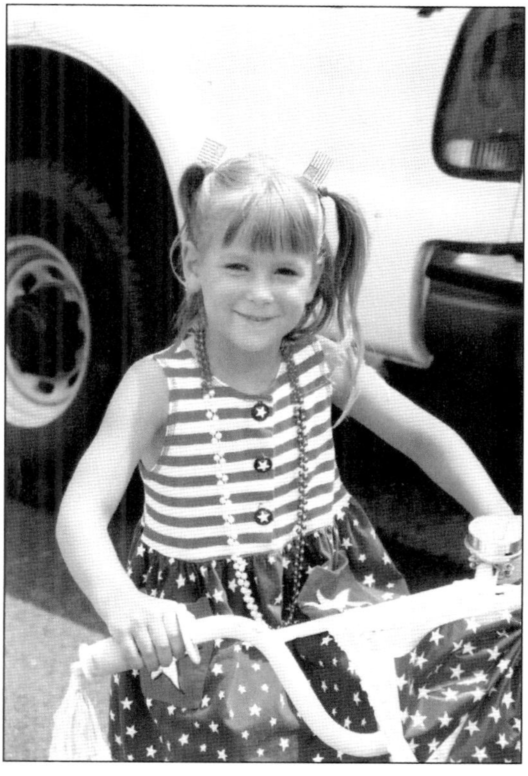

Holly Lehnertz wears her patriotism proudly in the annual Fourth of July parade. The traditional holiday parties are planned and hosted by resident volunteers, thanks to the efforts of individuals like Vicki Pesch, Tonia Gonzalez, Pete Gronset, Deanne Schmidt, and so many others who donate many hours of their time, creativity, and organizational skills to make these events such a success. (Photograph by Lorette Dodt.)

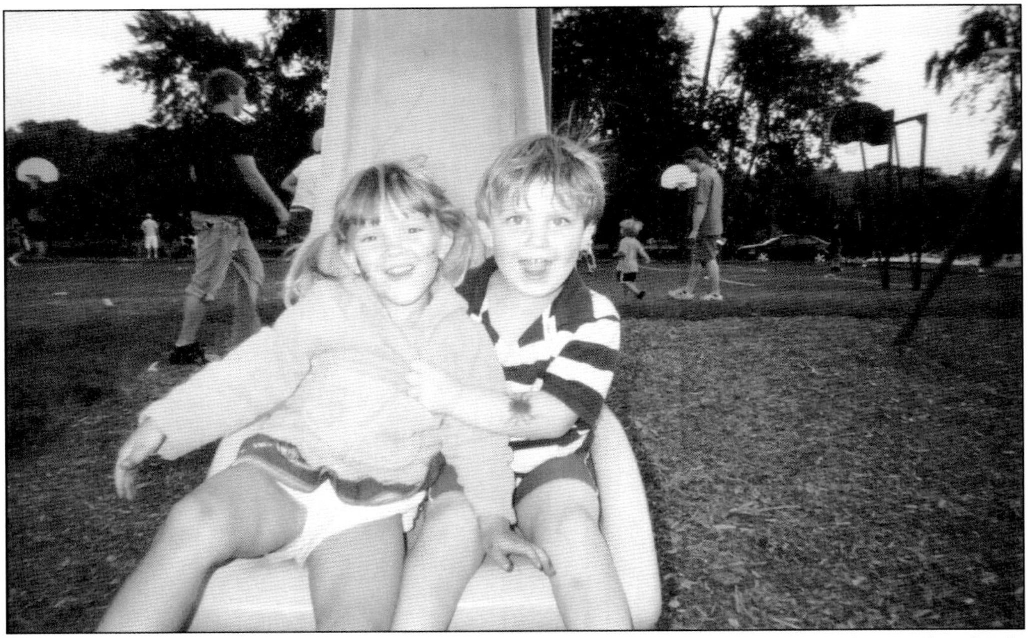

Kelly Henderson and Freddie Hall jockey for slide space during the annual Fourth of July picnic in Trout Park in 2007. Fourth of July activities include a potluck picnic and barbecue, a softball game, a parade, a band, crafts, and other family games. Some years have also featured an impressive fireworks display.

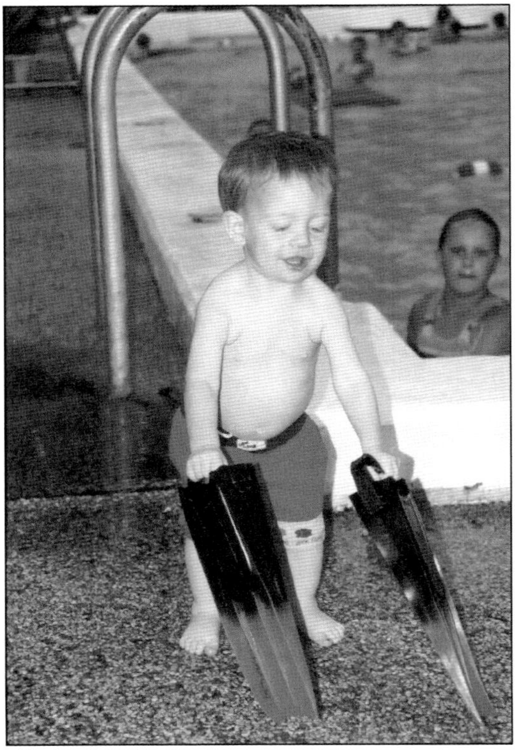

Young Matthew Cummings enjoys his flippers and the Trout Valley pool while Kelly Detman looks on from the water on a summer day in 1999. (Photograph by Lorette Dodt.)

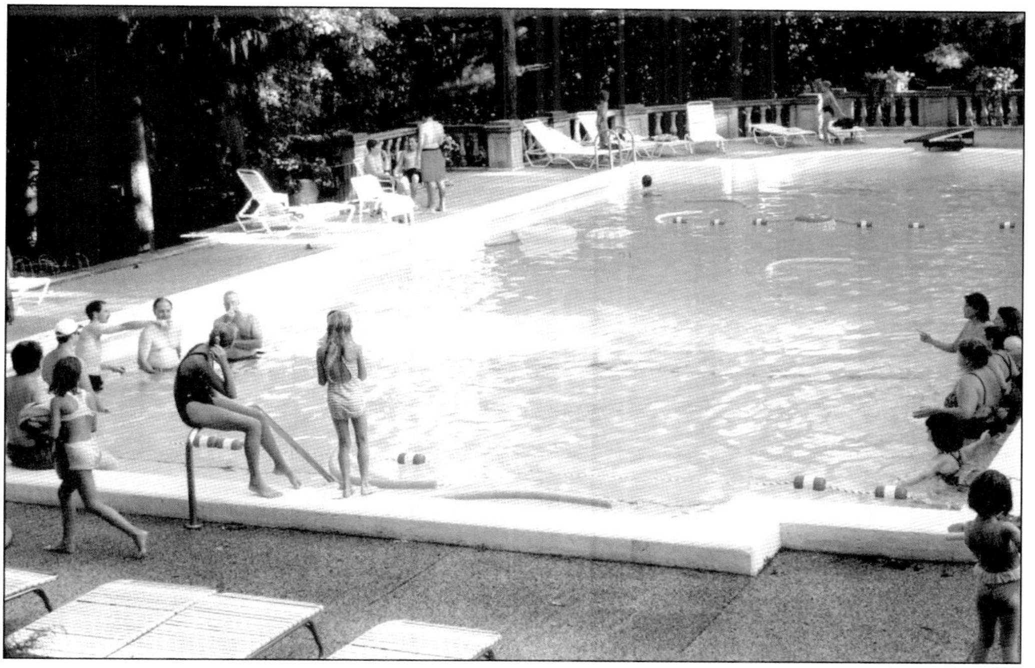

It is moms versus dads in this gutterball tournament during adult swim at the Trout Valley pool. (Photograph by Lorette Dodt.)

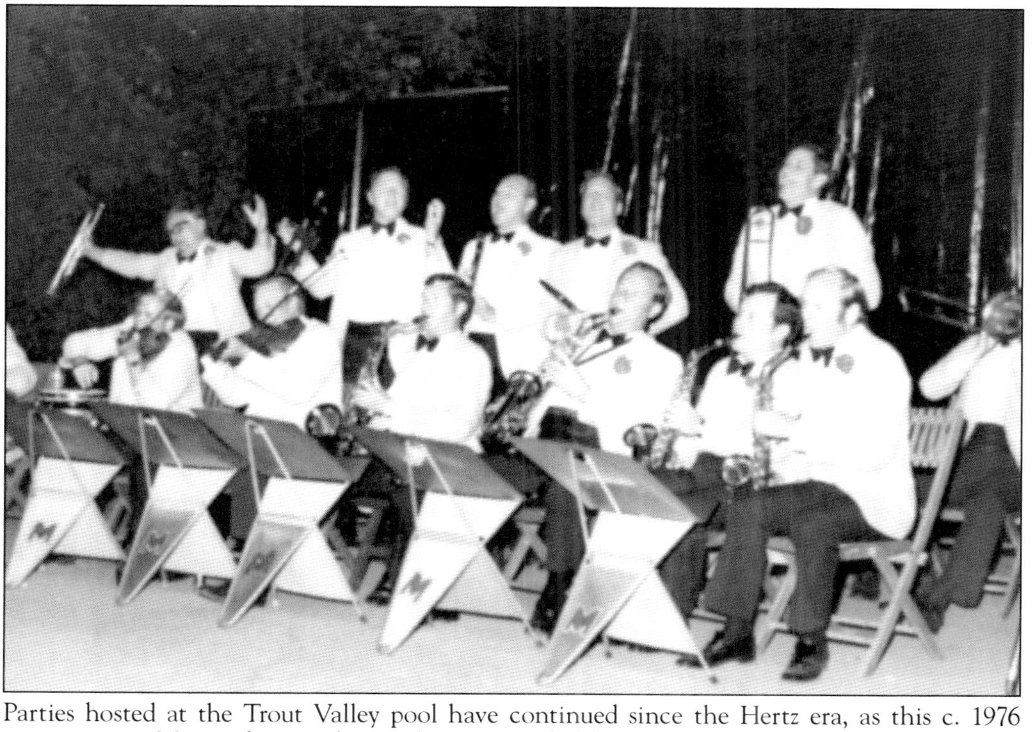

Parties hosted at the Trout Valley pool have continued since the Hertz era, as this c. 1976 event attests. Music, skits, and comedy are provided by Trout Valley residents. (Courtesy of Bud Himes.)

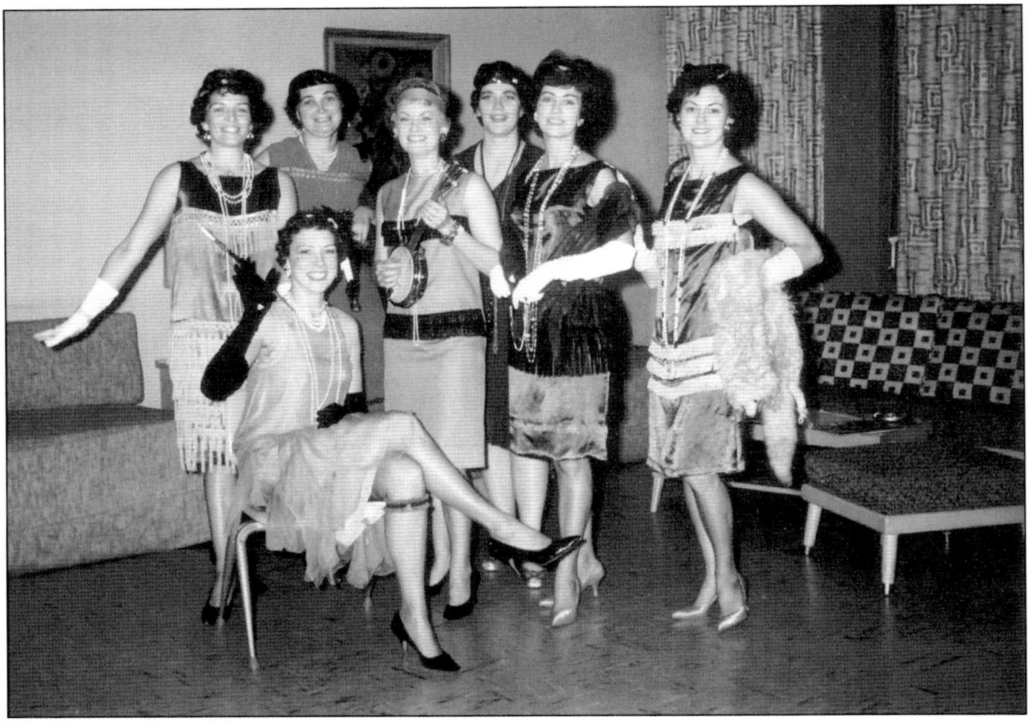

Trout Valley ladies dress in 1920s flapper attire for this party hosted at the Trout Valley pool in 1961. (Courtesy of Richard Trentlage.)

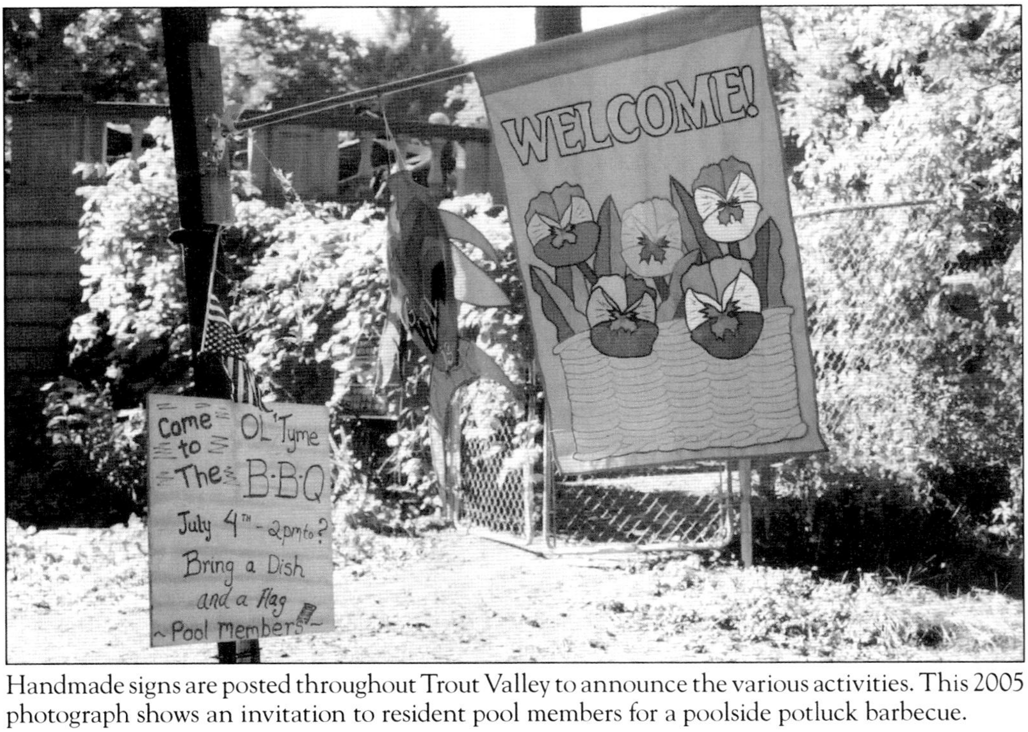

Handmade signs are posted throughout Trout Valley to announce the various activities. This 2005 photograph shows an invitation to resident pool members for a poolside potluck barbecue.

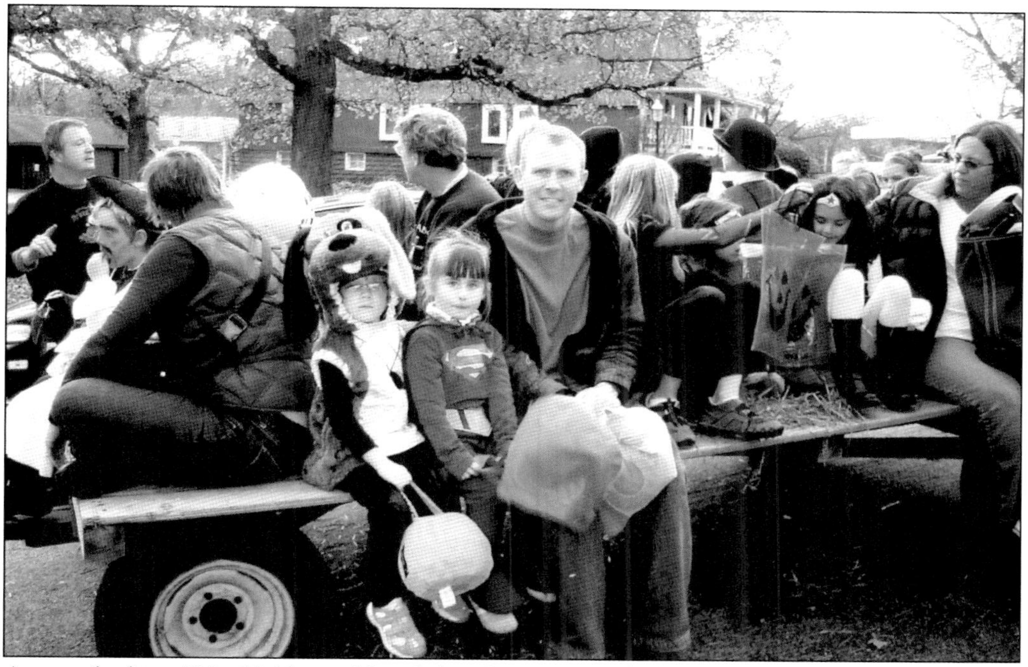

A super looking Talia Kidder and her father Steve are ready for the annual Halloween hayride. Her trusty canine companion Bridget Heinhold and others are prepared with treat bags in hand for the trick-or-treating ride through Trout Valley, driven by Mayor Bob Baker in 2007.

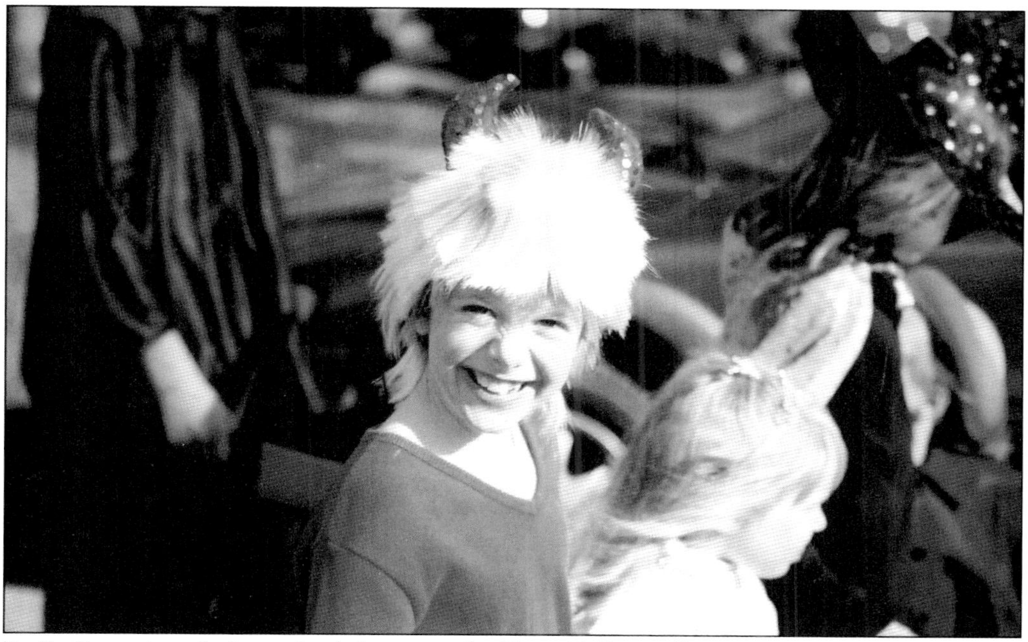

Emily Cummings flashes a devilish grin at the Trout Valley Halloween party in 2005.

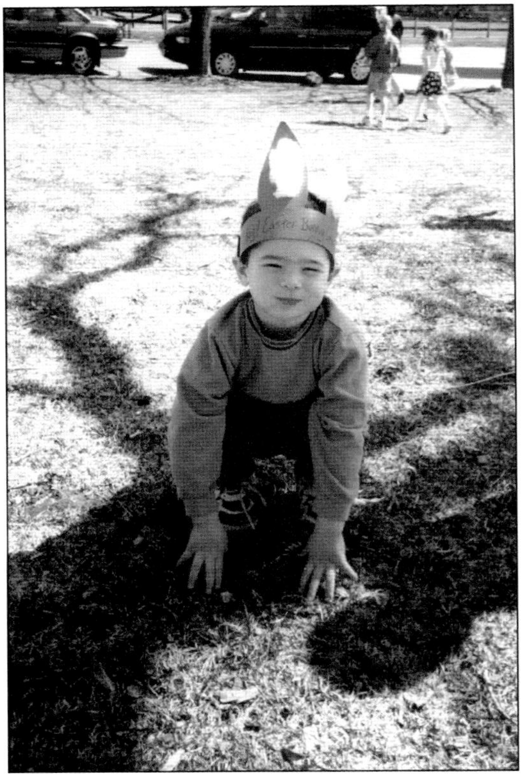

Quinn Baker is all ears at the annual Trout Valley Easter party in 1999. In years past, the Easter party has featured a petting zoo, children's crafts, a potluck brunch buffet, and an Easter egg hunt.

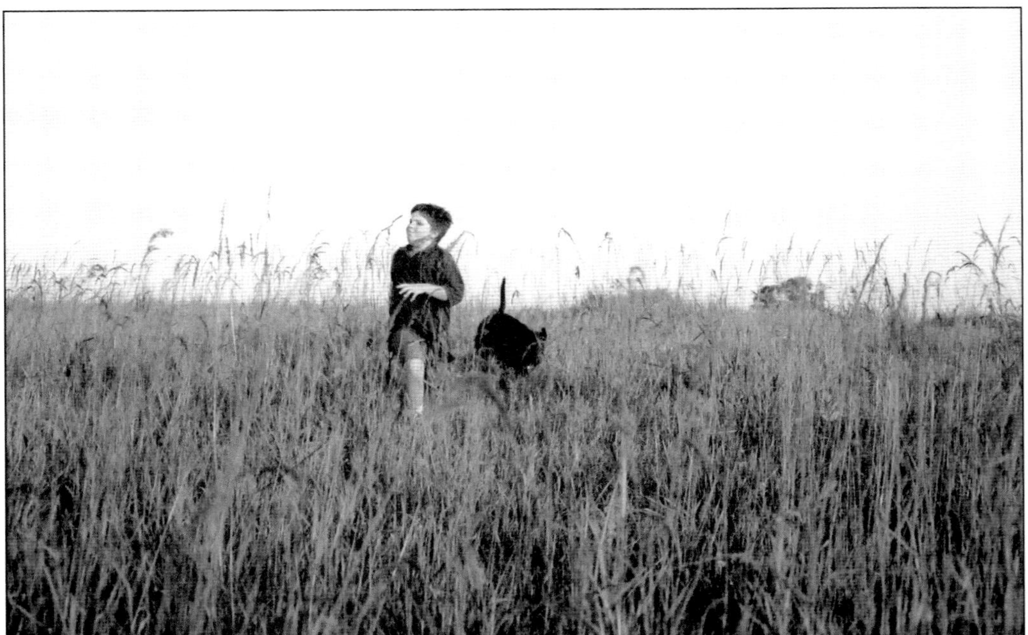

Colin Dodt and his dog Mocha race through the waist-high grass in the lower pasture field in 1999. (Photograph by Lorette Dodt.)

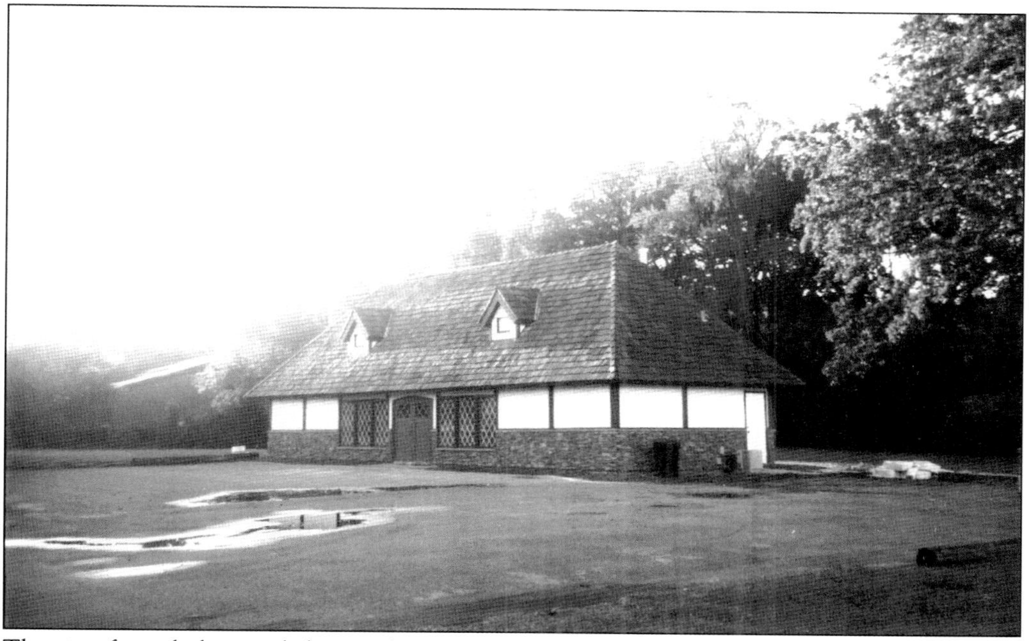

The riverfront lodge used during the Curtiss era originally stood on this same location. In the years 2000 and 2001, an all-volunteer force of Trout Valley neighbors built a new lodge in the same location where the original lodge once stood. The Riverfront Lodge now serves as a gathering space for community events and activities.

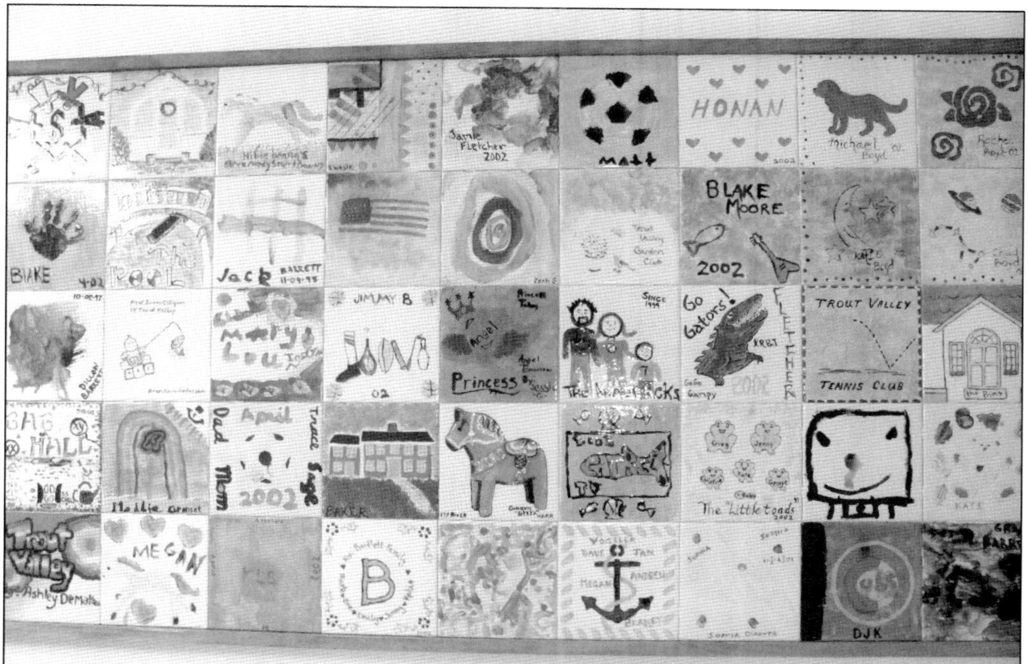

A collage of hand-painted tiles made by valley residents adorns the walls of the Riverfront Lodge, seen here in 2008.

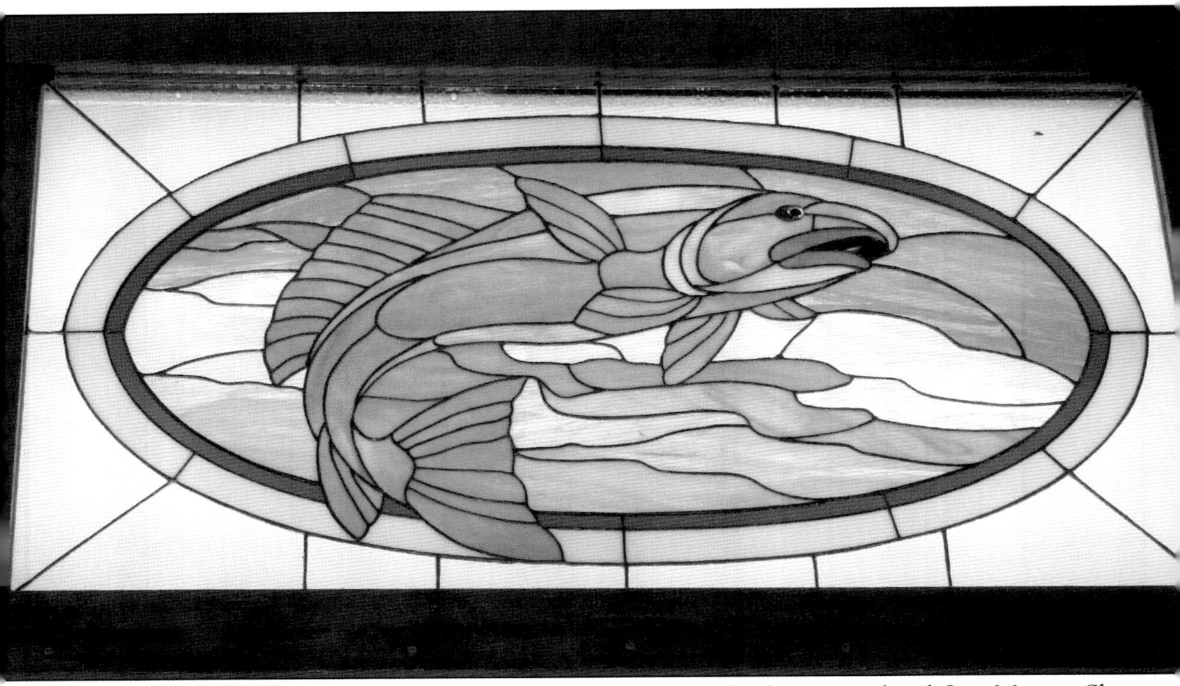

This hand-crafted stained glass window was designed by long-time local Jan Moore. She made this artwork specifically for Trout Valley, generously donating this product of her artistic talent made during her final years. It is on prominent display as a lasting legacy in the Riverfront Lodge.

AFTERWORD

Our photographic essay has provided a short timeline of the history of Trout Valley. Still in its infancy, the land has been witness to many interesting developments over time. It has seen the extravagant wealth and Hollywood glamour of the Hertz years, the scientific advances and farming innovations of the Curtiss era, and its rebirth as a self-governing community aiming to press forward to the future, but not break with the past.

We should all be so lucky to find a home that brings us satisfaction, pride, and pure enjoyment. In many ways, it is not the reality of our surroundings that we recall, but the memories that are created there. Trout Valley may be the place where we live, sleep, and work day-to-day, but in truth it is much more. It is beyond a physical space, but an ideal—a place where we can pass on the values we cherish and hold dear.

What makes this area so unique is its respect for traditions. We stay connected to our history by borrowing elements of it and passing them on to the next generation. We have familiar rituals that bring us together, and we share the experiences with our children. These traditions are simple yet powerful ways of expressing the unique character and heritage of an area. They help to create a bond that fosters a lifelong attachment to Trout Valley. Now more than ever, we understand the need to establish a strong foundation and respect for community.

Tradition is a powerful and significant aspect of life in Trout Valley. When residents reflect on favorite memories created while living here, they often describe the annual activities and celebrations. These familiar events are part of the glue that holds this closely knit neighborhood together. They provide a sense of belonging and help to define that special quality that makes up our hometown.

The strength of our community helps sustain us through many challenges of life, and is instrumental in teaching us to honor and support each other as neighbors. We watch as each new crop of children is raised, experiencing the joy of seeing Trout Valley through their eyes. Eventually these children grow and pass the torch to the younger friends who follow.

When asked what she had discovered in *The Wizard of Oz*, character Dorothy Gail responds "If I ever go looking for my heart's desire again, I won't look any further than my own back yard. Because if it isn't there, I never really lost it to begin with!" In the pure and honest voice of a child, she's right. There really is no place like home.

Bob Baker
Mayor of Trout Valley